KT-227-985

Understanding the Market

SECOND EDITION

ANDREW DUNNETT

LONGMAN

LONDON AND NEW YORK

Longman Group UK Limited,
Longman House, Burnt Mill,
Harlow, Essex CM20 2JE, England
and Associated Companies throughout the world.

Published in the United States of America
by Longman Publishing, New York

© Longman Group UK Limited 1987, 1992.

All rights reserved; no part of this publication may be reproduced, stored in a retrieval
system, or transmitted in any form or by any means, electronic, mechanical,
photocopying, recording, or otherwise without either the prior written permission of
the Publishers or a licence permitting restricted copying in the United Kingdom issued
by the Copyright Licensing Agency Ltd., 90 Tottenham Court Road, London W1P 9HE.

First published 1987.
Second edition 1992.
Third impression 1995.

British Library Cataloguing in Publication Data
A catalogue record for this book is
available from the British Library

Library of Congress Cataloging-in-Publication Data
Dunnett, Andrew, 1948–
    Understanding the market / Andrew Dunnett. — 2nd ed.
        p. cm.
    Includes index.
    ISBN 0–582–08375–3
    1. Economics.   2. Capitalism.   3. Oligopolies.   I. Title
    HB171.5.D846   1992   91–44524
    330—dc20   CIP

Set by 8 in 10/13pt Melior

Produced through Longman Malaysia, PP
LYP/02

Contents

E00047381290 01

Preface to the first edition

This book is directed towards first-year students doing economics either as a single discipline or as a part of a broader social science degree (such as business studies); at those students taking professional examinations (for example in accountancy); and at students of A-level economics. As such the market to which it is directed is the same as that for my earlier book *Understanding the Economy* which was an introduction to macroeconomics. *Understanding the Market* is an introduction to microeconomics.

The approach of this book reflects the belief that the teaching of microeconomic theory cannot be divorced from the real world to which that theory can and should be applied. It is thus a mixture of theory and application. Although the microeconomic theory presented is the bare minimum which the student needs to appreciate the applied material, it remains an unpalatable fact that this material is often difficult for students to grasp. In writing this book there were two possible strategies I could have adopted. Either I could 'fudge' the issues and spare the reader the mental effort involved in trying to fathom out exactly what was meant by long-run equilibrium, a Pareto optimal allocation of resources, and so on. Or I could do it 'properly' with a degree of rigour appropriate to the discipline of economics, sweetening the bitter pill where possible and rewarding the reader with applied material when the necessary theory had been covered. I took the second option. Notwithstanding this, however, the balance between theory and application in this book is heavily biased towards application, reflecting, I believe, the needs of students and teachers alike.

Chapter 5 epitomises this approach. The cost concepts therein are treated rigorously but there are numerous applied examples provided as illustrations.

Most markets in the real world are oligopolistic. Paradoxically it is in this area that neo-classical theory has least to say or has the fewest definitive predictions to make. My approach to this in Chapter 8 (9 in second edition), which is a major chapter, has been to take a number of cases, each one illustrating particular features of oligopolistic behaviour and public policy towards it.

In Chapters 10 (12) and 11 (14) I have presented a welfare-theoretic model of how markets allocate resources. This serves as a useful reference point in Chapter 12 (16) where I consider an alternative way of allocating resources – planning in command economies and in wartime. This chapter is an unusual but, I believe, valuable feature of this book. The welfare framework carries over to Chapters 13 (17) and 14 (18) where I consider state intervention in market economies in the form of the public provision of goods and services and the nationalised industry sector. The approach here is however essentially pragmatic and the issues discussed are those of contemporary relevance.

The theme which develops as the book progresses is the role of the state in mixed economies, a theme which is discussed in the concluding chapter.

The questions which follow each chapter are designed to highlight some of the points in that chapter. They are designed to make the reader think about what he has read and (where this book is being used as a textbook) to stimulate class discussion. There is no particular pattern to these questions, though they are all designed as 'short answer' questions. It must be emphasised, however, that in the multiple-choice type of question there is not necessarily any single correct answer – more than one answer could be considered correct or none could be correct. Complex issues cannot have simple definitive answers.

In writing this book I have received an enormous amount of support from my colleagues at Ealing. They have give freely of their time and much of the empirical material in this book has been contributed by them. Being economists, they understand that knowledge is one of the few things you can give away and still retain, and that social benefits over and above the private benefit flow from a project such as this.

In particular, I would like to thank Phillip Wyatt who is an inexhaustible font of knowledge and cuttings from the FT. The debt I owe him is enormous. I would also like to thank David Glen, Carol Rees, John Crowley, Andy Hartropp, Paul Cormack, Brian Ardy and Adrian Bourne. Thanks to all those friends who helped and supported me in the critical period during which this manuscript was in preparation.

Ealing, Summer 1986

Preface to the second edition

The first edition of *Understanding the Market* contained some significant omissions. The second edition is a more comprehensive text. Thus Chapters 7 on price discrimination, 10 on trade, 13 on factor markets, and 15 on income distribution are entirely new as are substantial parts of Chapter 9 on oligopolistic behaviour. In addition substantial parts of Chapters 2, 5, 11, 16, 17 and 18 have been re-written with the aim of increasing clarity. The objective throughout has been to get the reader to focus in more easily on the key issues.

As a result of all these changes the new edition is about 40 per cent longer than the original. This is probably an optimum size for a book of this nature: comprehensive and thought-provoking without being too daunting for the student. Knowing when to stop is part of the writer's art.

My thanks are due to Brian Ardy, Adrian Bourne, Paul Cormack, Andy Dennis, Shelagh Hewson, Stephanie Jenkins, Carol Rees and Phillip Wyatt and many others. My particular thanks are due to Michael Simpson, not only for reading the complete manuscript but for showing concern for my spiritual well-being, a debt which one day I shall repay.

Holland on Sea
10 September 1991

Acknowledgements

The publishers are grateful to the following for permission to reproduce copyright material:

Basil Blackwell Ltd for table 9.7; Central Statistical Office for tables 4.2, 4.3, 13.4, 15.1, 15.2, 15.3, 15.4, 15.5, 15.6, 15.7, 15.8, 15.9, 15.10, 15.11, 17.2, 18.1; The Economist for figs 5.6 and 5.12; Gerald Duckworth and Co. for tables 16.1 and 16.2; Her Majesty's Stationery Office for figs 5.8, 5.9, 5.10, 5.11, 9.3, 9.4, tables 9.1, 9.2, 9.4, 17.1, 18.2; The Independent for table 10.8; The Journal of the Economics Association for fig. 4.8, tables 5.4 and 5.6; McGraw-Hill Book Co. for table 9.10; The Ministry of Agriculture, Fisheries and Food for tables 2.2, 2.5, 2.6 and A2.8; The Observer Ltd., for table 11.3; The Office of Population, Censuses and Surveys for tables 13.2, 13.5; Retail Business, Economist Intelligence Unit for tables 2.3, 2.4, 10.3, 10.4 and 10.5; Times Books for table 11.1.

Whilst every effort has been made to trace the owners of copyright material, in a few cases this has proved impossible, and we take this opportunity to offer our apologies to any copyright holders whose rights we may have unwittingly infringed.

1 Introduction

1.1 What economics is about

Definitions are for dictionaries (or, more correctly, dictionaries are for definitions) but some definitions are so abstract and so conceptual that to the uninitiated reader they convey very little meaning. Economics as a discipline covers a broad spectrum of enquiry and hence its subject matter can only be defined in very broad terms. Using such broad terms, we could say that *economics is about making decisions*. The *economic problem* or *choice problem* consists, in its widest sense, of two elements. Firstly, there must be a scarcity of resources — money, labour, time, land and so on — secondly, because of the scarcity of resources, choices have to be made about how they are used. Defined in this way, of course, the scope of economics appears vast but this is no accident for the scope of economics *is* vast — it is the 'science of choice' and as such its subject matter covers almost every aspect of human activity.

The purpose of this present work is somewhat more modest. It concerns itself with how decisions are made but confines itself to a narrower range of decisions — they are the economic decisions taken by three principal agents, the producer, the consumer and the state. Taken together these decisions shape the sort of society in which we live. The producer decides what will be produced, in what quantities and by what methods, responding to a lesser or greater extent to the wishes of consumers on these same issues. The extent to which the consumer is *sovereign*, in the sense that ultimately producers merely respond to his wishes, will be an important theme in this book. The second key theme concerns the role of the state, the third member of the triumvirate. The state acts as both producer and consumer but, in addition, it determines the legal and institutional framework within which producers interact with other producers and with consumers. Thus, the role of the state is crucial in determining ultimately how society's resources shall be allocated.

Economics is conventionally divided into macroeconomics and microeconomics. Microeconomics concerns itself with individual decisions — the individual firm, the individual consumer and individual prices. In macroeconomics the subject of enquiry is the economy as a whole – thus problems of inflation, unemployment, the balance of payments and economic growth are studied. The reader will appreciate, however, that the study of macroeconomics is predicated upon a particular analysis of how the microeconomy works. This book provides such an analysis.

1.2 Some key words

One of the difficulties experienced by the student of economics is that certain key words used by the economist have a meaning and significance peculiar to economics itself and different from the everyday usage of the terms. In this section we shall introduce some of these key words while at the same time sketching out how these concepts relate to the wider whole. Our aim is to provide the reader with some sort of perspective – a large-scale map of the landscape of this book.

The word *market* refers to the totality of buyers and sellers (both actual and potential) of a particular *good* or commodity or service. Thus, for example, one can talk about the market for shoes, the housing market, the market for foreign exchange and the market for professional footballers. A few markets have a physical existence (for example, before deregulation the Stock Exchange was a place where buyers and sellers came together to trade shares) but most markets do not. When we are talking about a particular market it should be delineated with care. For example, in air travel the scheduled services market is distinct from the inclusive package tour market.

In any market there are those who wish to sell and those who wish to buy. The buyers constitute the *demand* side of the market, the sellers the *supply* side. The demand for shoes therefore means the total number of pairs of shoes people would be prepared to buy at a given price. Note that one can talk about an individual's demand for shoes (normally a few pairs per year) or the market demand for shoes (several million pairs per year in Britain). The concept of demand implies both willingness and ability to pay for a particular good – thus it is different from *need*. A poor man may need a new pair of shoes but unless he has the money to pay for them there will be no demand in the market.

The supply of shoes similarly implies willingness to sell at a particular price. Note that both demand and supply are dependent upon price. The price is the money or other consideration given when goods or services are exchanged. Note also that *price* rather than *value* is used since price is an objective datum whereas value is a subjective assessment of intrinsic worth. (In this respect we are in a world of cynics. Oscar Wilde, remember, defined a cynic as a man who knows the price of everything and the value of nothing.)

The prices paid by buyers and received by sellers can be considered to be *market prices*, that is, determined in some way by the *market forces* of demand and supply. In some situations, however, the price at which a particular good or service is sold is more or less set by the seller, for example, postal charges are set by the Post Office. In such a case where there is little interaction between demand and supply – or in other words where market forces are very weak – it is more realistic to talk about *administered prices*, rather than market prices.

In a Soviet-type *command economy* or *centrally planned economy* most prices are in fact administered prices, set by the state. The term *mixed economy* refers to an economy such as that of the UK, where some productive decisions are taken centrally by the state (for example, in the sphere of the National Health Service and defence) while other productive decisions are left to the market. Thus, some prices are administered while others are market prices. It is important to note however, that even where there is no state intervention, many prices are administered rather than determined by market forces. This is because the supply side of the market is dominated by a few large firms. Such firms set (or administer) prices. These prices can be considered as market prices only in the very general sense that demand conditions will ultimately determine whether the prices set are sustainable.

Markets that are dominated by a few large firms are known as *oligopolies* or oligopolistic markets. In some cases one firm, called a *monopolist*, supplies the whole market for a particular good or service, for example, British Rail is a monopoly seller of rail transportation services. Markets can in fact be classified according to the *degree of concentration* that they exhibit on the supply side. Markets which are highly concentrated on the supply side (monopoly, oligopoly) will typically exhibit different behaviour patterns from those low-concen- tration or *competitive* markets where market forces or the *forces of competition* hold greater sway. That is, the structure of a market will determine to some extent the *conduct* and *performance* of the firms within it. A market structure of extremely low concentration where there are many buyers and sellers, no one of whom is large enough to affect the market price, is known as *perfect competition*. Such market structures are seldom encountered in the real world, except perhaps for some agricultural products, and even here prices are often affected by state intervention.

The foregoing definitions are designed merely to prevent the confusion that might otherwise arise when the terms are encountered for the first time. Short definitions cannot hope to convey the full meanings of some of the terms since many of them carry deep philosophical and ideological connotations, the full import of which will become apparent only as the reader proceeds through the book.

It is hoped that this rather perfunctory introduction has served to steer the reader away from some of the more common areas of confusion. Economics is like any other discipline in that it needs its own jargon for its practitioners to function effectively and to communicate with one another. All too often, however, in economic discourse words are used in a confusing way, as when Humpty Dumpty in *Through the Looking Glass*, said: 'When *I* use a word, it means just what I choose it to mean.' Small wonder Alice was confused.

2 Market demand

2.1 Determinants of demand

In this chapter we shall discuss those factors which determine the demand for a good or service. In order to make the discussion somewhat less abstract we shall consider the demand for a particular good, say, lager.

The market demand for lager (which we can measure as so many million barrels per month) will be affected by a number of different factors, including:

1. *The price of lager*. Other things being equal, the higher the price of lager, the less will be demanded.
2. *The price of substitutes*, such as other beers, spirits, soft drinks, and so on. Other things being equal, if the price of substitutes goes up while the price of lager remains fixed, then there will be a tendency for people to switch to lager. That is, they will consume more lager and less of the higher-priced substitutes.
3. *The price of complementary goods*. Again, other things being equal, a rise in the price of a complementary good may affect the demand for lager. A rise in the price of crisps, for example, will tend to reduce the demand for lager. If we usually consume lager with crisps and we buy fewer crisps because the price has risen, this may result in us buying less lager. In practice of course only a very substantial increase in the price of crisps would produce a discernible impact on beer consumption. *A priori*, however, we could argue that if there is any effect at all we could *predict* the direction of that effect. That is, an increase in the price of crisps will tend to reduce (rather than increase) beer consumption.
4. *Income*. This may affect lager sales but we cannot predict *a priori* the direction of causation. That is, we cannot say for certain whether an increase in income will increase or decrease (or leave unchanged) consumption of lager. Normally however, we could expect higher incomes to increase demand for most goods including lager.
5. *Tastes*. This term tends to be used in economics to represent all

the other factors which influence demand other than those specifically mentioned above. In the context of our example there are many other influences on tastes. Successful advertising, for example, will increase the demand for lager. The weather may also have some effect (more is consumed in hot sunny weather) and changing social habits (for example, the emergence of wine bars, stricter drink/drive laws and increasing home consumption of alcohol) may also have some long-term influence on lager consumption.

We can summarise what we have said so far in symbols as follows:

$$q_d = f(P,P_s,P_c,Y,T) \tag{2.1}$$

This is simply a shorthand way of saying that the demand for lager (q_d) depends on, or is a *function* (f) of the set of variables within the brackets, namely, the price of a lager (P), the price of substitutes (P_s), the price of complementary goods (P_c), income (Y), and tastes (T). Equation [2.1] can of course be used to analyse the demand for any good or service – the demand for cars, foreign holidays, two-bedroom rented apartments, cinema tickets, window cleaners, economics textbooks, and so on. It is a completely general *model* which is universally applicable. All we have to do is to specify – carefully - what good or service we are considering and equation [2.1] will provide us with a framework (though nothing more) for considering what factors will influence demand. We must be careful, however, to specify exactly what good is being considered. For example, the demand for one particular brand of lager will be different from the demand for lager generally.

For the time being we shall just consider the relationship between the demand for lager and the price of lager. That is, we shall assume that all the other factors which influence the demand for lager are held constant. This is known as the *ceteris paribus* assumption, and it is a simplifying assumption which we need to make at this stage.

Ceteris paribus ('other things being equal') demand varies inversely with price – that is, when the price goes up the quantity demanded goes down. An example of this is shown in Fig. 2.1. Figure 2.1 illustrates a hypothetical *demand schedule*, or *demand function*, or *demand curve* (which may often be a straight line). The units of measurement of the axes are for illustrative purposes only. At a price of 70p a pint, market demand will be 1 million barrels per month. At a lower price of 50p, the quantity demanded will increase to 2.5 million barrels. Thus, the demand function shows the relationship between the quantity demanded and price. It is important to emphasise, however, that the demand curve such as that shown in

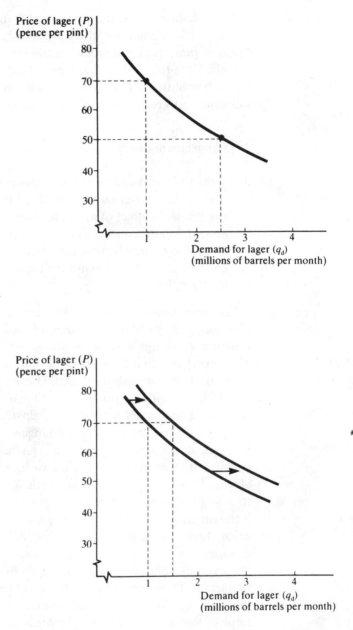

Figure 2.1

Figure 2.2

Fig. 2.1 is drawn on the assumption that all the other factors influencing demand are held constant (the *ceteris paribus* assumption). If these other factors are not constant (*ceteris non paribus*) then the demand curve will shift. For example, consider the probable effect of an increase in the price of whisky. Since whisky, in some situations, is a substitute for lager, this will cause some people to increase their demand for lager while reducing their demand for whisky. This is illustrated in Fig. 2.2.

The whole curve shifts to the right, indicating that, at each price, more will be demanded than previously. For example, at a price of 70p per pint, market demand increases from 1 million to 1.5 million barrels. Note that in Fig. 2.2 demand has increased because the whole curve has shifted. Thus we can see that the phrase 'an increase in demand' can mean one of two things depending on the context. Either:

1. a *movement along* the demand curve as a result of a drop in price, or
2. a *shift* of the demand curve to the right as a result of a change in one of the non-price factors. For example, we mentioned earlier the probable effect of an increase in the price of whisky. This, we argued, would cause a drop in the demand for whisky (movement along the demand curve for whisky) which, in turn, would cause an increase in the demand for lager (demand curve for lager shifts to the right).

You therefore need to be alert whenever the phrase 'an increase (decrease) in demand' is encountered. Either of these two very different meanings may be implied.

2.2 Demand and elasticity

The knowledge that the demand for lager will fall if the price goes up is not in itself particularly useful. However, it might be quite useful to know the *extent* of any fall in demand consequent upon a price increase. Economists use the term *elasticity* to describe the degree of sensitivity of demand to price changes.

Elastic demand

If a small increase in price causes a large fall in the quantity demanded, then demand is said to be sensitive to price changes or *elastic*. Similarly, if demand is elastic a small drop in price will result in a large increase in demand.

Inelastic demand

If the quantity demanded changes very little as a result of a change in price, then demand is said to be *inelastic* or insensitive to price changes.

Unit elasticity

If a given percentage fall in price leads to an equal percentage increase in demand then demand is said to be of *unit elasticity*. For example, if the demand for a particular commodity is of unit elasticity this implies that a 3 per cent rise in price will lead to a 3 per cent fall in demand.

Elasticity can be defined as:

$$e = \frac{\text{percentage change in quantity demanded}}{\text{percentage change in price}}$$

Its value (ignoring the sign, which will always be negative) varies between zero and infinity, as Table 2.1 illustrates.

Table 2.1 Elasticity definitions

Value of e	Description	Meaning
Less than one	Inelastic	Demand fairly insensitive to price changes
One	Unit elasticity	Demand changes by the same percentage as the change in price
Greater than one	Elastic	Demand sensitive to price changes

The concept of elasticity is an essential part of the economist's analytical apparatus – his bag of tools, as it were. The measure of elasticity we have just defined is, in fact, only one of a number of differing elasticities. The concept of elasticity just refers to the degree of sensitivity of one variable to another – in this case the degree of sensitivity of demand to price. In order to distinguish this elasticity from others, it is normally known as the *own-price elasticity of demand*.

2.3 Factors influencing the elasticity of demand

The elasticity of demand for any particular good depends primarily on the availability of substitutes. If close substitutes are readily available then demand will be elastic, implying that a small increase in price will cause many consumers to switch to the substitutes, resulting in a large fall in demand. If there are no close substitutes, on the other hand, demand will be much less elastic, that is, it will be much less sensitive to price changes.

This implies, in terms of the example we considered earlier, that the demand for a particular type of lager will be more elastic than the demand for lager in general. We can illustrate this diagrammatically in Fig. 2.3. The *slope* of the demand curve gives an approximate indication of its elasticity. (This is not strictly true because the scale used for the axes will affect the slope and, as we shall see later on, the elasticity varies at each point on a straight-line demand curve; but it will serve our purposes for the present.) For the moment assume that a steep demand curve indicates inelastic demand (as in Fig. 2.3a) whereas a less steep curve indicates a more elastic demand (Fig. 2.3b). We shall, for the purpose of this example, invent a new brand of lager. Any Scandinavian or Bavarian sounding name will do, so we shall call it 'Kronerbrau'. Hence we compare in Fig. 2.3 the effect of a price increase on the demand for Kronerbrau and the demand for lager generally.

For the purposes of comparison we have indicated the same percentage price increase in both parts of Fig. 2.3.

The demand for Kronerbrau is much more elastic than the demand for lager generally, since other brands are very close substitutes for

Figure 2.3(a) Demand for all lagers (b) Demand for Kronerbrau

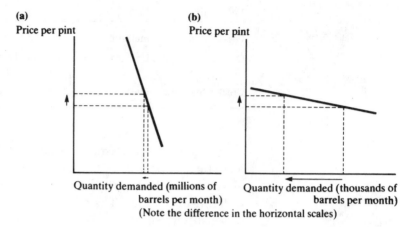

(a)
Price per pint

(b)
Price per pint

Quantity demanded (millions of barrels per month)

Quantity demanded (thousands of barrels per month)

(Note the difference in the horizontal scales)

Kronerbrau. Hence, if the price of Kronerbrau goes up while the price of other brands remains constant (remember, the demand curve is drawn on the *ceteris paribus* assumption), demand for Kronerbrau will drop sharply (Fig. 2.3b). The same percentage price increase applied to all lagers, however, will produce a much smaller percentage drop in demand since there are no close substitutes available (Fig. 2.3a).

2.4 Empirical estimates of price elasticities

Econometrics is the name given to the statistical estimation of economic relationships, such as demand parameters and elasticities. Econometrics involves rather complicated technical procedures – in fact the process of estimating demand elasticities is even more difficult than we suggest in the Technical Appendix to this chapter since there are additional statistical problems which have to be overcome. Econometric techniques have however been developed which allow estimates of demand elasticities to be generated, though these estimates should always be treated with care and used with caution.

One area in which copious amounts of data on consumption levels and prices have been collected is that of food. The Annual Report of the National Food Survey Committee publishes estimates of the price elasticity of demand for certain foods and a selection of these is given in Table 2.2. As one would expect, the demand for foods for which there is no close substitute – bread, milk, sugar – is rather inelastic. For example, a 10 per cent increase in the price of bread would reduce consumption by less than 1 per cent according to this estimate. Consumers are rather more price sensitive however when it comes to things such as cheese and meat, both of which have price elasticities in excess of unity, indicating that in the case of cheese for example a 10 per cent increase in price will reduce demand by 12 per cent. As with any commodity elasticity depends on the availability of substitutes. There are lots of things other than cheese you can put in your sandwiches.

Note also that the demand for convenience products, such as frozen peas, is relatively elastic. Cheaper substitutes exist and price sensitive consumers can be expected to switch to these substitutes when prices rise – and of course to switch back when prices fall. Note finally that not all meat exhibits price-sensitive demand characteristics. The demand for chicken for example is rather inelastic. Chicken perhaps now represents a rather cheap staple source of protein ($e = -0.13$) in contrast to other poultry (duck, pheasant) which is seen as an expensive luxury ($e = -0.85$).

The figures in parentheses in Table 2.2 are the *standard errors* of the parameters. They give an indication of how reliable the estimates are. If the ratio of the parameter estimate to its standard error is more than 1.96 (say roughly 2) then we can be reasonably confident in the estimate. Thus some of the estimates shown in Table 2.2 appear to be rather unreliable, though others appear fairly stable.

2.5 The problem of defining a market: goods and characteristics

Up to now we have glossed over the problems of delineating the market we are studying. The demand for a particular brand of lager is,

Table 2.2 Estimates of the price elasticity of demand for certain foods, (figures in parentheses are standard errors – see text)

Bread	−0.09 (0.18)
Milk	−0.19 (0.19)
Sugar and preserves	−0.24 (0.23)
Fresh potatoes	−0.21 (0.07)
Other fresh vegetables	−0.27 (0.15)
Processed vegetables of which:	−0.54 (0.19)
frozen peas	−1.12 (0.30)
Fruit juices	−0.80 (0.27)
Cheese	−1.20 (0.43)
Carcass meat	−1.37 (0.24)
Other meat and meat products	−0.49 (0.27)
bacon and ham	−0.70 (0.29)
chicken (not free range)	−0.13 (0.27)
other poultry	−0.85 (0.29)
frozen convenience meat and meat products	−0.94 (0.20)

Source: *Annual Report of the National Food Survey Committee*, MAFF, 1989, Table 5.2. These estimates are derived from survey data for the period 1984–89.

of course, part of the demand for lager generally, which, in turn, is part of the overall demand for beer. This much is reasonably obvious. What is less obvious is that lager is sold in two quite distinct situations – firstly in pubs for consumption on the premises and secondly in supermarkets and off-licences for home consumption. These two segments of the lager market are sufficiently distinct for us to be justified in treating them as if they were two separate markets. Ostensibly the product being sold is the same in both situations but this overlooks the point that when people buy things they are expressing a demand for certain characteristics which that good possesses. (This was the insight into consumer behaviour provided by the economist K. Lancaster.)[1] People drink lager in pubs as part of a wider social experience – in other words they go to pubs not just to drink but also to meet their friends, to make new contacts, and so on. When they buy drinks in a pub they are purchasing all these attributes or characteristics. When they buy lager in a supermarket they are purchasing different characteristics since the product will be consumed in a different set of circumstances, even though the product itself may be the same wherever it is purchased.

This has important implications. We could argue for example that the elasticity of demand for lager sold in pubs may be different from, and probably lower than, the elasticity of demand for lager sold in supermarkets. In other words, people are more aware of, and more responsive to prices when those prices are prominently displayed, as in a supermarket. This in itself might tend to increase the elasticity of demand for supermarket lager above that of pub lager. Moreover, the decision to buy drinks in a pub may be taken when one has already 'had a few' which may itself influence the consumption decision. In the cold light of the supermarket shelves you might see things in quite a different way. The fundamental point, however, is that when you go to a pub you are expressing a demand for certain characteristics – company, conversation, pleasant surroundings, a chance to make new friends and influence people. These are, in effect, included in the price of the drinks. One's demand for these things (these characteristics) may be much less elastic than the demand for the thirst-quenching properties of beer.

2.6 Characteristics: the demand for ice-cream

An excellent example of the way in which characteristics may delineate distinct market segments is provided by the market for ice-cream. Table 2.3 shows that in the UK the market for ice-cream is dominated by two firms – Wall's and Lyons Maid – who together account for over 50 per cent of the market.

However putting together all ice-cream sales as if they constituted a single market obscures an important truth, namely that there are two distinct market segments. The first is the 'impulse' purchase, where the consumers (often children) buy ice-cream for immediate consumption, usually outside the home. The second is the 'take-home' purchase, where consumers (often parents!) buy ice-cream in bulk from supermarkets to take home and put in their freezer for consumption at some later date. Table 2.4 shows that market shares in these two segments are very different. In the impulse sector the long-established duopoly of Wall's and Lyons Maid accounts for almost 90 per cent of sales. In the take-home market, in contrast, there is much more competition and although Wall's is still clearly the market

Table 2.3 Ice-cream market: manu-facturers' market shares (% of value) 1988

Wall's	42
Lyons Maid	10
Own-label	29
Other brands	19
	100

Source: *Retail Business*, No. 383, January 1990.

leader the largest market share is supplied by the supermarkets' own-label products. (Wall's is a subsidiary of Unilever and Lyons Maid is part of the Allied Lyons group, both major conglomerates.)

Table 2.4 Ice-cream market: manufacturers' shares by sectors (% of value) 1988

	Wrapped impulse	Take home
Wall's	66	30.0
Lyons Maid	23	4.5
Own-label	11	42.5
Other brands	—	23.0
	100	100.0

Source: as for Table 2.3.

Clearly the product being purchased once it reaches the mouth of the consumer is the same whether it is purchased on impulse or from the supermarket. The circumstances surrounding its purchase – and ultimate consumption – are very different however. Prices are much lower for take-home products reflecting differences in the elasticity of demand.

2.7 Income elasticity of demand

Up to now our discussion has been conducted within the *ceteris paribus* assumption – that is, we have assumed that the other factors which influence demand have been held constant. We now turn to a consideration of the non-price factors which influence demand.

The responsiveness of demand to changes in income is known as the income elasticity of demand. The formula is

$$e_y = \frac{\text{percentage change in quantity demanded}}{\text{percentage change in income}}$$

The value of the income elasticity of demand (e_y) can be either positive or negative or zero. If a rise in income results in a fall in the quantity demanded (e_y negative) then the good in question is termed an *inferior* good. Classic textbook examples of inferior goods are such things as black-and-white television sets, white bread and holidays in Southend. Actually there is nothing wrong with Southend (apart from the fact that the tide goes out rather a long way) but the argument runs that the result of an increase in income will be to make people buy fewer rather than more holidays in Southend as their increased affluence allows them to switch to higher-priced substitutes (for example, holidays in Spain). Most goods are *non-inferior* – that is, the income elasticity of demand is positive, implying that an increase in income leads to an increase in demand.

Table 2.5 Estimates of the income elasticity of demand for certain foods (1989)

Liquid whole milk	−0.40 (0.05)
Margarine	−0.44 (0.09)
Potatoes	−0.48 (0.07)
Sugar and preserves	−0.54 (0.08)
Bread	−0.25 (0.03)
Cakes and biscuits	0.02 (0.5)
Tea	−0.56 (0.09)
Instant coffee	0.23 (0.09)
Cheese	0.19 (0.06)
of which:	
natural	0.22 (0.06)
processed	−0.12 (0.15)
Fruit juices	0.94 (0.08)
Yoghurt	0.58 (0.08)
Fresh vegetables other than potatoes and green vegetables	0.35 (0.04)

Source: as for Table 2.2. Figures in parentheses are standard errors.

Table 2.5 gives some empirical estimates of the income elasticity of demand for a number of different foods. Some foods are inferior in the sense that as income rises consumers switch to a superior product. All the staples – milk, fats, potatoes, sugar and so on – exhibit this characteristic. Similarly processed cheese is inferior but natural cheese is not. As income rises consumers buy less of the cheaper processed cheese and more of the superior more expensive natural cheese.

Note that the demand for bread has a negative income elasticity but the demand for cakes is normal, in the sense that its income elasticity is positive. This points up how out of touch Marie Antoinette was when told that the poor people of Paris had no bread. She replied: 'Qu'ils mangent de la brioche' (Let them eat cake) – a somewhat insensitive remark.

Note finally, that more affluent middle-class households tend to consume more 'healthy' foods like yoghurt and fresh vegetables whereas lower income households, like the poor people of Paris, fill their bellies with bread and margarine and chips, washed down with a mug of tea, while the middle classes sip their cup of Nescafé.

It is important to note that the *income* elasticities shown in Table 2.5 measure something quite different from the price elasticities of Table 2.2. Price elasticities show the responsiveness of demand to changes in *price*. Income elasticities show the responsiveness to changes in *income*. Price elasticities are always negative. Income elasticities can be positive, negative or zero.

2.8 Cross-price elasticity of demand

The demand for some goods is sensitive to changes in the price of other goods. For example, the price of holidays in Spain will affect the demand for holidays in Greece, Italy and the UK. Such goods are clearly substitutes. The cross-price elasticity of demand measures the responsiveness of demand to changes in the price of other goods. The formula is

$$e_x = \frac{\text{percentage change in the quantity of good A demanded}}{\text{percentage change in the price of good B}}$$

Table 2.6 Estimates of cross-price elasticities

Cross-price elasticity of demand for	With respect to the price of	
Beef and veal	Mutton and lamb	0.13 (0.10)
Beef and veal	Pork	0.03 (0.10)
Apples	Pears	0.01 (0.06)
Pears	Apples	0.08 (0.34)
Butter	Bread	−0.22 (0.10)

Source: as for Table 2.2 except for the estimate relating to bread and butter which is taken from the 1980 Report. Estimates for later years have failed to find statistically significant estimates of the coefficients both for substitutes and complements. All the 1989 estimates shown in this table are statistically not significant, as judged by the standard errors shown in parentheses.

Pairs of goods which are *substitutes* have a positive cross-price elasticity of demand. As one would expect, and as can be seen from Table 2.6, the demand for beef is sensitive to changes in the price of other meats – if the price of mutton rises by 10 per cent then the demand for beef will rise by about 1 per cent.

Some other pairs of goods have a cross-price elasticity of demand which is negative. Such goods are termed *complements* or *complementary goods*. Examples of complementary goods are video recorders and video tapes (if the price of video recorders goes down the demand for video tapes will go up) and, as can be seen from Table 2.6, bread and butter.

2.9 Technical Appendix: Estimating the elasticity of demand

Economics cannot proceed very far unless it can make *quantitative* predictions based on empirical estimates of parameters such as demand elasticities. For example, it is not very useful to be told that if the price of milk goes up then the demand will go down. However, a prediction that the demand for milk will drop by, say, 5 per cent following a 10 per cent increase in price is a very useful piece of information, always provided of course that it is more or less correct.

To make such a prediction, however, it is necessary to have an (accurate) estimate of the price elasticity of demand for milk, derived from data which records consumers' responses to changes in the price of milk in the past. Obtaining reliable estimates of such elasticities is by no means a straightforward task. What we shall do here is to illustrate how such estimates could, in principle, be derived, glossing over some of the more intractable problems which are beyond the scope of this book.

As the reader will by now be aware, the elasticity of demand is dependent on the slope of the demand function. Hence we shall discuss initially the way in which the demand function is estimated. Suppose you wish to estimate the elasticity of demand for Kronerbrau, and that you have available information from previous months on the sales of Kronerbrau (q_d) which were achieved at a number of different prices (P). This information is given in Table 2.7 and the same information plotted in Fig. 2.4. As you can see, there is a clear tendency for demand to increase as price falls, that is, there is an

Table 2.7 Price/quantity of Kronerbrau

Price per pint (P)	Quantity demanded (q_d) (thousands of barrels per month)
65	120
55	150
51	200
45	210

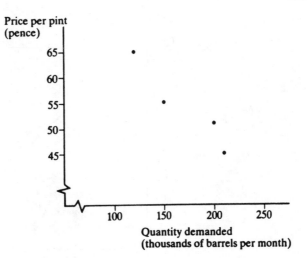

Figure 2.4

inverse relationship between price and quantity demanded.

We argued above that demand will depend on price plus a number of other factors. That is:

$$q_d = f(P,P_s,P_c,Y,T) \qquad [2.1]$$

We will therefore have to assume that all these other factors were constant during the period to which our data relate if we are to estimate the relationship between demand and price. The simplest form of such a relationship is a straight-line demand 'curve' of the form

$$q = a - bP \qquad [2.2]$$

where a and b are known as the *parameters* of the equation. It would be nice if we could straightforwardly translate equation [2.2] into a

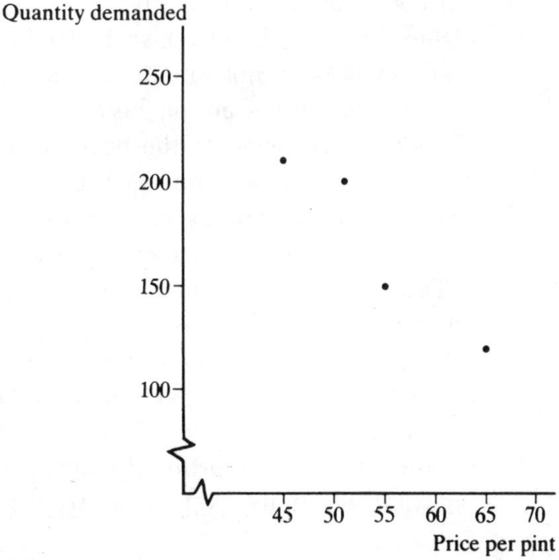

Quantity demanded

250 —

200 —

150 —

100 —

45 50 55 60 65 70

Price per pint

Figure 2.5

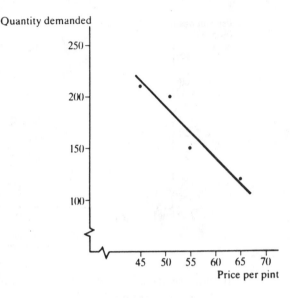

Figure 2.6

line on a graph in Fig. 2.4. To do this, however, it is preferable to rotate Fig. 2.4 through 90° so that price is now plotted on the horizontal axis and quantity on the vertical axis, as in Fig. 2.5.

The reason for this is that when we plot functional relationships it is a convention in mathematics that the *dependent* variable should be measured on the vertical axis and the *independent* variable on the horizontal axis. The quantity demanded depends on (or is a function of) price – hence quantity is the dependent variable and price is the independent variable. It is merely a convention – like driving on the left-hand side of the road in Britain – but Alfred Marshall (1842–1924), one of the founding fathers of modern economics, appears not to have known this. Hence he drew his diagrams the 'wrong' way round as in Fig. 2.4, and since then everyone in economics has followed suit. To be consistent with the way that mathematicians plot functional relationships, however, we shall – in this section only – adopt the mathematical convention as in Fig. 2.5. Thereafter we revert to the normal Marshallian treatment.

To the scatter of points in Fig. 2.5 we can fit a line such as that in Fig. 2.6. The technique used to fit such a line – which we shall not discuss here – is known as regression analysis.

The slope of the estimated demand curve shown in Fig. 2.6 gives us an indication of the elasticity of demand. Consider Fig. 2.7.

The slope of the demand curve q/P shows the ratio of the change in quantity q to the change in price P. This is not quite the same as the elasticity which shows the ratio of the *proportional* change in quantity to the *proportional* change in price. Because of this it turns out that elasticity is in one way a rather inconvenient measure,

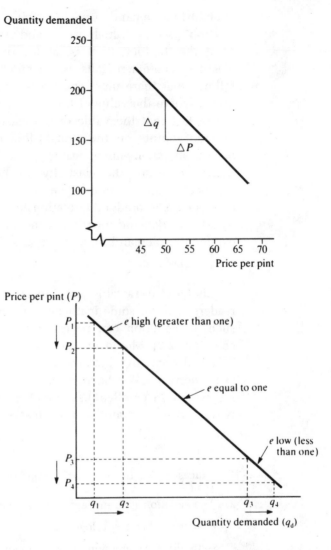

Figure 2.7

Figure 2.8

because the value of the elasticity is different at each point on a straight-line demand curve.

This is illustrated in Fig. 2.8 (where we have reverted to the standard Marshallian treatment). The fall in price from P_1 to P_2 is the same in absolute terms as the fall from P_3 to P_4 and it produces the same absolute increase in quantity demanded. However, when price falls from P_1 to P_2 the *proportional* fall in price is quite small but it produces a large *proportional* increase in demand – hence the elasticity of demand is high.

Conversely, the fall in price from P_3 to P_4 represents a large proportional drop in price but it produces a small proportional increase in demand, hence elasticity here is low. Thus, given a straight-line demand curve, elasticity is high (that is, more than 1) at the 'top' (that is, at high prices) and elasticity is low (that is, less than 1) at the 'bottom' (that is, at low prices). Since the value of the elasticity coefficient falls as we move 'down' the demand curve, it follows that there must come a point, roughly in the middle of the curve, where the value of the coefficient is equal to unity.

The fact that the value of the elasticity coefficient is different at different points on the straight-line demand curve is, as we said before, an inconvenient feature. Clearly we would prefer to have a single value for the elasticity coefficient rather than an infinite number of such values. The way that this problem is normally overcome is to model the relationship between demand and price not by a linear demand function such as that in equation [2.2], but by an exponential demand function such as

$$q_d = aP^b \tag{2.3}$$

This looks intractable (and indeed it may look incomprehensible to readers without some mathematical knowledge) but it turns out that such an equation can be estimated almost as easily as the linear equation [2.2]. Moreover, such an equation has a constant elasticity.[2] This is the way in which the estimates of elasticity in section 2.6 have been derived. We have of course glossed over the problems of estimation. In practice these problems are considerable, so the reader is warned to treat any such estimates with caution.

Notes

1. Lancaster, K., *Introduction to Modern Microeconomics*. Rand McNally, 1974.
2. The equation is 'transformed' by taking logarithms of both sides, thus:

   $$\log q_d = \log a + b \log P$$

   so that linear regression techniques can still be applied. Equation [2.3] has a constant elasticity since

   $$e = -\frac{dq}{dp}\frac{p}{q} = -abp^{b-1}\left(\frac{P}{ap^b}\right) = -b$$

Questions

2.1 In terms of elasticity how would an economist describe the following:

    (a) 'quantity demanded fell very little as a result of a substantial rise in price.'

    (b) 'a large increase in demand resulted from a small reduction in price.'

(c) 'quantity demanded fell by the same percentage as the rise in price.'

2.2 What are the most important factors affecting the elasticity of demand for a product?

2.3 How elastic do you expect the demand for the following goods to be? Give an inspired guess in each case and explain the basis of your guess.

(a) salt   (b) cigarettes   (c) Lambert and Butler King Size cigarettes   (d) first-class letter services

2.4 Why might the demand for coal be more elastic in the long run than in the short run?

2.5 State whether you would expect the cross-price elasticity of demand between the following goods to be positive, negative or zero, and explain why.

(a) margarine and butter   (b) petrol and motor vehicles
(c) coffee and cocoa   (d) motor cycles and motor cycle helmets

2.6 In the last three years sales of natural gas have risen despite an increase in its price. Does this mean that the demand curve for natural gas is upward sloping? How else could you explain the phenomenon?

2.7 On the Friday of each week a petrol-filling station cuts the price of petrol from £2.00 to £1.90 per gallon. Sales on Fridays rise to 1200 gallons per day, which compares with an average of 1000 gallons per day during the rest of the week. Calculate the price elasticity of demand facing the filling station. Give two reasons why this estimate may not be valid.

2.8 After Easter most Easter-eggs remaining unsold in the shops tend to be marked down in price. This is not generally true of Cadbury's Creme Eggs (the small chocolate eggs filled with a sweet glutinous mass which sell for about 20p). Can Lancaster's 'characteristics' approach to demand theory help explain this?

3 Market supply

3.1 Market structures

In the previous chapter we considered the demand side of the market. We now turn to a consideration of the factors influencing the supply of a particular good or service, the so-called supply side of the market.

In a particular market the degree of concentration on the supply side – that is, the number of firms who together make up the market supply – will be an important influence on the behaviour we can expect to find in the market. Consider two extreme cases, on the one hand atomistic or perfect competition and, on the other, monopoly.

3.2 Atomistic competition

The term atomistic competition, or perfect competition, refers to a situation in which the market is supplied by many small firms, no one of whom is large enough to have any influence on prices. That is, each individual firm constitutes such a small proportion of total market supply that it cannot affect the price it receives for its product. If it were to substantially increase or decrease the amount it produces, the effect on total market supply would still be negligible because the firm is but a tiny part – a tiny atom – of the overall market supply. Such a firm is known as a *price taker* because it has no influence on market price but must accept it as a given datum. Such a firm, in effect, faces a demand curve for its product which is perfectly elastic, as in Fig. 3.1. It can sell as much as it likes at the market price, P_m, but any attempt to charge a higher price will result in all the firm's customers switching to a rival supplier. It is worth emphasising that atomistic

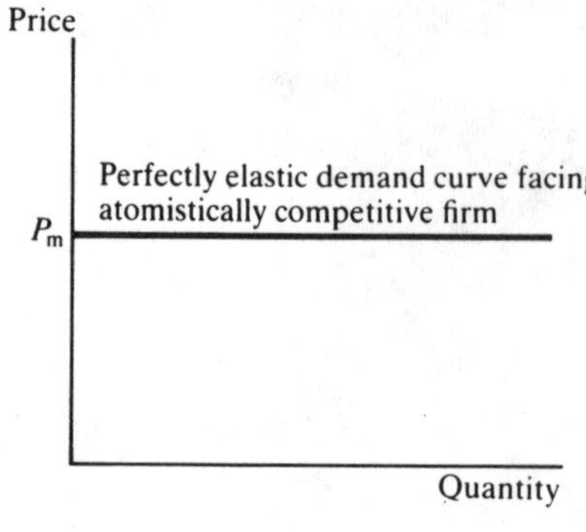

Figure 3.1

competition can only exist in markets where the good or service is *homogeneous* – that is, the output of one seller is indistinguishable from that of other sellers.

This condition is more or less satisfied in the market for some agricultural products. If the requirement that there should be a large number of sellers is also satisfied then we can legitimately describe such markets as being atomistically competitive. A better example, however, is the foreign exchange market where the commodity being traded is foreign currency. This is completely homogeneous (Belgian francs being sold by individual A are indistinguishable from those being sold by individual B) and the multiplicity of traders ensures that none of them can have an appreciable impact on market supply (nor, in this case, an appreciable impact on market demand).

The terms perfect competition and atomistic competition are here used interchangeably. The use of the term 'perfect' is not meant to imply that there is anything particularly meritorious about this form of market structure. It does imply, however, that this represents an extreme case – or polar case. Perfect competition then, is the most unconcentrated form of market structure that can be conceived of. At the opposite extreme, the most highly concentrated form of market is one in which a single firm supplies the entire market for a particular good or service – a monopoly.

3.3 Monopoly

Monopoly literally means 'single seller'. Since the firm is the sole supplier of a particular good the demand curve facing that firm is the market demand curve. The degree of elasticity of this demand curve depends among other things on the extent to which substitutes are available even though, by definition, there are no close substitutes. Thus, for example, British Rail is a monopoly seller of rail transportation services, but substitutes do exist in the form of transport by private car, bus, air, bicycle, and so on. The degree to which one or more of these alternative modes of transport is an acceptable alternative – that is, a close substitute – will determine the elasticity of the demand curve facing British Rail.

Unlike the perfectly competitive firm which is compelled to accept the ruling price as a given datum, the monopolist is a *price maker*. He is free to charge whatever price he likes though he cannot, of course, force consumers to buy at these prices – the higher the price he sets the less will be the market demand – and in determining what price to charge the monopolist will have regard to the elasticity of demand for his product.

The model of perfect competition and that of monopoly may be seen as representing two ends of a spectrum. They are polar cases. Although there are markets in the real world which approximate closely to one or other of these polar cases, most markets exhibit a

3.4 Imperfect competition

degree of concentration which would place them somewhere in between these two extremes. Such market forms are known as imperfect competition (or monopolistic competition) and oligopoly.

An imperfectly competitive market is similar to a perfectly competitive market in that a large number of sellers supply the market. However, unlike the perfectly competitive market where the product is homogeneous, in imperfect competition the output of each firm is differentiated in some way from that of other firms – the product is *heterogeneous*. This is achieved mainly through branding which emphasises in the mind of the consumer the distinguishing characteristics of each firm's product. Thus, for example, soap was at one time sold by weight. It was a homogeneous product in much the same way as salt or sugar are now. In the post-war period, however, soap manufacturers began to differentiate their product from that of rivals by marketing techniques which included distinctive packaging, colour and scent and extensive advertising expenditure designed to accentuate the special characteristics of their product and to promote its brand image. This product differentiation is partly real and partly imaginary. There may be some real differences between the various brands of soap but these differences are not as great as the advertisers would have us believe. Often however the advertising does not emphasise any real distinguishing attributes of the firm's product, since these are minimal anyway. Rather, it seeks to establish in the mind of the consumer a favourable product image by associating it with vitality, luxury or sexual success. 'Use Acme soap and famous film stars will lust after your body.'

Extensive advertising expenditure is a feature of imperfectly competitive markets. It is one of the most important forms of *non-price competition*. Competition by price becomes less of a feature since the product has been rendered non-homogeneous and the fact that it is not sold in standard weights or sizes makes it more difficult for the consumer to compare the value for money he is getting from the various brands.

Imperfectly competitive firms are no longer price takers though the amount of discretion they have in setting prices is not as great as that of the pure monopolist. The demand curve for their product is, however, downward sloping and the elasticity of demand for their product will depend upon how successful they have been in differentiating their product from that of rivals. A successful advertising campaign which convinces consumers that Acme soap (and no other brand) brings vitality, luxury and sexual success will render the demand for Acme soap inelastic since other brands (substitutes) do not have these desirable attributes – at least, not in the mind of the consumer. The important implication of this, of course, is that if the Acme Soap Co. can establish a brand loyalty for its product and thereby render the demand inelastic, it can increase prices without suffering a large drop in demand and can thereby increase its sales revenue and profits.

Such product differentiation through advertising is an important form of non-price competition since it allows firms who are selling what is essentially a homogeneous product to enjoy the same quasi-monopolistic market conditions as those firms selling a heterogeneous product. Examples of successful attempts at product differentiation abound. Unsuccessful attempts are less common but one such is the retailing of petrol. In the early 1960s each of the oil companies attempted to differentiate its product from that of its rivals by extensive advertising suggesting that its brand was superior in terms of power generated and miles per gallon delivered. The introduction in the mid-1960s of the star octane rating system (by which the petrol was graded by a star system corresponding to its octane rating) made it more difficult for the oil companies to pursue these claims so that they abandoned the attempts at product differentiation. The advertising which still goes on is designed to promote the overall image of the oil company rather than directly to promote its particular brand of petrol.

3.5 Oligopoly

In imperfect competition firms are selling similar but differentiated products. Strictly speaking, to be classified as an imperfectly competitive market the number of supplying firms should be large. An oligopolistic market, by contrast, is one in which the number of supplying firms is, by definition, small. (Oligopoly means literally 'a few sellers'). Thus it is a market form in which a few firms supply the entire market for a particular good or service. An extreme form of oligopoly is known as duopoly – that is, just two firms supply the entire market or, at least, the vast bulk of the market. Of necessity oligopolistic firms are large, sometimes very large. Such highly concentrated market structures are common and, in fact, represent the dominant mode of organisation in the manufacturing sector of the economy. The degree of concentration of a particular market can be measured – albeit somewhat imperfectly – by so-called *concentration ratios*. The five-firm concentration ratio, C_5, shows the proportion of the market for a particular good supplied by the five largest firms in the industry. Table 3.1 shows such concentration ratios for seven product groups in Europe.

Before proceeding, we note a number of difficulties associated with the estimation and use of concentration ratios lest the unwary reader be misled into thinking that they provide an unambiguously accurate measure of concentration. Firstly, data on sales are not generally available in the form in which the researcher would like them. He is

Table 3.1 Concentration ratios (C$_5$) (European Community 1986)

	%
Office equipment	65.3
Machine tools	12.5
Electricity	40.4
Motor vehicles	51.0
Textiles, leather, clothing	3.7
Chemicals	41.5
Tobacco	43.7

Source: 'Horizontal Mergers and Competition Policy in the EC', *European Economy*, No. 40, May 1989.

therefore often forced to use data on *employment* (which are more readily available) as a proxy for sales data and the resulting estimates are known as employment concentration ratios. Whether employment or sales are used as the basis for calculation, the choice of the top five firms, rather than three or seven, is essentially arbitrary. The five-firm ratio is however the most widely used. The second problem with concentration ratios is that they relate to sales of *home-produced* goods only. Some of these home-produced goods will be exported. More importantly, some domestic markets will be supplied partly by importing firms. If an attempt is made to take account of such imports, the measured degree of concentration would fall for most industries. It has been argued[1] however, that to do so would produce an unrealistic picture of the extent of competition. The reasons for this are that, firstly, many imports are inputs into domestic production. For example, Ford makes extensive use of imported components in its 'UK produced' cars. Secondly, many imports which are nominally competitive are, in fact, complementary since they are resold by major domestic firms under their own brand name. For example, Vauxhall (a subsidiary of the American firm, General Motors) imports Cavaliers and sells them under the Vauxhall name. These are both features of the activities of multinational companies, a major theme which will be taken up again in a later chapter.

The final caveat that one should note in connection with concentration ratios is that *firm* concentration ratios are not the same as *plant* concentration ratios. For example, a given firm, even though it dominates the market for a particular product, may be supplying that market from a number of small plants rather than from one large one. There may be considerable economies (for example, savings in transport costs) to be gained from multi-plant operation. However the existence of such multi-plant operations significantly weakens the case for the social benefits that are claimed to flow from the existence of large firms with market power.

3.6 Oligopolistic behaviour

Oligopolistic firms enjoy a protected position in much the same way – though not to the same extent – as monopolistic firms. This protection is afforded by barriers to the entry of new firms (commonly called simply *barriers to entry*) which prevent newcomers entering the industry to take for themselves part of the profits enjoyed by oligopolists by virtue of their protected market position. Such entry barriers take a variety of forms. There may be legal barriers – the Post Office for example enjoyed, until recently, a monopoly position protected by law. Alternatively, the barriers may be conferred by sheer size alone – the oil companies, for example, make large profits which are undoubtedly the envy of other firms. These other firms find it difficult to break into the oil business, however, because it is difficult to start small in the oil business. Large amounts of capital and expertise are needed to compete on equal terms with the existing oil companies.

In oil exploration and exploitation the nature of the entry barrier is essentially technical: the technology involved is such that only very large-scale operations can be profitable since the set-up costs involved are large. In other industries, however, low unit costs can be achieved with quite small production. Oligopolistic firms in such industries are potentially vulnerable to attack from outsiders, but such firms have evolved a number of defensive strategies designed to exclude interlopers by the erection of artificial entry barriers. Advertising expenditure is one such barrier to the entry of new firms since any potential entrant cannot penetrate the market unless he is prepared to spend large sums on advertising. Thus, even though there are no technical reasons on the production side to deter new entrants, they are prevented from entering the industry by the high cost of advertising necessary to gain a foothold in the market.

A particularly effective entry barrier is provided by the marketing strategy known as *brand proliferation*. This is practised with particular effectiveness by the tobacco industry. This industry is a duopoly in the sense that just two firms dominate the market – Imperial Group (part of Hanson Trust) and Gallagher (part of American Brands). In the cigarette market in 1989 these firms taken together had 77 per cent of the market with a third firm (Rothmans) having 14 per cent. There is, however, a multiplicity of *brands*, many of which are heavily advertised and promoted through sports sponsorship. Given the multiplicity of brands, a new entrant into the cigarette industry can hope to pick up only a small fraction of brand switchers at any one time, and then only if his new brand is heavily

Table 3.2 Degree of concentration, market structure and characteristics

Perfect *(atomistic)* *competition* (Many sellers)	*Imperfect* *(monopolistic)* *competition* (Several sellers)	*Oligopoly* (A few sellers)	*Monopoly* (One seller)
Example			
Agricultural produce (but marketing boards introduce imperfections	Eggs	Cars	London Transport (but may be in competition with British Rail)
Features			
Homogeneous product	Product differentiated by branding	Differentiated product	Exclusive product
←————— No entry barriers —————→		←————— Entry barriers —————→	
Price taker	←————— Price maker —————→		
	←————— Advertising —————→		
	Additional forms of ←———— non-price competition ————→		

3.7 Summary: aspects of market structure

promoted. Thus new entrants are deterred from attempting to break into the industry.

We have in this chapter considered a number of different aspects of market structure which are summarised in Table 3.2.

The most obvious aspect of market structure is the degree of concentration, but the presence or absence of entry barriers and the degree of product differentiation are also important. These things, then, determine the structure of the industry. The conduct of the firms within the industry will be determined to a large extent by this structure. Thus, for example, in industries of high concentration we would expect to find significant amounts of advertising and other forms of non-price competition. Price competition, if it does occur, will tend to be in industries where the product is homogeneous.

It is important to emphasise at this point that what we have provided is four different *models* of market structure – atomistic competition, monopolistic competition, oligopoly and monopoly. In analysing any particular market situation one should be careful to select the appropriate model with which to analyse the situation. If one considers the market for petrol, for example, then the choice of the appropriate model of market structure will depend upon what aspect of that market we are considering. The major oil companies, once called the Seven Sisters, are clearly oligopolistic. At the retail level, however, since there are many retail outlets – lots of individual filling stations and garages – the market is clearly an imperfectly competitive one. Moreover, we could even argue that since the product being sold is perceived as being homogeneous then the degree of imperfection is slight, that is, the market is almost perfectly competitive. The implication of this is that price competition between garages will tend to result in them all charging the same price, since each garage in effect faces a perfectly elastic demand curve. On the other hand, certain garages may enjoy an element of monopoly by virtue of their geographical location – a garage which is the only one within a 50 miles radius is unlikely to engage in price competition to attract custom.

Notes

1. See: Hart, P. E. and Clarke, R., *Concentration in British Industry 1935–75.* NIESR Occasional Paper 32, 1980, App. 1A; Monopolies and Mergers Commission, 1978, Green Paper, *A Review of Monopolies and Merger Policy*, p. 57.

Questions

3.1 Economists are fond of analysing market situations in terms of models which correspond to certain 'ideal types' – perfect competition, monopoly, oligopoly, imperfect competition and duopoly. Which of the above models would you choose to analyse the following markets?
(a) the market for air-travel
(b) food retailing
(c) the foreign exchange market for sterling
(d) the market for ice-cream (in the UK)
(e) the market for rail transport (in the UK)
(f) tobacco and tobacco products (UK)
(g) the 'rag trade'
(h) oxygen and industrial gases (UK)
(i) the market for germanium (a metal)
(j) fireworks
(k) long-life fruit juices (e.g. 'Just Juice')
(l) eggs

3.2 State which of the following firms are price takers and which are price makers.
(a) a perfectly competitive firm
(b) a monopolist
(c) an oligopolist
(d) an imperfectly competitive firm

3.3 Would a firm operating in a perfectly competitive market be likely to:
   (a) combine with other firms to advertise the industry's product?
   (b) advertise its own product?

3.4 Coca Cola and Pepsi Cola jointly have about 40 per cent of the soft-drinks market. They both spend large amounts on advertising. What form does this advertising take? Why do they not engage in price competition? What is the intended effect (on the elasticity of demand for Coke) of slogans such as 'It's the real thing' and 'Coke is it'?

3.5 Why has the EC sought to introduce common standards for items such as cauliflowers, apples and sausages?

3.6 An oligopolistic firm suspects that if it cuts prices its rivals will follow suit. How will this action on the part of the rivals affect the elasticity of the demand curve facing the firm?
   (a) it will make the firm's demand curve more elastic
   (b) it will make the firm's demand curve less elastic
   (c) it will not affect the elasticity of the firm's demand curve

4 The market price

4.1 The determination of market price

Chapter 2 looked at the demand side of the market. Chapter 3 considered the supply side of the market by looking at those factors affecting the structure of the market for a particular good or service. In this chapter we shall put these two things together to study how prices are determined in competitive markets.

It is possible to conceive of an industry supply curve or market supply curve – in many ways analogous to the market demand curve – such as that in Fig. 4.1.

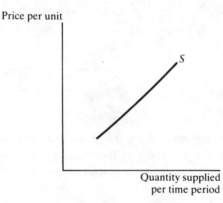

Figure 4.1

Like the market demand curve it is drawn on the *ceteris paribus* assumption and its upward slope illustrates the general proposition that more will be supplied (that is, offered for sale) at higher prices than at lower prices. This makes sense because the higher the price per unit, the easier it will be for firms to make a profit and more firms will be attracted into the industry, thereby expanding industry supply. A point to be emphasised is that supply conditions in any particular market will depend to a large extent on the structure of that market. Initially it will be convenient to think in terms of perfectly competitive markets for here there are no barriers to the entry of new firms. Moreover, in atomistic competition no one firm is large enough to significantly influence market supply. Thus prices are determined

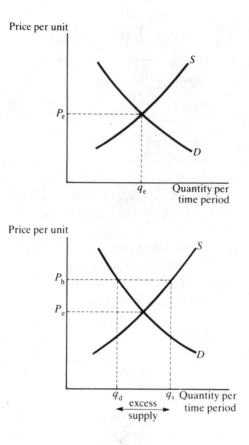

Figure 4.2

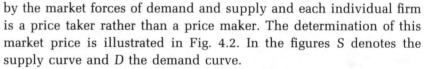

Figure 4.3

by the market forces of demand and supply and each individual firm is a price taker rather than a price maker. The determination of this market price is illustrated in Fig. 4.2. In the figures S denotes the supply curve and D the demand curve.

Price P_e is an equilibrium price in the sense that at this price the amount being offered for sale is exactly equal to the amount consumers are prepared to purchase. This is the *market clearing* price at which there is neither excess demand nor excess supply. In Fig. 4.3, however, at price P_h there is excess supply since the quantity which firms would like to sell (q_s) is greater than the amount consumers are prepared to buy. The existence of this excess supply will tend to depress prices, driving them down towards the market clearing level P_e. Note that there is an automatic tendency for this to happen; that is, in the absence of any factors to prevent it, price will tend to move towards the equilibrium level. Similarly, if there is an excess demand as in Fig. 4.4, the efforts of buyers to secure for themselves the available supply will push up prices towards the equilibrium level where both buyers and sellers are satisfied. Note that as price increases from P_L to P_e two things happen. Firstly, the increase in

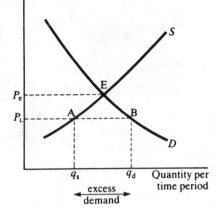

Figure 4.4

price encourages firms to supply more; that is, there is a movement along the supply curve from point *A* to point *E*. Secondly, the increase in price discourages consumers. In effect some purchasers who would have bought at the lower price P_L are not prepared to buy at the higher price P_e. Thus there is a movement along the demand curve from point *B* to *E*.

4.2 Shifts in supply

If we continue to think in terms of perfectly competitive markets we can analyse the effect on market price of shifts in the supply curve. As we shall show in Chapter 5, the industry supply curve will depend upon the costs (both production and selling costs) of the firms in the industry. A reduction in costs will cause the industry supply curve to shift to the right, indicating that more will be supplied than previously at each price. Similarly, an increase in costs causes the supply curve to shift to the left. This is shown in Fig. 4.5 as a shift from curve *S* to curve *S'*. As a result of the shift in supply, excess

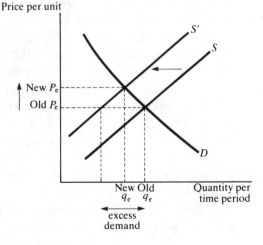

Figure 4.5

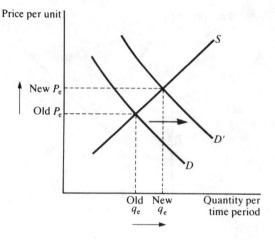

Figure 4.6

demand will emerge at the old equilibrium price and the existence of this excess demand will drive up the price to a new equilibrium.

The quantity traded also falls. Thus the market moves from one equilibrium position (old P_e, old q_e) to a new equilibrium (new P_e, new q_e).

The effect of shifts in demand can be analysed in a similar manner. In Fig. 2.2 we showed that the effect of an increase in the price of a substitute would be to make the demand curve shift to the right. As Fig. 4.6 shows, this will result in an increase in market price and an increase in the quantity traded.

4.3 Elasticity of supply

In section 2.2 we introduced the concept of elasticity – the responsiveness of one variable to changes in another. The own-price elasticity of supply is defined as:

$$e_s = \frac{\text{percentage change in quantity supplied}}{\text{percentage change in price}}$$

If supply is elastic, therefore, this means that a relatively small change in price will result in a relatively large change in the quantity supplied. On the other hand, if supply is inelastic it will be relatively unresponsive to price changes. Obviously, supply elasticities are positive, an increase in price leading to an increase in supply and a fall in price leading to a fall in supply.

4.4 Price in non-competitive markets

Strictly speaking, industry supply curves such as those shown in Figs. 4.1 to 4.6 only make sense in the context of perfectly competitive markets where firms are price takers. In markets where a degree of monopoly exists (that is, in all markets other than perfectly competitive ones) we can no longer talk about market price since prices are set by sellers. We shall use the term *administered price* to distinguish this situation from the competitive situation for which we reserve the term market prices. Administered pricing will be analysed in detail in Chapter 9.

There is, however, a less rigorous and more general sense in which to interpret Figs 4.2 to 4.6. This interpretation is that in all markets, regardless of market structure, the price of a particular good or service will depend upon relative scarcity, that is, how much buyers are prepared to pay relative to how much sellers are prepared to accept. In other words, there exists a market clearing equilibrium price which is determined by demand and supply. This proposition is, in a fundamental sense, correct but it is too general and non-specific to take us very far in analysing real-world situations. Moreover, it tends to obscure certain aspects which may be important features of the real world. For example, price may be administered (as it is in non-competitive markets) and any excess demand or supply may be eliminated by quantity adjustments rather than price adjustments.

We have also ignored the possibility of trading taking place at prices other than equilibrium prices, a possibility we explore in the following section.

4.5 The stability of equilibrium

We have assumed up to this point that equilibrium prices are stable equilibria in the sense that the actual market price automatically tends to move towards the equilibrium price. In certain markets, however, for reasons explained below, prices tend to be rather unstable, oscillating from a high price to a low price but never converging on an equilibrium. The markets for certain agricultural products exhibit this tendency, the market for pig meat being a well-documented example.

The market for pigs is fairly competitive on the supply side, though becoming less so as factory-farming methods become increasingly more common with the decline in the number of producers and the increase in the average size of pig unit. In pig production there is a biologically determined production period of a more or less fixed length which means that supply reacts to price changes only after a time lag. In addition, farmers have historically responded to price information in a rather naive way, not realising that high prices which encourage lots of farmers to move into pig production will, after a certain time lag, lead to a glut of pig meat and hence a slump in pig prices. These two factors can produce cycles in pig prices such as that illustrated in Fig. 4.7.

Suppose the initial equilibrium price of £50 is disturbed by some random shock – perhaps an outbreak of foot-and-mouth disease – which causes the quantity supplied to fall from 4000 to 2500. The price immediately jumps to £60 per pig and this encourages more farmers to move into pig production. After a time lag, supply therefore expands to 5000 but the market will only absorb this amount if prices drop to £40 per pig. This causes some producers to switch away from pig production, and after a time lag output therefore drops to 2500,

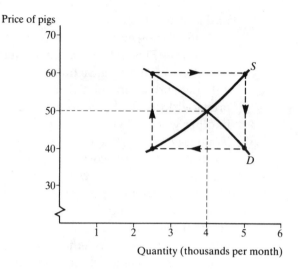

Figure 4.7

4.6 Market prices and administered prices

and the cycle starts all over again.

In competitive markets, where price is determined by the market forces of demand and supply, prices often fluctuate much more than they do in those markets where prices are administered by firms. That is, markets where firms are price makers will exhibit more price stability than markets where firms are price takers.

Compare, for example, the market for cadmium with that for germanium. Both metals are in fact produced as by-products in the production of other metals but supply conditions are very different in the two cases. Cadmium is a by-product of zinc production which is

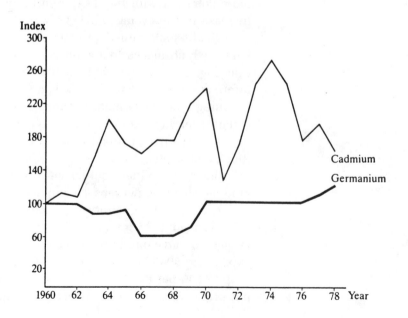

Figure 4.8 Price-relative index for cadmium and germanium (Source: T. Wilkinson 'The economics of mineral byproducts and co-products' *Economics*, Journal of the Economics Association Vol. XIX, Part 3, No. 83, Autumn 1983 p. 85)

fairly widely diffused among a number of firms. Hence the supply of zinc is fairly competitive, with no single producer or group of manufacturers being in a position to control the market. It follows therefore that the market for cadmium is also competitive with each firm being a price taker.

In contrast, the market for germanium is a producer-controlled oligopoly. There are only thirteen producers worldwide, five of whom produced 78 per cent of total world output in 1977/78. The producers of germanium would therefore be in a much better position to control germanium prices than the cadmium producers who would have to accept passively the market prices. Figure 4.8 shows this to be the case. In the competitive industry (cadmium) prices fluctuated in response to changes in demand brought about by changes in worldwide economic activity. In the oligopolistic market (germanium) producers achieved a much greater degree of price stability over the period.

4.7 When is a market not a market?

Why should there be greater price stability in producer-controlled markets than in competitive markets? There are two possible explanations. The first is that in producer-controlled markets the market is brought to equilibrium by movements in quantity rather than by movements in price. That is, producers affect and control the market price by restricting supply when prices are tending to fall and by expanding supply when prices are tending to rise. The second explanation is rather different. This is that in producer-controlled markets there is no such thing as a market price, that is, an equilibrium price determined by the forces of demand supply. The price is simply that determined by the producer. This is clearly the case in monopolistic markets, but the same may also be true for oligopolistic markets, particularly where one producer is a dominant firm within the oligopoly. This possibility is explored in Chapter 9.

Questions

4.1 Consider the market for cocoa beans. What will be the probable effect on equilibrium price and quantity of the following?
(a) a successful advertising campaign for Cadbury's drinking chocolate
(b) a drought in the cocoa-producing areas
(c) an increase in the price of coffee and the introduction of a new high-yield strain of cocoa bean

4.2 For a particular week in June, three families – Smith, Jones and Brown – have the demand schedule for strawberries shown in Table 4.1. Assuming these three families comprise the whole market, calculate the market demand for strawberries and plot it on a graph. On the same graph plot the supply function using the

Table 4.1 Strawberries

Price per punnet	Quantity demanded			Market demand	Quantity supplied	
	Smith	Jones	Brown		A	B
35	3	5	5		8	11
40	3	5	4		9	12
45	2	4	4		10	13
50	1	4	3		15	18
55	0	3	2		20	23

data in column A. What are the equilibrium price and equilibrium quantity?

Now suppose that favourable weather conditions produce a bumper crop. Growers will now be willing to sell more at each of the old prices. This causes a shift of the whole supply function. Plot this new supply function from the data in column B. What are the new equilibrium price and quantity?

4.3 Table 4.2 shows production levels and prices for oilseed rape (used in the production of margarine, etc.)

Table 4.2 Price and output of oilseed rape

	Quantity harvested	Price
1973	31	79
1974	55	172
1975	61	128
1976	111	136
1977	142	162
1978	155	182
1979	198	215
1980	300	230
1981	325	255
1982	581	270
1983	563	310

Source: *Annual Abstract of Statistics 1985*, Tables 9.4 and 18.10.

Consider the validity of the following statements, amending or deleting where necessary.

(a) Over the period the percentage increase in output was much more than the percentage increase in price. Therefore the supply of this commodity is shown to be very inelastic/ elastic.

(b) The easier it is to switch from growing one crop to growing another, the more elastic/inelastic will be the supply.

(c) Any estimate of the elasticity of supply is valid only if we are prepared to accept the assumption of *caveat emptor/ceteris paribus/per ardua ad astra*. In practice other things may not remain the same. For example, the price of cereals and vegetable crops may also have increased.

(d) Switching from wheat production to rape production depends on relative prices/absolute prices – that is, the price of rape relative to the price of wheat.

4.4 House prices in Ealing, West London, as elsewhere, are determined by market forces. What will be the probable effect on house prices of the following? (Assume *ceteris paribus* throughout and explain your answer.)

(a) The Building Societies adopt a more generous attitude to borrowers when granting loans for house purchase.

(b) Mortgage interest tax relief is abolished.

(c) A new motorway is built linking Ealing with Central London.

(d) The local authority relaxes planning restrictions on new housing development.

(e) House prices in Acton (near Ealing) rise.

(f) The cost of building new houses increases.

(g) Banks start to give mortgages for house purchase.

Table 4.3 Potatoes

	Price (£ per tonne)	Land in potato production	Output ('00 000s tonnes)
1973	20.7	224	68
1974	23.6	216	68
1975	56.8	204	45
1976	143.4	222	49
1977	69.9	233	66
1978	40.0	214	73
1979	58.9	204	65
1980	51.2	206	71
1981	63.3	191	62
1982	78.5	192	69
1983	85.5	195	48

Source: *Annual Abstract of Statistics 1985*, HMSO, Tables 9.3, 9.4, and 8.10.

4.5 Table 4.3 shows for the UK the price per tonne of potatoes, the amount of land devoted to potato production and the annual output of potatoes. Consider the extent to which the data for the mid-1970s shows evidence of a 'cobweb' type reaction in this market, similar to the pig cycle in section 4.5.

5 Costs

5.1 Cost concepts

'Costs', as one of my colleagues once remarked, 'is difficult'. Despite the seemingly ungrammatical nature of this remark, it illustrates that what is apparently an unambiguous and straightforward concept turns out to be much less straightforward on closer examination. To take a simple example: say one wished to know the cost of driving from London to Birmingham in order to make a comparison with the cost of doing the same journey by train. The total cost of car ownership can be broken down into three main headings:

1. *Variable costs*: that is, those costs which are directly related to distance travelled, in this case petrol and oil.
2. *Fixed costs*: those costs which are incurred whether the car is used or not, in this case insurance premiums, road tax and the depreciation in the value of the car that occurs solely on account of its ageing.
3. *Semi-fixed costs* (or semi-variable costs): the depreciation that occurs in the value of the car by virtue of use rather than ageing, for example, tyre and brake pad wear, engine wear and general mechanical deterioration.

In practice it may be quite difficult to measure what we have called semi-fixed costs and to distinguish them from truly fixed costs since the market value (that is, the second-hand value) of a car is determined almost exclusively by age rather than by distance travelled.

What then is the cost of driving from London to Birmingham? If we assume that you already have a car and a current driving licence, then there are essentially two ways of looking at the cost of such a journey. One could argue in a certain context that the only cost that should be taken into consideration is the variable cost, that is, the cost of petrol, since the other costs (fixed costs) would be borne anyway whether or not you drove to Birmingham. The extra cost that is incurred as a result of the trip (that is, the cost of 4 gallons of petrol, or whatever) is called the *marginal cost* of making the trip. It is the increase in the total costs of car ownership which results from making the journey.

On the other hand, one could argue, in a different context, that the real cost of driving from London to Birmingham is seriously underestimated if one only takes into account the marginal cost of the journey. If, for example, one is contemplating buying a car in order to make this journey every week for a year, and one wishes to compare the annual cost of travelling by car with the annual cost of doing the same number of journeys by train then, for a valid comparison to be made, the cost of travelling by car should include some, if not all, of the fixed costs. Since these fixed costs constitute a substantial part of the total cost of car ownership this will clearly materially affect one's assessment of the relative cost of travelling by car as opposed to rail. In this context the relevant cost is not the marginal cost but rather the average cost of doing the journey, that is, the total annual cost divided by the number of journeys.

Clearly, therefore, the context in which one is assessing the costs will determine what should be included and what should be excluded. The first context we considered – in which the fixed costs would be borne irrespective of whether the car was used for the trip or not – we will term the *short-run* context. The short run, in economics, is defined as a situation in which there are fixed factors. In this case, the car is a fixed factor. On the other hand, the second context we considered in which one was contemplating the purchase of a car in order to make repeated journeys, we will call the *long-run* context because here there are no fixed factors.

It is very important to note that the terms 'long run' and 'short run' do not refer to time periods. They refer only to the fixity or non-fixity of factors. The long run can, in fact, be extremely short in terms of time. Consider the situation where you are contemplating making a single trip to Birmingham but you do not own a car. The cost of driving to Birmingham then is the cost of petrol plus the cost of hiring a car for a day. Is this a short-run or a long-run context? Well, in terms of our definition (which is the standard definition) this is a long-run context because there are no fixed factors. In this long-run context, however, the marginal cost of the trip will be much higher than it would have been if you already owned a car – that is, the long-run marginal cost will be much higher than the short-run marginal cost.

The concept of marginal cost (along with similar concepts such as marginal revenue) is central to traditional neo-classical analysis, yet, initially it can be a difficult concept to grasp. Marginal cost is the increase in total cost which results from the additional activity being considered. It is not the same as variable cost (though it is similar). Nor is it the same as short-run cost because the short run is a *context* within which various cost concepts are considered. We shall go on in

Table 5.1 Cost concepts

Context	Example	Relevant cost	Features
Short run	Single trip to Birmingham (already owns car)	Extra cost incurred, i.e. marginal cost. Short-run marginal cost is cost of petrol	Fixed factor, i.e. the car
Long run	Weekly trip to Birmingham for one year	Average cost over 12 months, i.e. total cost divided by number of trips	No fixed factors, i.e. can decide whether or not to buy car and, if so, what type
Long run	Single trip to Birmingham (but has to hire car)	Extra cost incurred, i.e. marginal cost. LRMC more than SRMC	Defined as being a long-run situation because there are no fixed factors
Very long run	Repeated trips to Birmingham (but has to learn to drive first)	Average cost	All factors variable including 'technology' (that is, the skill with which you use those factors). When you have done it once it becomes easier to repeat it. 'Learning effect'

section 5.2 to explain the concept more formally. Table 5.1 may also help to summarise what we have said so far.

Note that for the sake of completeness we have included in Table 5.1 yet another context in which we could assess costs. This we call the *very long run*. Here there are no fixed factors but more importantly *technology* is also variable. 'Technology' is the skill with which you use those factors. Without straining the analogy too much it could, for example, correspond to a situation in which one has neither car nor driving licence, yet one is contemplating the cost of repeated trips by car as opposed to rail. A valid comparison would therefore have to take account of the additional cost of acquiring a driving licence. Once this has been acquired, however, we move from a very long-run context to a different context. This is known as a 'learning effect' and will be explained in section 5.6. In sections 5.2, 5.3 and 5.4 we shall look at cost in a short-run context. In section 5.5 we move to the long run and in section 5.6 we consider learning effects.

5.2 The variation of costs with output in the short run: the special case

What we shall do initially is to describe a special case to illustrate how unit costs (average costs) may vary as output varies in the short run. In the following section we explain the technical relationship between the various cost concepts and then, in section 5.4, consider a more usual example of how unit costs vary with output in the short run.

The special case is taken from the shipping industry and the context we shall consider is a short-run context in which the only variable factor is the amount of fuel used. The rate at which fuel is burnt, of course, determines how fast the ship steams. All other factors – depreciation of the vessel, insurance, crew's wages, and so on – are fixed. So these are fixed costs which remain the same regardless of the speed at which the ship steams. The faster the ship steams therefore, the more these fixed costs can be spread. The 'output' being produced in this example is a service – transportation of cargo. Output is measured in tonne-kilometres transported and one unit of output is one tonne of cargo transported one kilometre. If the ship steams faster it will therefore be increasing output since it will cover a greater distance in a given time. Since this allows the fixed costs to be spread more thinly, we can say that average total costs (or unit costs) are falling as output increases. This explains the downward sloping part of the average total cost curve, shown in Fig. 5.1.

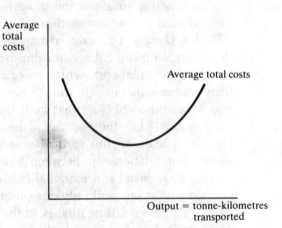

Figure 5.1

However, Fig. 5.1 shows that average total costs do not decline continuously as output increases. Rather, they begin to level off after a certain while and then start to increase. That is, in this special case, the short-run average total cost curve is U-shaped. The reason why average costs start to increase beyond a certain point is that the speed of the ship is not linearly related to the amount of fuel used. For example, steaming at 14 knots requires more than twice as much fuel as steaming at 7 knots. In fact there is a sort of 'cube law' governing the relationship between speed and fuel used: the fuel used is proportional to the cube of the speed,

$$F = kS^3$$

A similar physical law applies to the speed at which a car is driven and the amount of fuel used: driving at 80 mph takes more than twice as much petrol as driving at 40 mph, and the reasons are similar in both cases. Water resistance (in the case of the ship) and wind resistance (in the case of the car) is related to speed in a non-linear fashion.

This explains why, beyond a certain point, average costs start to increase as shown in Fig. 5.1. At fairly low speeds the increased fuel cost resulting from faster steaming is more than offset by the cost reduction resulting from spreading the fixed costs more thinly. Thus, as output increases, average total cost falls. However, because of the 'cube law' alluded to above, at higher speeds the increased fuel costs resulting from faster steaming more than outweigh the benefits of spreading fixed costs. The resultant short-run average total cost curve is U-shaped.

5.3 The technical relationship between average cost and marginal cost

This section illustrates graphically the relationship between the various cost concepts. Though useful, it is not essential to an understanding of subsequent sections and could be omitted by those readers wishing to avoid the more technical aspects of the subject. They should proceed to section 5.5.

With a U-shaped average cost curve such as that shown in Fig. 5.1 there exists a technical relationship between total costs, average total costs and marginal costs which owes more to the laws of mathematics than to economic laws (if, indeed, there be any). This is illustrated in Figs 5.2a and 5.2b. Note that both figures have the same horizontal scale (output) but the vertical scales are different. We have put an (arbitrary) scale on the vertical axes to emphasise this. Figure 5.2a shows the relationship between average costs (SRATC: short-run average total costs) and marginal cost (MC). Marginal cost is equal to average cost at one and only one point, namely where average cost is neither rising nor falling (that is, at the bottom of the U-shaped curve). The marginal cost curve cuts the average cost curve from below at its lowest point.

To appreciate why this should be so, consider an analogous example, namely that of a football team whose average height is six foot. If an extra player comes along (the marginal player) whose height is 6 ft 1 in. then the average height of the twelve players must rise. Thus if marginal is greater than average then average is rising. Similarly, if the new player is only 5 ft 11 in. then the average height of the team will fall. Thus, if marginal is less than average then

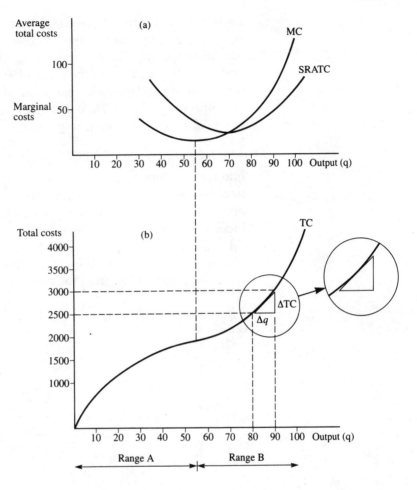

Figure 5.2 (a) and (b)

average is falling.

By looking at this in reverse it is clear that if the average is falling then marginal must be less than average and if the average is rising then marginal must be greater than average. As with the football team, so with the cost curves shown in Fig. 5.2a. And, of course, if the extra player's height is exactly 6 ft then the average height of the team will not change (that is, marginal and average are equal when the average is not changing).

Figure 5.2b shows how total costs (TC) rise as output rises. The slope of the total cost curve in fact measures marginal cost. To see why this should be so, consider what happens as output rises from 80 to 90 units. (This change in output is marked as Δq on the inset diagram.) As can be seen, costs rise by 500 ($\Delta TC = 500$). Thus:

$$\Delta TC = 500 \quad \Delta q = 10$$

This is the change in total costs that results from producing 10 more units of output. Strictly speaking, marginal cost is the change in total costs that results when output increases by a very small amount. As the inset in Fig. 5.2b emphasises, $\Delta TC/\Delta q$ only measures this approximately since with the slope of TC changing the triangle is only tangent to the TC curve at one point. If we make Δq small, however (say one unit), then ΔTC will be 50. That is, at this level of output marginal cost is approximately equal to 50 (as can be seen from Fig. 5.2a).

We have drawn Fig. 5.2 so that the slope of TC (that is, MC) falls into two distinct regions. In range A (up to about 55 units of output) total cost is increasing at a decreasing rate (that is, the slope of TC is decreasing). Hence MC is decreasing. In range B the slope of TC is increasing; hence MC is increasing.

Finally consider Figs 5.3a and b. This is identical to the previous Figure except that here we highlight the relationship between TC and ATC. Note that the ray from the origin is tangent to the TC curve at an

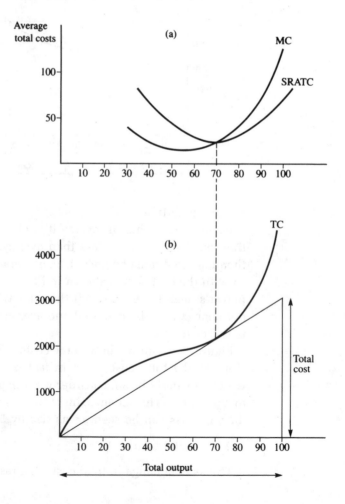

Figure 5.3 (a) and (b)

output level of 70 units. This corresponds with the level of output where SRATC is at a minimum. The slope of the ray is of course equal to average cost (TC/q) as can be seen.

5.4 The variation of costs with output in the short run: the normal case

In section 5.2 we showed how the short run average cost curve would be U-shaped. We emphasized, however, that this was a special case. A more normal short run situation would be one in which average costs stay constant over a range of output before eventually starting to increase. This is illustrated in Fig. 5.4.

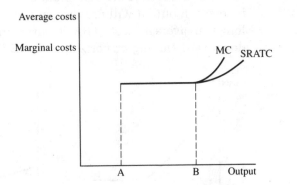

Figure 5.4

Given the relationship between average cost and marginal cost explained in section 5.3, it follows that if average cost is constant then it will equal marginal cost, that is, between output levels A and B marginal cost and average cost are the same, as illustrated in Fig. 5.4.

At output levels beyond B, average costs are shown to rise. The reason for this is that we are illustrating a short-run situation, that is, one in which there are fixed factors of production. It is obvious that if more and more units of the variable factor are applied in a situation in which other factors are fixed then, eventually, the returns to this variable factor will start to diminish. Take for example the manufacture of a particular product, where the fixed factors can be considered as the floor space in the factory and the machines within it, and the variable factor can be considered to be the amount of labour employed. If the amount of labour employed increases there is some scope for increasing output without increasing unit costs. Beyond a certain level of output, however, average costs will start to rise because the combination of factors (labour, machines, floor space) is non-optimal. In practice the range of output over which short-run average costs are constant may be quite small because many production processes are characterised by *fixed factor proportions*. For example, say a capstan lathe requires a single operator. The employment of a second operator to take over when the first has a break would probably raise output a little but would add a lot to the costs. Thus average costs would rise sharply. Obviously, with a given technology, in this situation only one combination of factors is sensible (one operative to each machine).

The short-run situation is in fact a very restricted context. In general, the long-run context in which the number and type of machines, the number of men and even the size and number of factories can be varied is a more valid and interesting context in which to investigate the variation of costs with output. This is discussed in the following section.

5.5 The variation of costs with output in the long run

Once all the factors are variable there is no reason to suppose that an increase in output will produce an increase in average costs. Thus the long-run average cost (LRAC) curve in most industries would be downward sloping or horizontal, as in Fig. 5.5.

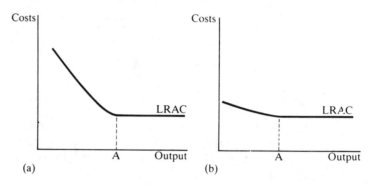

Figure 5.5 (a) and (b)

If increased output results in lower unit costs, we say that there are *economies of scale*. Scale economies, or *returns to scale*, are almost universally present. For example, to build a double garage is not twice as expensive as building a single garage. Running a double-decker bus is cheaper than running two single deckers. Two can live as cheaply as one (almost). It may be, however, that beyond a certain level of output all the benefits of economies of scale have been reaped. Beyond this point the long-run average cost curve becomes horizontal. Figure 5.5 illustrates a situation in which there are economies of scale up to point A. Beyond point A there are constant returns to scale.

The levels of output labelled A in Fig. 5.5 would be called the *minimum efficient scale* (MES) or *minimum efficient plant size* (MEPS) because firms or plants operating below this level of output are too small to reap all the benefits of economies of scale. One should be careful to distinguish between firm size and plant size, since a large firm may, for example, operate a number of small production units. Firm size in itself may confer benefits but these tend to be *financial* economies of scale rather than *technical* economies of scale. For example, by virtue of its size, the large firm may be able to borrow more cheaply or buy its raw materials more cheaply because its buying power enables it to exert influence over suppliers. Unlike technical economies, which benefit society as a whole, these financial

Table 5.2 Minimum efficient plant size

Industry	MEPS as % of UK output	MEPS as % of EC output	% increase in costs at one-third of MEPS
Oil refining	14	2.6	4
Integrated steel plants	72	9.8	>10
Bricks	1	0.2	25
Cement	10	1.0	26
Petro-chemicals	23	2.8	19
Paint	7	2	4.4
Nylon/acrylic	4	1	9.5–12
Ball-bearings	20	2	8–10
Cylinder blocks	3	0.3	10
TV sets	40	9	—
Washing machines	57	10	7.5
Marine diesels	30	5	8
Beer	12	3	5
Cigarettes	24	6	2.2

Note: the last column, the percentage increase in costs, shows the cost penalty suffered by a plant whose size is only one-third of the MEPS (except for bricks, nylon, cylinder blocks and diesels where the size of the hypothetical plant is one-half of the MEPS).

Source: C. F. Pratten, *Costs of Non-Europe* Vol. 2, 1989, European Commission. This is a collection of estimates brought together by Pratten. Some of the estimates can be regarded as more reliable than others.

economies benefit the firm at the expense of other sections of society. Whereas technical economies of scale may provide a valid justification for the existence of large firms, often with monopoly power, financial economies do not.

Estimates of the MEPS are available for a number of industries and these are shown in Table 5.2. These are so-called 'engineering type' estimates since they attempt to estimate costs which could be achieved in plants of various sizes using the best technology currently available. Note from Table 5.2 that in some industries, for example bricks, the MEPS is quite small, or rather it is a relatively small proportion of the total UK produced sales (only 1 per cent of UK sales). In other industries however, the MEPS is a large proportion of UK produced sales. In steelmaking for example, the MEPS represented over 70 per cent of total UK produced sales.

In assessing the benefits of large size, one must take into account not only the estimated MEPS but also the cost penalty incurred from operating below this MEPS. For example, any firm operating in an industry with the cost conditions illustrated in Fig. 5.5a would be at a clear disadvantage if its plant size were less than that producing output level A. In Fig. 5.5b however, although the MEPS is the same, the cost penalty for operating below it is minimal.

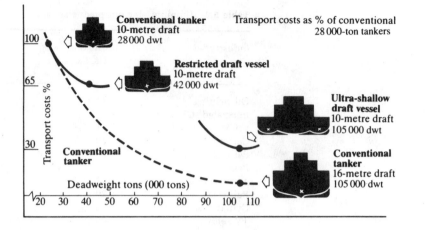

Figure 5.6 Transport costs as percentage of conventional 28 000 ton tankers (Source: *The Economist*, 20 February 1982)

Table 5.2 also gives an estimate of the cost penalty suffered by a firm operating below the MEPS. In some cases this cost penalty is small (for example in cigarette manufacture). In other cases it is much larger (for example, in the manufacture of cement).

There may be some instances in which MES is so large that it may be difficult to operate at such a scale. An example of this is provided by the tanker industry. Other things being equal, the larger the tanker, the lower the unit costs of transporting crude oil. This is illustrated in Fig. 5.6, where the dotted line shows the LRAC curve of conventional tankers. Unfortunately, when conventional tankers become very large their increased draught prevents them from entering shallow ports and this tends to restrict their usefulness.

As can be seen from Fig. 5.6, a compromise solution is the proposed ultra-shallow draft vessel (USDV) which is as large as a conventional supertanker but being much wider has a smaller draught. The costs per ton of oil transported of such a vessel would be higher than a conventional supertanker but much lower than conventional small tankers, and it would be able to enter ports previously restricted to small vessels.

Diseconomies of scale: Chiefs and Indians

Most of the empirical evidence supports the proposition that unit costs fall as output rises. However, it is popularly believed by people who work in organisations that the number of administrators responsible for running the organisation seems to increase at a much faster rate than the number of people actually carrying out the tasks for which the organisation was established. That is, there is a natural law of organisations which states that the larger the organisation the greater the number of Chiefs relative to the number of Indians. If this were indeed the case this would be some sort of evidence for the existence of diseconomies of scale.

Table 5.3 presents some evidence from UK manufacturing industry.

Table 5.3 Number of Chiefs per Indian, by firm size

Firm size (employment)	Managers per operative
1– 99	0.39
100– 199	0.42
200– 299	0.43
300– 399	0.44
400– 499	0.50
500– 749	0.47
750– 999	0.51
1000–1499	0.51
1500–1999	0.60
2000–2499	0.59
2500–2999	0.67
3000–3999	0.51
4000–4999	0.56
above 5000	0.62

The ratio 'managers per operative' shows the number of administrative, technical and clerical employees per operative.

Firm size relates to firms rather than plants, except that where a business engages in a number of separate manufacturing activities these are treated as separate businesses.

Source: derived from *Business Monitor*, PA 1002, 1988, Table 6. The nomenclature 'operative' is that used in the *Business Monitor*.

What it seems to show is that as firm size increases the number of administrative, technical and clerical employees increases relative to the number of operatives. That is, the firm becomes top heavy.

It is of course possible that there is some alternative explanation for this empirical finding. It could be for example that the ratio of managers to operatives depends on the sub-sector of manufacturing that is being considered. However, the evidence from the *Business Monitor* suggests that even within a particular sub-sector the ratio increases as firm size increases.

5.6 Learning effects

Large firms may have significant cost advantages over small firms not just because of the current scale of their activities, but also because of the accumulated experience they have in a particular industry. This experience can only be gained by operating in the industry and it gives rise to what is known as *learning by doing*. Such learning effects produce cost savings, the magnitude of which is well documented in a number of studies. So-called learning curves have been drawn up for a number of different industries and three examples are shown in Figs. 5.7, 5.8, and 5.9.

Note that unlike the LRAC curves of Figs 5.4 and 5.5 which measure the current scale of output on the horizontal axis, the learning curves

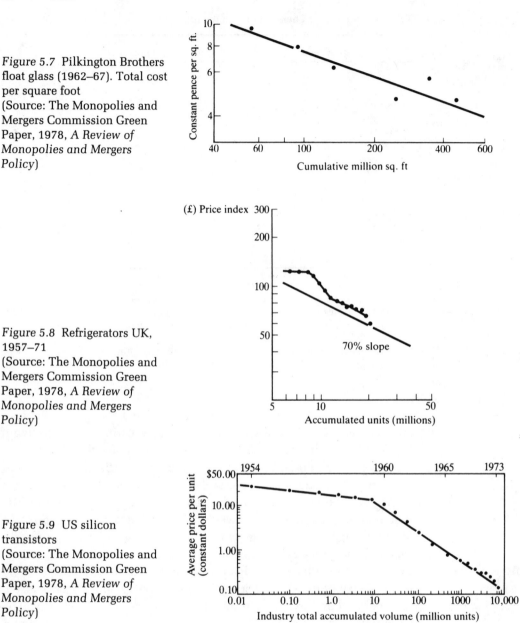

Figure 5.7 Pilkington Brothers float glass (1962–67). Total cost per square foot
(Source: The Monopolies and Mergers Commission Green Paper, 1978, *A Review of Monopolies and Mergers Policy*)

Figure 5.8 Refrigerators UK, 1957–71
(Source: The Monopolies and Mergers Commission Green Paper, 1978, *A Review of Monopolies and Mergers Policy*)

Figure 5.9 US silicon transistors
(Source: The Monopolies and Mergers Commission Green Paper, 1978, *A Review of Monopolies and Mergers Policy*)

of Figs 5.7, 5.8, and 5.9 relate unit cost to *accumulated* output.

Accumulated experience and scale tend to go hand in hand of course, the one reinforcing the other so that large firms have a cost advantage by virtue of the large scale of their plants, but the ability to design and run such plants in a cost-effective way only comes with experience. Figure 5.10 shows the combined effects of scale and experience in the manufacture of a plastic resin. The learning effect is

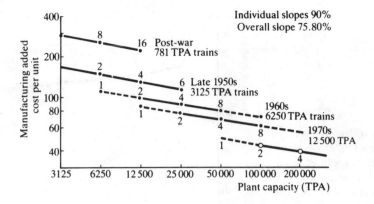

Figure 5.10 Scale evolution over time – A plastic resin (Source: The Monopolies and Mergers Commission Green Paper, 1978, *A Review of Monopolies and Mergers Policy*)

embodied in the acquired technology necessary to construct and run larger plants.

Figure 5.10 is very much a hybrid. It illustrates the short-run, the long-run and the very long-run contexts which we considered at the beginning of this chapter. At any particular time, for example in the late 1950s, with a given plant size we are in a short-run situation since we have a fixed factor (the size of the plant). Even with a given plant size, however (for example, the 3125 TPA trains typical in the late 1950s), cost reductions can be achieved by operating the plant at a higher level of capacity utilisation (each of the short-run average cost curves is downward sloping). However, for a given plant capacity (measured along the bottom axis), for example, 12 500 TPA, experience enables it to be run more efficiently. For example, the four firms operating plants of this size in the 1950s had average costs of 140p per unit whereas the single firm operating a plant of this size in the 1970s had average costs of 90p per unit. This is the effect of learning. Learning also enables bigger plants to be built, and this is the effect of scale.

5.7 A case study on costs: the motor industry

Some of the cost concepts we have introduced in this chapter will be illustrated in this section in the context of the motor industry, both in Britain and Europe and worldwide. The data are drawn from a variety of sources but the reader should be reminded that data on costs are no more reliable – and in some cases may be less reliable – than data in the social sciences generally. It is not so much the case that, as Disraeli claimed, 'there are lies, damned lies and statistics'; rather the reader should try to develop respect for the data, a respect which is only gained by careful consideration of how the data involved could have been collected and what they are intended to show. For example, many studies of minimum efficient plant size cite the pioneering but now somewhat dated work of Pratten whose estimates of the variation of costs with output were of the 'engineering' type. That is, they were not based on the costs of plants actually in existence but, rather, they

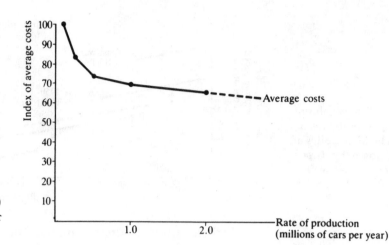

Figure 5.11
(Sources: Cost data derived
from Pratten's (1971) estimate
cited by D. G. Rhys in P. S.
Johnson *The Structure of
British Industry*. Granada 1980
and Rhys in *Economics* Winter
1988 Vol. xxiv Part 4 No. 104)

were based on the estimates of engineers, skilled in their particular field, of the costs of operating plants of various sizes. Figure 5.11 shows the cost advantages enjoyed by the larger firms in the motor industry. As can be seen, severe costs penalties would be incurred by firms producing less than 500 000 units per year. A firm producing only 100 000 units for example, would have average costs some 25 per cent higher than one producing 500 000 units. Beyond this level however the advantages of large scale production are not so marked.

Table 5.4 shows the output levels achieved by the major car makers in the 1980s. As can be seen Rover, the only British volume car manufacturer, operates on a scale where it cannot achieve the full benefit of large scale production. It is awkwardly placed between the true volume manufacturers like Ford and Fiat and the luxury car manufacturers like Saab and Rolls Royce whose value-added originates from their exclusivity.

However, the total number of cars produced by a particular manufacturer may be a poor indicator of the potential for scale economies. The number of units of any particular model and the extent to which common components can be fitted to a number of different models should also be taken into account. This is because the volume required to achieve the potential cost reductions varies considerably from one operation to another, as Table 5.5 illustrates.

Note particularly from Table 5.5 that the MES for some operations is very much larger than it is for others. In final assembly for example minimum costs are achieved at an output level of only 250 000 units a year but in the casting of the engine block an output level of four times this much is required to minimise unit costs – a full one million units per year. This helps to explain why manufacturers choose to use common components (engines, gearboxes) across a range of cars and why manufacturers may buy in major components from other

Table 5.4 Worldwide car output of selected manufacturers (thousands of units per year. Representative figures for the 1980s)

General Motors	4800
Ford	3000
Toyota	2700
Nissan	2100
Renault	2000
Volkswagen-Seat	2400
Peugeot-Citroën	1800
Fiat	1700
Chrysler	1400
Honda	1000
Toyo Kogyo	850
Lada	800
Mitsubishi	600
Daimler Benz	550
BMW	450
Rover	**400**
Volvo	400
Alfa Romeo	200
Saab	110
Jaguar	50
Rolls Royce	3

Source: G. Rhys, 'Economics of the motor industry', *Economics*, Journal of the Economics Association Vol. XXIV, Part 4, No. 104, Winter 1988, p. 162.

Table 5.5 Minimum efficient scale (MES) of different manufacturing operations

Manufacturing operation	MES (units per plant per year, thousands)
Casting of engine block	1000
Casting of various other parts	100–750
Power train (engine, transmission) machining and assembly	600
Pressing of various panels	1000–2000
Paint shop	250
Final assembly	250

Source: as for Table 5.3, p. 161.

manufacturers (Rover for example uses Volkswagen gearboxes in its Maestro range).

Note also that the MES in the pressing of body panels seems to be very large indeed – one to two million units per year. This helps explain why even very large manufacturers like Ford of Europe produce only four basic models – Fiesta, Escort, Sierra and Granada, even though there may be numerous variations to trim levels and engine capacities for each of these basic models.

It is worth considering the impact of the 'new technology' on the motor industry. This technology consists basically of replacing labour by intelligent robots. Some authors have argued that this is a flexible technology which lends itself well to small scale production, effectively lowering the MES and enabling medium size producers to operate as efficiently as very large ones. However the latest estimates by Garyl Rhys, on whose work Table 5.5 is based, suggest the opposite. Earlier estimates cited in the first edition of this textbook gave an MES for the casting of engine blocks of 100 000 units per year. Latest estimates suggest a figure ten times larger – one million units. The same seems to be true for other aspects of production. New technology appears to raise rather than lower the MES.

Table **5.6** MES. Non-technical economies of scale minimum output of the firm required to achieve minimum average costs (thousands of units per year)

Advertising	1000
Sales	2000
Risks	1800
Finance	2500
Research and Development	5000

Source: G. Rhys, 'Economics of the motor industry', *Economics*, Journal of the Economics Association Vol. XXIV, Part 4, No. 104, Winter 1988, p. 161.

Finally note that there are non-technical economies of scale in car production. These of course are to do with firm size rather than plant size. Estimates are given in Table 5.6. Note in particular that the MES is huge when R & D expenditures are considered – a full five million units. This suggests that companies like Rover are hugely uncompetitive when it comes to developing new models, which explains of course why they choose to embark on joint ventures with companies such as Honda. In future it is likely that no new models will be developed by Rover which do not feature some collaboration with other manufacturers. Many collaborative ventures already exist among the world's car makers. These are shown in Fig. 5.12 together with some of the equity holdings which certain car makers have in other car makers.

Costs in the short run

The discussion so far has been about minimum efficient scale. That is, in terms of the nomenclature we introduced earlier, it has been about costs in the long run. However in the short run, costs also vary

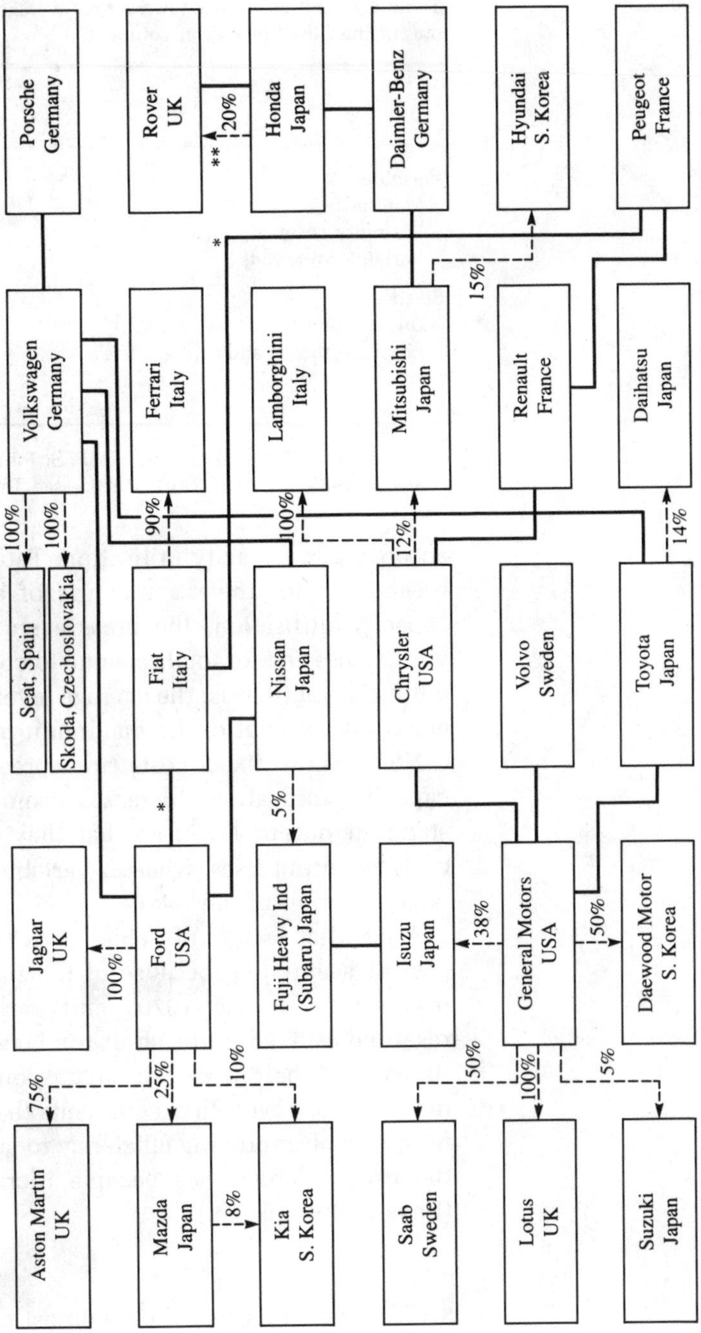

Figure 5.12 Principal links between car makers (solid lines) and equity stakes (dotted lines)

(Source: *The Economist*, 24 February 1990)

*Commercial vehicles

** Rover also owns 20% of Honda's British manufacturing operations

Table 5.7 Unit cost breakdown for an average car (standard output is a higher level of output than the break-even volume)

	At break-even volume (%)	At standard output (%)
Variable		
Materials	53	62
Warranty costs	2	4
Variable overheads	7	10
Fixed		
Direct labour	12	8
Fixed overheads and capital costs	26	16
	100	100

Source: derived from D. G. Rhys in P. S. Johnson, *The Structure of British Industry*, Granada, 1980 and from Rhys (1988) – see Table 5.4.

according to capacity utilisation. Table 5.7 gives estimates of the cost breakdown for the manufacture of an average car at two levels of capacity utilisation, the break-even volume (that is, the minimum volume needed for total revenue to cover total costs) and the 'standard output' level (that is, the average level of capacity utilisation, which is about 80 per cent of the maximum possible).

Notice how fixed costs are spread more thinly as the level of capacity utilisation increases from the break-even level to the standard output level, so that they constitute a smaller fraction of costs as output rises, whereas variable costs like materials constitute a larger fraction of the total.

A peculiar feature of Table 5.7 is the treatment of labour as a fixed cost. It seems that because of the impact of employment protection legalisation in the 1970s and early 1980s labour costs became regarded as fixed in the short run because firms were reluctant to vary the size of their workforce in response to short-term fluctuations in demand. However Rhys comments that 'as the 1980s unfolded and the necessity of improving efficiency to survive became more pressing, so the use of labour has become increasingly "variable" once again' (Rhys (1988) op. cit.).

Questions

5.1 A firm finds that the total cost of producing 1000 units is £400. The cost of producing 1001 units is £405. Therefore marginal cost at this level of output is:

(a) £1   (b) £5   (c) £405   (d) £1000

5.2 If British Rail is running half-empty trains, what is the marginal cost of carrying extra passengers?

5.3 Which of the diagrams in Fig. 5.13 are logically incorrect?

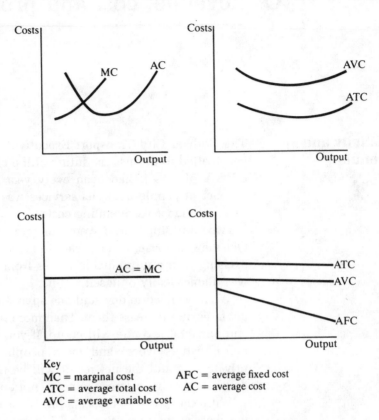

Key
MC = marginal cost   AFC = average fixed cost
ATC = average total cost   AC = average cost
AVC = average variable cost

Figure 5.13

5.4 Give examples of the following types of scale economy:
(a) technical   (b) financial   (c) managerial
(d) marketing and research and development   (e) risk bearing.
Which of the above do not represent real savings of resources from society's point of view?

5.5 A seaside hotel has fixed costs of £1000 per month. During the winter it makes a loss since in addition to its fixed costs it has variable costs (heating, lighting, staffing, food) of £5000 per month, whereas its revenue from guests is only £5100 per month. Should the hotel close during the winter?

6 Revenue, cost and profit

6.1 Elasticity and revenue

The Gotham City Transport Executive was worried. A meeting had been called to discuss the future of the city bus service which was in crisis again, as it had been every year for the past few years. The number of people using its services was dwindling and it was again unable to meet its operating costs.

Two opposing views were emerging in the Transport Executive. One view advocated an increase in fares, possibly accompanied by the excising of the unprofitable routes from the system. The other view was diametrically opposed to this.

'What we need to do,' said one advocate of the opposing view, 'is to *cut* fares, not increase them. Then more people will use the City buses and our total revenue will go up. If you raise fares again it will only make matters worse and more people will switch to using their private cars and the net result will be that our fare receipts will go down. It's a cut in fares we need, not an increase.'

'With the greatest respect, Mr Chairman,' said one of the other members of the Executive, 'that is complete and utter nonsense. If we cut fares the numbers of extra passengers we shall attract onto the system will be minimal. Since all the existing passengers will be paying less than before the net result will be a fall in our revenue. Anyway, people like using their cars. It's more convenient so that even if the bus were cheaper they would still use their cars.'

'Rubbish,' said the first speaker. 'For most journeys the bus is a perfectly acceptable substitute. I say cut fares and increase revenue.'

At that very moment Batman and Robin arrived in the nick of time to prevent the members of the executive coming to blows.

'Well, Caped Crusader,' said the chairman of the executive, 'What's the answer? If we want to increase our revenue should we cut fares or increase them?'

'It depends,' said Batman, 'on the elasticity of demand.' If demand for bus services is inelastic, he went on to explain, this means that it is insensitive to price changes so that an increase in fares will result in only a small drop in demand. Hence total fare receipts will rise. If,

Table 6.1 Variation of revenue with price

q	P	TR	MR
0	40	0	
1	36	36	36
2	32	64	28
3	28	84	20
4	24	96	12
5	20	100	4
6	16	96	−4
7	12	84	−12
8	8	64	−20
9	4	36	−28
10	0	0	−36

q = quantity, P = price, TR = Total revenue, MR =
marginal revenue.

on the other hand, demand is elastic, an increase in fares will cause
lots of people to switch to their cars and total fare receipts will fall.

This can be illustrated with a numerical example. Table 6.1 shows
the number of passengers (q) who would be prepared to travel at each
of the flat fares (P). The data from Table 6.1 are plotted in Fig.6.1. As
can be seen, if the bus service was free (P = 0) then the number of
passengers who would use it would be ten (that is, ten thousand
passengers per day). At the other extreme, a flat fare of 40p (P = 40)
chokes off demand completely (q = 0). From the data given in
columns 1 and 2 of Table 6.1 we can work out the total fare receipts

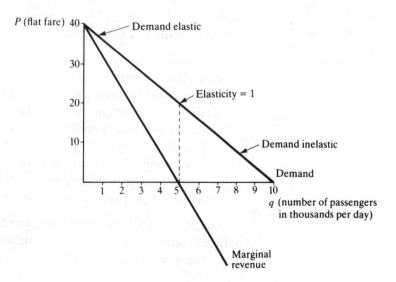

Figure 6.1

(total revenue) which will accrue at each price. This is shown in column 3. As can be seen, revenue is maximised at a price of 20p, where the number of passengers will be 5000 per day. This corresponds, not coincidentally, to a point half-way down the demand curve shown in Fig.6.1 where elasticity is equal to unity.

This can be further illustrated by considering the *marginal* revenue that results when output is increased. Marginal revenue is a concept similar to the concept of marginal cost introduced in section 5.1. It measures the change in total revenue when output is increased by a small amount (in our example this small amount is one unit of one thousand passengers). As can be seen, marginal revenue declines as output increases but as long as marginal revenue is positive this means that the increase in output has increased total revenue. As soon as marginal revenue becomes negative, however, this means that the increased output results in a reduction of total revenue. The data in column 4 of Table 6.1 are also plotted in Fig. 6.1 and they trace out the marginal revenue curve. As can be seen, the marginal revenue curve cuts the 'quantity' axis at $q = 5$. At this point, marginal revenue is zero. This point on the marginal revenue curve corresponds to a point on the demand curve where price is equal to 20. This, as we saw before, is the point at which revenue is maximised.

It is worth noting a few technical details illustrated by our numerical example. Firstly, marginal revenue measures the change in revenue when output changes by a small amount. Hence, for example, we have shown marginal revenue to be equal to 36 when output increases from 0 to 1 and this can be read off from the graph (MR = 36 when output = 1/2). Secondly, note that the marginal revenue curve cuts the quantity axis half-way along from where the demand curve cuts the axis. This is not an accidental occurrence but results from the mathematical relationship between the two curves.

Summarising the main points:

1. If marginal revenue is positive this implies that demand is elastic and that therefore a cut in price will lead to a more than proportional increase in demand, thus increasing total revenue.
2. If marginal revenue is negative this implies that demand is inelastic and that therefore a cut in price will lead to a less than proportional increase in demand, thus decreasing total revenue.
3. Where marginal revenue is zero, elasticity is equal to unity. At this point revenue is maximised since a change in price will lead to an equal proportionate change in demand.

Thus, a firm wishing to increase, or maximise, its sales revenue has only to estimate the elasticity of demand for its product and then apply the simple rules set out above. Unfortunately, when we leave

Gotham City and return to the real world we have to recognise that the problem of estimating the elasticity of demand may be inordinately difficult, for reasons sketched out in section 2.9. Often an indication of the elasticity of demand can only be obtained by trial-and-error experimentation. This yields an estimate after the event which, had it been available before the event, would probably have led the firm not to undertake the experiment. For example, in 1981 London Transport cut fares on its bus and underground services by 30 per cent, anticipating that this would lead to a sizeable increase in traffic (measured by passenger-miles). However, traffic increased by only 11.5 per cent, leading to the eventual abandonment of the policy.[1]

In practice, of course, the demand curve would not be defined over its entire range as it is in Fig. 6.1. Rather an estimate of the demand curve (and hence of its elasticity) may be available for only a small range of price/output combinations near to the existing price/output combination.

6.2 Elasticity in the short run and the long run

It is worth noting that the elasticity of demand in the short run may be less than that in the long run. Note that here we are using the terms 'short run' and 'long run' to refer to periods of time rather than to situations in which there are fixed factors (short run) or in which all factors are variable (long run). In a sense, however, the two definitions run together, that is, the elasticity of demand for a particular good tends to be low in the short run (time period) because of the existence of fixed factors; and higher in the long run (time period) because there are no fixed factors. Consider, for example, the elasticity of demand for petrol. An increase in price will lead to only a small drop in demand initially (that is, the elasticity of demand is low in the short run) because people's consumption patterns are to a large extent determined by their own particular circumstances. For example, if they live a long distance from their work and no public transport is available they will have no alternative but to drive to work, at least in the short run, because of the existence of the fixed factors – location of home and job and type of car. In the long run, however, they could get another job nearer their home, or move nearer to their work, or buy a smaller, more fuel-efficient car. In the still longer run of course the increased demand for fuel economy in cars will result in manufacturers developing more fuel-efficient vehicles, thereby further reducing the demand for petrol. Thus, in the long run, the elasticity of demand for petrol is higher than in the short run.

Estimates of such elasticities are of course difficult to obtain in practice because other factors have a nasty habit of not remaining constant. The demand for petrol will obviously be affected by income so that, over time, if incomes rise this will induce a rise in the demand for petrol which will partially or totally offset the effect of the

Table 6.2 Elasticities of demand for petrol in the EEC

Short run	Price	−0.23
(1 year)	Income	0.53
Long run	Price	−0.75
	Income	1.73

Source: G. J. Kouris, 'Price sensitivity of petrol consumption and some policy implications', *Energy Policy*, Vol. 6 No. 3, September 1978.

price increase. Statistical techniques are, however, available which can separate out the effects of a price change from the effects of an income change. Thus, estimates of both price and income elasticities for both the short run and long run can be obtained. One such set of estimates is shown in Table 6.2.

Note that, as one might expect, the demand for petrol is rather unresponsive to price changes in the short run, but rather more responsive in the long run. Even in the long run, however, demand is still price inelastic – a 10 per cent increase in price will lead to a fall in demand of only 7.5 per cent.

6.3 Profit maximisation

In section 6.1 we showed how a firm would maximise its sales revenue. However, most firms take account not only of the revenue to be gained from a certain level of output but also of the costs of producing that output. Thus profit, which is the difference between revenue and costs, will be an important consideration. In this section we shall illustrate the rule that should be applied by the firm wishing to maximise profits.

In Fig. 6.2 we take the example of a firm facing a downward-sloping demand curve for its product (that is, any firm other than a perfectly competitive firm). The associated marginal revenue curve is also

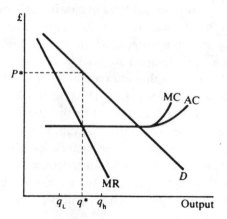

Figure 6.2

shown (the relationship between the demand curve and the marginal revenue curve was explained in section 6.1). We have assumed that the cost conditions facing the firm are such that average costs remain constant over a wide range of output. Thus the average cost curve is shown as being horizontal over the relevant output levels. It is important to note that this implies that marginal cost will also be constant and equal to average cost over this same range (for reasons explained in section 5.3).

A firm facing these demand and cost conditions has to decide two things – how much to produce and what price to charge, but the two decisions are not independent. Once the level of output has been determined, the maximum price the market will be prepared to pay to take up this level of output will be determined by demand conditions, as summarised in the demand curve facing the firm.

First the firm decides on the profit-maximising level of output. This is q^* in Fig. 6.2. At this level of output marginal cost equals marginal revenue. The reason why this level of output should yield maximum profit can be demonstrated by considering other possible output levels – a lower level of output (q_L) and a higher level of output (q_h). At q_L marginal revenue is greater than marginal cost (the MR curve is above the MC curve). This means that, if one considers a small increase in output, the resultant increase in revenue (MR) will be more than the resultant increase in cost (MC). Since revenue is increasing more than costs, profit must also be increasing. The same must be true for all levels of output below q^* – an increase in output adds more to revenue than to costs, hence increasing profits. For similar reasons, at levels of output greater than q^*, such as q_h, the opposite is true. MC is above MR, hence a reduction in output reduces costs more than it reduces revenue, and hence profits increase. Thus q^* is the profit-maximising level of output.

Having decided on the level of output, the profit-maximising firm

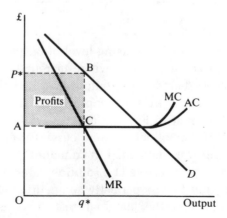

Figure 6.3

then charges the maximum price per unit that the market will bear. This is given by the demand curve and is labelled P^*.

Figure 6.3 illustrates the amount of profits achieved by such a firm. Profits are the difference between total revenue and total costs. The rectangle OP^*Bq^* represents total revenue since it is the price per unit (OP^*) multiplied by the number of units sold (Oq^*). Total costs are represented by the rectangle $OACq^*$ since this is the average cost per unit (OA) multiplied by the number of units sold (Oq^*). The difference between the two – the shaded rectangle AP^*BC thus represents profits.

6.4 Profit maximisation in perfect competition (short run)

Unlike the monopolist and the monopolistically competitive firm, the perfectly competitive firm faces a demand curve for its product which is perfectly elastic – that is, a horizontal line. The perfectly competitive firm is a price taker. It can sell as much as it likes at the prevailing market price. This means it can sell additional units without reducing the price on all units sold. Thus marginal revenue and price are the same thing. In Fig. 6.4 therefore we show the demand curve facing the competitive firm and label it to indicate that it is equal to price, marginal revenue and, also, average revenue.

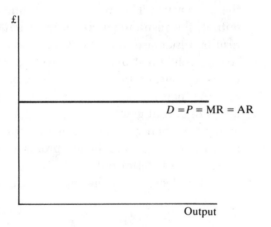

Figure 6.4

The profit-maximising level of output for the perfectly competitive firm, like any firm, is where marginal cost and marginal revenue are equated. This level of output is only defined therefore if the marginal cost curve is upward sloping since a horizontal marginal cost curve such as that in Figs 6.2 and 6.3 would have no point of intersection with the marginal revenue curve (or an infinite number of points if MC and MR happened to coincide).

In order to arrive at a solution value for the profit-maximising level of output for the perfectly competitive firm we will therefore have to assume that the marginal cost curve is upward sloping. In effect,

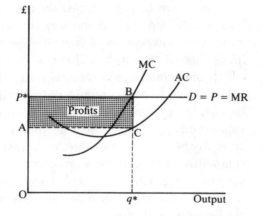

Figure 6.5

therefore, we are considering a short-run (fixed factor) context such as that of section 5.2. In such a context a U-shaped short run average total cost curve implies that marginal cost will eventually start to rise as in Fig. 6.5. The profit-maximising level of output – the level of output where marginal cost equals marginal revenue – is again labelled $q*$. As before, the level of profits is AP*BC since this is the difference between total revenue (OP*Bq*) and total costs (OACq*). (Re-read the relevant parts of section 6.3 if you are unsure of the reasoning behind this.)

6.5 Super-normal profits and the entry of new firms

In Fig. 6.5 the level of output labelled $q*$ is an equilibrium level in the sense that there will be no tendency for it to change. It is important to emphasise, however, that it is short-run equilibrium in two senses of the term 'short run'. Firstly, it is short-run in the sense that there are fixed factors of production. Secondly it is short-run in the sense that the existence of these 'profits' can only be a transient phenomenon. The reason for this is that these 'profits' are above average, that is, they are *super-normal profits*. This, in turn, is due to the fact that the costs we have been talking about include a normal return to capital. In other words, part of the legitimate costs of the firm, from the economist's point of view, is the return which the capital tied up in the firm could earn in an alternative use. Economists call this the *opportunity cost* or *transfer price* of capital. For example, if the amount of capital tied up in the firm is, say, £10 000, then any evaluation of the firm's costs should include the interest that could be gained by investing this sum of money in some alternative way – for example, by purchasing government securities or other securities which yield a relatively riskless return.

In this respect the economist's treatment of costs may differ from that of the accountant. For example, if a firm is owned by an individual who has invested his own capital in the firm there will be no monetary cost attached to the use of that capital. He will not, for example, have to pay interest on money he has borrowed since no loan is involved. This is the way that accountants treat cost. For the economist, however, even though there is no monetary cost involved in the use of the capital, there is an opportunity cost – the return which the capital could otherwise earn in the best alternative use.

Therefore, since economic costs include the opportunity cost of capital, the profits shown in Figs 6.3 and 6.5 should be regarded as super-normal profits – that is, profits in excess of those that can currently be earned elsewhere, in similar risk industries. In a perfectly competitive market these super-normal profits can only be short-lived because their existence will encourage other firms to enter the industry. This will cause an expansion of market supply, and the market price will drop. This process, in theory, will continue until all the super-normal profits have been eliminated by the entry of new firms. This is illustrated in Fig. 6.6. Industry supply increases from S to S′ with the entry of new firms, and equilibrium market price thus falls from P_1 to P_2. Each firm in perfect competition takes the market price as a given datum and equates marginal cost to marginal revenue in order to maximise profits (or minimise losses). When market price has been driven down to P_2 an individual firm's most profitable level of output will be q_2^*.

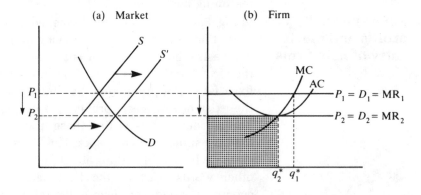

Figure 6.6 (a) and (b)

The shaded area represents both total costs and total revenue: thus there are no super-normal profits. Thus, Fig. 6.6b shows a competitive firm in equilibrium when all super-normal profits have been eliminated. This is sometimes called a *post-entry equilibrium*, that is, the equilibrium that results after new firms have entered the market to earn for themselves some of the super-normal profits. It could also be termed a long-run equilibrium where the term 'long run' refers to the absence of super-normal profits. Thus we have yet another interpretation of the terms 'long run' and 'short run'. We now have three different definitions of the terms short run and long run, and they are summarised in Table 6.3.

Table 6.3 Summary – short run and long run

As applied to	Short run	Long run
Time period	Less than 1 year or whatever arbitrary cut-off is chosen	More than 1 year
Costs	Fixed factors	All factors variable
Equilibrium	Presence of SNP (also called 'pre-entry' equilibrium)	Absence of SNP (also called 'post-entry' equilibrium)

SNP = super-normal profits.

6.6 The elusive long-run equilibrium

To recap, the profit-maximising level of output, q^*, shown in Fig. 6.5, is a short-run equilibrium level of output both in the sense that it exists in a short-run (fixed factor) context and also in the sense that it gives rise to super-normal profits, the existence of which triggers off responses from other firms which will eventually undermine this equilibrium, that is, change it from an equilibrium to a disequilibrium position. What of the long-run equilibrium position? Like the pot of gold at the end of the rainbow, the long-run equilibrium position does not exist. From a certain spot you can see the rainbow but you can never reach the crock of gold. The reason for this is not the ephemeral nature of the rainbow but that it only exists when viewed from afar. Close to, it vanishes. The same applies to the 'long run' in economics. From a particular short-run perspective you can contemplate the long run, but when you arrive at what you thought was the long run you find you are in another short-run position. You are always in the short run in the sense that the factors you are using are fixed at that particular point in time. You can change these factors but in so doing you do not move to the long run; you merely move to another short-run position.

Consider the example of a farmer producing, say, oil-seed rape, the raw material of margarine and other foods. If he is a profit maximiser he will expand production up to the point where the cost of the last tonne produced equals the market price. With a given area under cultivation (that is, in the short run) this is a profit-maximising equilibrium level of output. If the demand for margarine and hence for oil-seed rape is high this may result in super-normal profits being earned, and if it does, then next season other farmers may switch into rape production, expanding supply, depressing market price and eroding the profitability of rape production – a process which will continue until all the super-normal profits have been eliminated. Each individual farmer, however, always operates in a short-run context, aspiring to a short-run (profit maximising) equilibrium position. The concept of long-run equilibrium therefore should be seen as a description of a process (involving the entry and exit of other firms) rather than as a static point of equilibrium. Figure 6.6 therefore should be seen as a description of this process.

6.7 The industry supply curve in perfect competition

We talked in section 4.1 about how price is determined in perfect competition by the intersection of the demand curve and the supply curve, and we showed in Fig. 6.6 the interaction between the market and the individual perfectly competitive firm. We are now in a position to describe formally how that market supply curve is formed. This is merely an extension of the process described in Fig. 6.6. Suppose the industry is composed of just two firms, as in Fig. 6.7 – clearly a contradiction in terms since we assumed that in perfect competition there are many small firms, but an expedient assumption that we must make for purposes of exposition.

At a price of P_1, firm A will produce nothing since it has a higher cost structure than firm B and, at this price, it cannot produce at a profit. Only firm B will supply, at an output level of q_1, and this therefore is the market supply at this price. At a higher price of P_2 however, firm A will also find it profitable to produce (at output level q_2) and firm B will expand its output to q_3. Thus market supply at price P_2 is equal to the sum of firm A's production plus firm B's production $(q_2 + q_3)$.

In a similar way, by considering other prices we can trace out a market supply curve. This market supply curve is the horizontal summation of each individual firm's marginal cost curves – or, more specifically, that portion of the marginal cost curve which is above the average cost curve.

It is worth emphasising two points. The first is that each firm is in a position of short-run equilibrium. Thus, the industry supply curve should properly be interpreted within a short-run context – that is, we have derived a short-run market supply curve. The second point which should be reiterated is that an industry supply curve is only defined in the context of a perfectly competitive market structure. In

Figure 6.7

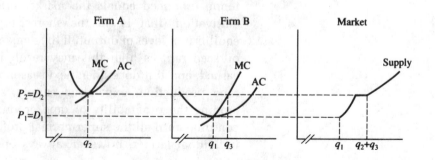

other market structures the 'supply curve' – if it exists at all – is the firm's marginal cost curve.

Note

1. London Transport Executive. Annual Reports.

Questions

6.1 A monopolistic firm can affect the price at which it sells. If it wishes to increase total revenue will it raise, lower or leave unchanged its price if it believes that demand for its product is elastic?

6.2 If a price-making firm wants to maximise its sales revenue it should:
 (a) set the highest price it can get
 (b) set the lowest price which covers its costs
 (c) choose a selling price at which the elasticity of demand for its product is unity
 (d) choose a selling price where the extra revenue received from the last unit sold exceeds the extra cost of making that unit.

6.3 'London Transport should cut fares to increase its revenue.' Do you agree? What effect might an increase in demand have on London Transport's costs?

6.4 How does the concept of opportunity cost help to evaluate the cost of a training scheme which uses skilled workers to train apprentices?

Table 6.4 Profitability of six firms

	Price (£/p)	Marginal revenue (£/p)	Output	Total revenue (£)	Total cost (£)	Profit	Average costs (£/p)	Marginal cost (£/p)
A	1.00	0.80	3000	3000	2500			0.75
B	1.50	1.20	5000				1.50	1.20
C		0.90	5000			Zero SNP	1.00	0.90
D	1.20	1.50	4000					1.50
E	1.00		4000	4000	2500		62.50	1.00
F	0.90	0.75	4000	3600	2000		At a minimum	

Table 6.4 contains information on six firms, all of whom are monopolists who wish to maximise profit. Complete the table and advise in each case whether the firm should:
 (a) increase price (and reduce quantity produced and sold)

(b)   reduce price (and increase quantity produced and sold)

(c)   remain at present position

(d)   none of the above: the figures supplied cannot be correct.

7 Case studies in pricing

Pricing and elasticity

Economics is all around us. You have only to open your eyes to see it, provided of course that it's part of your perceptive set. In this chapter we look at a number of examples that illustrate a fundamental point: the elasticity of demand for a product is an important influence on the price charged.

7.1 Price discrimination

Walk into your local travel agent and pick up a few brochures. They usually have lots to spare. Then take them home and study how the prices for a particular package holiday or a particular trip vary according to the time of year it is taken. Table 7.1 shows fares for a four-berth couchette on the DFDS ferry sailing from Harwich to Esbjerg in Denmark, though we could of course have given thousands of similar examples. As one might expect the highest fare is charged in the peak holiday season, between 17 June and 2 September. This peak fare of £82 is considerably higher than the fare of £50 charged during the low-season period. Note however that the ferry company does not simply divide the year into high season (or on-peak) and low season (or off-peak) segments. Rather it divides the market in a more complex way, identifying four levels of demand – pink, yellow, green and blue. The customer may well be confused by the complexity of all this – hence the use of colour coding in the brochure which unfortunately we cannot reproduce here. The lowest level of demand

Table 7.1 Price of a single fare (£)

Pink	1 January–14 January	66
Yellow	15 January–31 March	50
Green	1 April–16 June	70
Blue	17 June–2 September	82
Green	3 September–30 September	70
Yellow	1 October–12 December	50
Green	13 December–31 December	70

The table shows the price of a single fare in a 4–berth couchette on the Harwich–Esbjerg route.

Source: *DFDS (Scandinavian Seaways) Brochure*, 1990.

is coded yellow – it starts on 15 January, after the Christmas and New Year period has (mercifully) ended, and ends on 31 March when people start to think about an Easter holiday. It is followed by a green period when prices are 40 per cent higher (£70 instead of £50). The blue high-season period (price = £82) lasts from 17 June to 2 September covering the period when most people traditionally want to go on holiday. After this prices fall back to a green £70 and then, after 30 September, to a yellow £50 again. Many people however need, or want, to travel over the Christmas period so the ferry company charges a higher pink price of £70 for the period 13 December to 31 December.

It is very important to note that the variations in the price set by the ferry company have nothing to do with variations in cost. The cost to the company of running a ferry between England and Denmark is the same on 15 February as it is on the 15 August – yet in August they charge 64 per cent more than they do in February (£82 rather than £50). The price differentials reflect differences in the level of demand – or more precisely the *elasticity of demand* at different times of the year. This is an example of what economists call *price discrimination*. The price set depends upon the elasticity of demand – the more inelastic the demand the higher the price and vice versa.

We should perhaps pause and ask ourselves what determines the elasticity of demand for ferry trips between England and Denmark. We need to look at consumer motivation. Ferry trips to Denmark are mostly taken because people *want* to do them rather than *need* to do them. They are for most people a leisure activity, a holiday. Economic theory tells us that the elasticity of demand for any good or service depends upon the availability of substitutes. What we need to look at therefore is the other ways in which the consumer could spend his surplus income. Most people find the prospect of bobbing about on the North Sea for eighteen hours on a winter's night rather unattractive. Hence other forms of leisure activity, even staying at home and watching television, seem preferable. There are, in short, plenty of other things for the consumer to spend his money on – there are plenty of substitutes. In winter therefore the demand for ferry trips to Denmark is elastic – high prices will simply put people off altogether, so the ferry company charges a low price in an attempt to stimulate demand.

Note what happens at Christmas, however. At this time people's desire to travel is stronger so prices go up but prices are not as high as they are in summer. This is because the motivation for taking a ferry trip at Christmas is different from that in the summer. In the summer people enjoy the trip itself. Sitting out on deck breathing lungfuls of sea air is a pleasurable experience. But at Christmas time people may feel they need to travel to be reunited with their families. The primary motivation is to get there – the trip itself is probably rather irksome. And of course if the motivation is primarily to arrive, then better substitutes are available in the form of air travel which is considerably quicker and no more expensive.

Consumer motivation is complex. The underlying reasons why consumers purchase a particular service rather than spending their money on some other good or service will however, influence the elasticity of demand. It is this elasticity which is important to the ferry company. DFDS will not of course know exactly what this elasticity is. Indeed they may never even have heard of the concept of elasticity, but they will, by long experience, know that they can charge higher prices in the summer than in the winter. Years of experience with various sets of prices will have told them that consumers are less price sensitive in the summer than they are in the winter.

7.2 Price discrimination and profit maximisation

We should perhaps ask ourselves why DFDS chooses to discriminate. The answer quite simply is that by so doing they make larger profits than they would do if they charged the same price all year round. Figure 7.1 illustrates this.

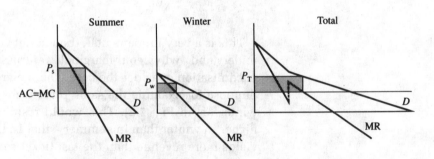

Figure 7.1

In Fig. 7.1 we assume that unit costs are constant and that there are just two market segments, summer and winter. In summer, there is more demand than in winter and demand is more inelastic – consumers are not discouraged by higher prices. We have chosen to illustrate this by drawing summer demand as a steeper curve than that for winter (see technical note at the end of this section). Total demand will be the sum of these two. In our diagram this will be the horizontal summation of the two curves. If the same price were charged all year round the profit maximising price would be P_T and the profit accruing to the company is represented by the shaded area. If on the other hand the company separates the two market segments, equating marginal cost to marginal revenue in each of the sub-markets the price charged in winter will be P_w while that in summer will be

P_s. The total profit will then be the sum of the shaded 'winter' area and the shaded 'summer' area which is greater than the shaded 'total' area. Thus discrimination increases the overall profitability of the company.

The key point to note relates to what the economist calls *equi-marginal returns*. To maximise its profit the firm must ensure that its marginal returns – in this case its marginal revenue – are the same in each market segment. Figure 7.1 shows this to be the case since at a price of P_s in summer marginal revenue is the same as that in winter when the price is only P_w (that is, marginal revenue is the same in summer and winter, even though price is different). If the same price were charged in summer and in winter marginal revenue would be different, given the difference in demands. This is illustrated in Fig. 7.2.

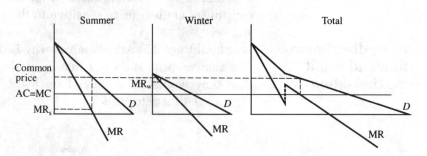

Figure 7.2

This is a very fundamental, though not very obvious, conclusion. To understand why equi-marginal returns are necessary for profit maximisation consider the case where marginal returns are not equal. Suppose for example the same price were charged in summer and in winter (as in Fig. 7.2). This would result in marginal revenue being higher in winter than in summer – that is, the last ticket sold in winter yields more revenue than the last ticket sold in summer. If there were some way in which the company could transfer this demand from summer to winter it would increase its overall profitability because the reduction in revenue resulting from the loss of the last ticket sold in summer would be more than offset by the increase in revenue resulting from the extra ticket sold in winter (because MR in the winter exceeds MR in the summer). The company should continue to persuade passengers to switch their demand from summer to winter as long as this holds true. But of course as the number of units sold in winter increases so the MR declines (there is a movement down the MR curve) and as the number of units sold in summer decreases so the MR increases (there is a movement up the MR curve). Thus the company should continue its persuasion by adjusting prices – until MR in summer equals that in winter as in Fig. 7.1. Thus we have demonstrated that equi-marginal returns are necessary for profit-maximisation.

There are a couple of additional points that need to be made. First to be able to discriminate a firm needs market power. A perfectly competitive firm in contrast, faces a perfectly elastic demand for its product (horizontal demand curve) and therefore by definition cannot identify different market segments and discriminate between them. For this reason, some textbooks refer to price discrimination as *monopolistic* price discrimination. What is required however, is not that the firm is a true monopolist but simply that it faces a downward sloping demand curve. DFDS is incidentally the only company operating the Harwich–Esbjerg route.

Second, successful discrimination requires that consumers cannot switch from one segment to the other. To take a rather far-fetched example suppose that Fig. 7.1 related not to the demand for trips but to the demand for baked beans. That is, the demand for beans is lower and more price-sensitive in the winter. If the baked beans manufacturer attempted to charge a higher price in summer than in winter, consumers would simply buy beans for the whole year in winter and store them until they required them in summer. In short, beans can be stored, trips cannot and it is this that enables discrimination to take place.

Technical note to Figures 7.1 and 7.2

Note: Students attempting to replicate this diagram should note that it must be drawn accurately. The only way to do this satisfactorily is on graph paper. The total curve must be the horizontal summation of the 'summer' and 'winter' curves and the MR curves must bear the correct relationship to the demand curves to which they relate.

Where the demand curve kinks there is a discontinuity so MR is undefined at this point – hence the 'break' in the MR curve.

To satisfy yourself that in Fig. 7.1 the sum of the shaded summer and shaded winter areas exceeds the shaded total area you need to measure them. In fact, in our diagram, profit is about 15 per cent greater with discrimination than it is without – measure it to satisfy yourself.

Note also that we have assumed that the slope of the demand curve is indicative of its elasticity, a shallow demand curve being more elastic. This is only approximately correct since a straight line demand 'curve' exhibits a different elasticity at every point.

7.3 Super Savers

In the previous section we saw how the prices set by DFDS varied according to the time of year. In common with other transport operators however DFDS has a complex rate structure which offers amongst other things:

(a) concessionary fares to retired people ('Senior Citizen Savers')
(b) concessionary fares to students
(c) return fares which cost less than the price of two single fares.

The rationale for the cheaper fares available to retirement pensioners and students is straightforward. It is another example of price discrimination. Students, and to a somewhat lesser extent retirement pensioners, form a low-income group who would be put off by high prices. Moreover in comparison to ordinary passengers they generally have more free time and enjoy greater flexibility about when to travel and hence can more easily be persuaded to take the mid-week sailings by the concessionary fares available for mid-week crossings. In short the ferry company has distinguished a market segment – pensioners and students – whose demand for trips is more elastic than that of ordinary passengers and it sets its prices accordingly.

The rationale for the Super Saver Return is perhaps not so straightforward. No matter what time of year the trip is made the price of a return fare is approximately one and a half times the price of a single fare (rather than twice the price of a single fare). This is the sort of pricing policy which is very familiar to all travellers – a return ticket normally costs less than the price of two single tickets.

On DFDS as we have seen there is a constant ratio of about 1:1.5 between the cost of a single and a return ticket. On British Rail, in contrast the ratio varies. For some types of fares it may be as low as 1:1.1. That is, the return fare is only 10 per cent higher than a single fare.

It is tempting to try to explain this as an example of monopolistic price discrimination between two market segments characterised by a difference in the elasticity of demand. To some extent this is legitimate but for a full understanding we also need an additional concept – that of peak load pricing, to which we now turn.

7.4 Peak-load pricing – Beattie calling

British Telecom is a near-monopoly supplier of telephone services in the UK though it now faces some slight competition in the provision of long-distance calls. In common with all telephone companies its cost structure is rather unusual in that its fixed costs are high and its variable costs are very low. In other words once the capital equipment – the cables, the exchanges, the satellites and so on – have been installed the cost of using that equipment is very low indeed. Marginal costs, that is, are very low provided there is sufficient capacity in the system to deal with the demands made on it at any one time. And therein lies the problem. The demand for telephone services varies according to the time of day. Demand is at its highest during the working day and particularly during the morning, but in the evening and at night the level of demand is much less. In economists' terminology this is a classic *peak load problem*.

As we shall see, however, the peak load problem facing BT has many of the same features as the problem facing the ferry operator DFDS. Similarly the way in which BT tackles the problem is to engage in price discrimination.

Consider the key features common to the two examples. For BT, as

Table 7.2 BT rate structure – local and national calls (time allowed in seconds for each dialled call unit fee of 5.06 p (September 1990))

Type of Call	Cheap rate Mon–Fri 6pm–8am Sat and Sun all day	Standard Rate 8am–9am and 1pm–6pm	Peak Rate Mon–Fri 9am–1pm
Local	240	85.0	60.0
Semi-local (up to 56.4km outside local call area)	81.8	35.1	26.25
National	51.5	31.0	23.25

Source: information sent to all BT subscribers, September 1990.

for DFDS and for the consumers of the services, output is not storable. Demand however varies in a predictable way. It is possible to identify different market segments, corresponding in BT's case to different times during the day. These segments are characterised by different levels and elasticities of demand and because BT is a price maker rather than a passive price taker it can discriminate by setting different prices for different times during the day.

These prices are illustrated in Table 7.2 which shows the number of seconds which can be purchased per unit. The Table indicates for example that a local call made during the peak rate period costs four times as much as if it were made during the cheap rate period. Thus 240 seconds can be purchased for 5p during the cheap rate whereas only 60 seconds can be purchased at peak rate.

A number of points need to be re-emphasised. Firstly for any firm the price set is influenced by both the costs of providing the service and the demand for it. For BT marginal costs – the cost of providing an extra unit of output – are very low in the short run provided there is spare capacity. If capacity is fully utilised, however, then in the short run the cost of providing an extra unit of output is very high.

Figure 7.3 represents this diagrammatically. In the short run, that is, with a given amount of capacity, the cost of producing an extra call is only Oa. However once the system becomes fully utilised at its full capacity Ox the cost of producing additional calls, given the fixed capacity, becomes infinitely large, so the SRMC curve becomes vertical at that point. The long-run marginal cost curve includes not only the running costs Oa but also the costs of providing additional units of capacity, by installing extra lines, larger switching complexes and so on. This is represented in the diagram by distance ab giving an

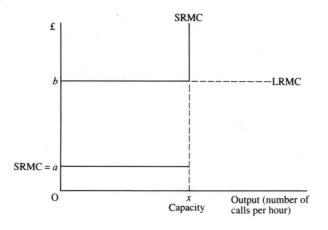

Figure 7.3

LRMC of O*b*.

In a sense the prices charged by BT reflect these differences in the costs of providing an extra unit of output. The low price charged off-peak reflects the low-to-negligible short-run marginal costs when demand is below capacity. The higher price charged on-peak reflects the higher SRMC when demand pushes up against the capacity constraint.

However we can also interpret BT's pricing structure as an example of monopolistic price discrimination. Even if costs did not differ between the on-peak and off-peak periods the profit-maximising objective would require a higher price to be charged on-peak where demand is higher and more inelastic. Analytically, that is, the situation is identical to that shown in Fig. 7.1 where the ferry company sets a higher price on-peak even though costs do not vary between high and low season.

BT of course is able to monitor the exact time during the day in which calls are made. It knows that during working hours demand is much less elastic. The reasons for this are complex but they include *inter alia* the fact that many business calls are made by employees on their employers' behalf. Employees are likely to be much less careful about how they spend their employers' money than about how they spend their own.

Prices will however affect demand. Although subscribers will probably be unaware of the details of BT's rate structure they will, to a lesser or greater extent be aware that savings can be made by using the phone off-peak rather than on-peak. This will tend to reduce the peak demand and boost the off-peak demand which is exactly what BT wants. In economists' terminology this is an example of a *shifting peak*.

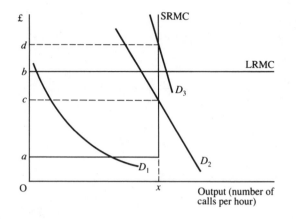

Figure 7.4

Pricing and capacity decisions

For a firm faced with a peak-load problem the pricing decision is complex since it is related to the decision about how much capacity to install. In Fig. 7.4 we have superimposed demand curves onto the cost curves we showed earlier in Fig. 7.3. We have identified, for the purposes of exposition, three levels of demand D_1, D_2 and D_3. The lowest and the most elastic demand is represented by D_1, corresponding to an off-peak demand. A low price of Oa will be charged at this time to encourage people to use the phone more. Even at this low price of Oa however there still remains substantial excess capacity on the system.

At the levels of demand labelled D_2 and D_3 however the demand for telephone services is pushing up against the limits posed by the capacity of the system. Demand will always be related to price however and a high price will choke off demand so that it can be kept within the capacity of the system. But what price should the firm charge when faced with demands such as D_2 or D_3?

For reasons which will be explained later economists have argued that public utilities, if operated in the public interest, should set prices which reflect marginal costs, since this, it is argued is what competitive firms do. It is unclear however which marginal costs – short run or long run – should determine price. Consider the situation that would exist if demand were at D_2. Clearly price must be higher than Oa because at this price demand would be far in excess of the capacity of the system. But how high should the price be – Oc or Ob? At Oc the price is just high enough to keep demand within capacity. At a higher price Ob, demand would be restricted so that spare capacity would emerge but here the firm is asking consumers to pay the cost of installing additional capacity (LRMC) even though spare capacity already exists (and incidentally violating the $P = $ SRMC rule for price setting).

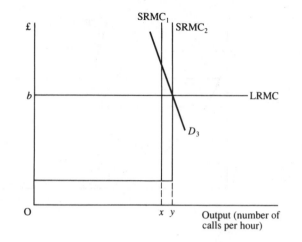

Figure 7.5

If demand were D_3 there are again two options for the firm. It can charge a high price of O*d* in order to keep demand within capacity. But this seems a very high price because it exceeds LRMC – in other words it is higher than the cost of providing the service even taking into account the cost of providing the capital equipment in the first place. The alternative is to charge O*b* and simply let people wait: 'Sorry. All lines are engaged. Please try later.'

This strategy does however produce extreme customer dissatisfaction, and while a monopolist may be able to shrug off customer complaints a competitive firm is likely to lose business to rivals.

There is no easy solution to this problem. The text book solution (and this is a textbook) is shown in Fig. 7.5 where the firm has expanded its capacity from O*x* to O*y* so that at a price of O*b* price is equal to both short-run and long-run marginal cost. In other words the price that a firm charges will be related to the capacity that it has installed. The two decisions – how much to invest in increasing capacity and what price to charge – are thus related.

It must be admitted that the textbook solution is an ideal which is unlikely to be achieved in practice. The reasons for this are that there are time lags involved in the installation of new capacity and that the demand function will not be perfectly predictable and stable.

There is one final but very important point. In Figs 7.3, 7.4, and 7.5 we have sketched cost curves which, we argued, characterised those facing BT. In fact they are a rather poor caricature, drawn this way merely for simplicity. In telecommunications there are massive scale economies particularly in satellite communications and other high technology systems. The long-run average cost curve must therefore be steeply downward sloping and for reasons discussed earlier the long-run marginal cost curve is therefore likely to be downward sloping as well. The implication of this is that extra capacity is likely to reduce unit costs – and perhaps prices.

7.5 Down to the sea again: Super Savers revisited

In section 7.2 we saw how the return fares offered by DFDS were on average only about 50 per cent higher than the price of a single fare. We also noted that such a pricing policy is normal practice for transport companies. The rationale can only be fully understood when the fine detail of those concessionary fares is studied. Detailed examination reveals that the cheap return fares are only available for certain mid-week crossings. The rationale then becomes clear. They are the response of the ferry company to a peak-load problem. No matter what the time of year, the localised peaks in demand occur at weekends, the troughs mid-week. The prices set are designed to encourage passengers to switch their journeys from week-ends to mid-week. Similarly British Rail's cheap return tickets can only be used for off-peak travel – normally after 10 o'clock in the morning and at week-ends.

8 Objectives of the firm

8.1 Do firms maximise profits?

In Chapter 6 we set out the rules to be followed by the profit-maximising firm: expand output up to the point where the last unit sold adds as much to revenue as it does to cost – that is, equate marginal revenue (MR) and marginal cost (MC) – and then charge the maximum price the market will be prepared to pay for this level of output. The question which occurs to everyone sooner or later is – do firms actually behave in this way? Do they maximise profit? Do they equate marginal cost and marginal revenue?

The notion that firms maximise profits seems on the face of it to be an overly simplistic view of behaviour. Moreover, it apparently fails to take account of certain important features of firms in the real world. The first of these is the so-called divorce of ownership from control. The dominant form of industrial organisation, as we have already noted, is the large firm. Such firms are run by managers who are not themselves the owners of the firm. The owners of the firm are shareholders and it is to this group that profits accrue. Since the shareholders in a public company are normally a widely dispersed group they will find it difficult to exert effective influence on the managers who will therefore be able to pursue whatever objectives they see fit. Therefore, it is said, there is no logical reason to argue that the objectives pursued will be those of profit maximisation since profits *per se* do not benefit the individuals who make the pricing and output decisions. Thus the divorce of ownership from control makes the assumption that firms maximise profits seem less plausible.

Secondly, the process of profit maximisation apparently requires firms to equate marginal cost with marginal revenue – two magnitudes which the firm may find it difficult or impossible to measure. In other words, firms will typically not possess the information necessary for them to follow the rules for profit maximisation; nor can they acquire such information except, possibly, at prohibitively high cost. We shall investigate the implications of these two points below, in sections 8.2 and 8.3.

8.2 The implications of the divorce between ownership and control

If the managers of large firms are not motivated by the desire to maximise profits – because they themselves do not receive such profits – then what does motivate their behaviour and what are the implications of this for their pricing and output decisions? A number of plausible hypotheses exist. One such is that firms (in the person of the managers who make the decisions in such firms) attempt to maximise something other than profit. They may for example attempt to maximise the firm's sales revenue or the long-term growth of the firm. Such hypotheses are associated respectively with Baumol[1] and Marris.[2] Generally speaking a firm which pursues sales revenue maximisation as an objective will sell a larger quantity at a lower price than the profit-maximising firm (the rules for achieving sales maximisation are explained in section 6.1). However, their basic objective may have to be tempered by the necessity to attain a certain minimum level of profitability, so that in practice the price and output level may be somewhere between the profit-maximising level and the sales revenue maximising level. Note also that sales revenue maximisation as an objective is similar – though not identical – to the maximisation of market share.

The growth of the firm is the objective pursued by managers in the Marris model. By considering the fortunes of the firm in the longer term, Marris attempts to lift the theory of the firm from its traditional static context into a more dynamic setting. The implications for price and output decisions are by no means clear cut, however. The necessary finance to fund the long-term expansion of the firm can most readily be obtained internally through retained profits. Thus growth maximisation is not necessarily inconsistent with profit maximisation. It could also be consistent with the Baumol model of sales revenue maximisation, however, since the managers could equate the growth of sales with the growth of the company.

A slightly different approach associated with Williamson[3] is to argue that managers attempt to maximise their *utility*, that is, the intrinsic satisfaction they get from their work. Managers derive utility from a number of different aspects of their job. They may, for example, derive satisfaction from the status that they have within the company and from the company's status within the wider corporate environment (that is, relative to other firms) and in society generally. Their personal status within the company will depend on the number of staff for whom they are responsible – the size of their department within the company – and the amount of managerial perks they can acquire – company car, expense account, trips abroad, and so on. Thus one might expect that, if such managers attempt to maximise anything, they would, within the limits of their discretion, attempt to maximise expenditure on staff and managerial 'slack' (that is, perks).

Their standing in the world outside the company, however, will depend on the image that the company presents. Thus, other things being equal, one would expect the managers to promote not just the growth of the company but, more importantly, to promote those activities designed to enhance its corporate image. Thus sports sponsorship, sponsorship of the arts and expenditure on lavish office buildings can be seen as having a dual role. Not only do such expenditures assist the company in marketing its products by promoting a favourable image of the company to the consumer, they also increase the utility of its managers – the status of the manager depends on the status of the firm. Such expenditures would be termed *discretionary investment*. They are expenditures over and above that necessary to maximise the firm's profits or its sales revenue.

Williamson formalised his model of managerial behaviour in terms of a utility function. Subject to a minimum profit constraint, managers attempt to maximise their utility (U) which depends on expenditures on staff (S), discretionary investment (I_D) and managerial slack (M).

$$U = f(S, I_D, M)$$

Because of these expenditures such firms have operating costs in excess of those which are strictly necessary to promote the firm's growth or profitability. In a sense, therefore, such firms are inefficient, but they are deliberately inefficient through choice. The term *X-inefficiency* was coined by Leibenstein[4] to describe such a situation in which a firm suffered from – or enjoyed – a cost structure which had built into it an allowance for these non-necessary expenditures. X-inefficient firms can still be profit maximisers, however, so in this sense the Leibenstein model is rather different from that of Williamson.

Up to now all the models we have discussed have an explicit maximand: profits, sales revenue, growth or utility. Some authors would argue, however, that typically firms do not attempt to maximise anything. These are the so-called *behavioural theories of the firm*. Such theories, associated with a number of writers including Cyert and March,[5] and Simon,[6] analyse or describe the process by which decisions are arrived at in the firm. It is important to recognise, they argue, that the firm is an organisation composed of a number of groups with different and possibly opposing interests. For example, the sales department may be pursuing market share or sales revenue as an objective: the stock control department may be anxious to avoid stock-out situations even if this means the maintenance of uneconomically high levels of stocks; the marketing department may be concerned with product innovation; the directors and shareholders with the profitability of the company; and the technical department (if there is one) with the technical excellence of the product. The decisions which emerge from behind the closed doors of the company are the net result of the interplay between these various interest groups, the outcome obviously being influenced by the relative strengths of each group.

Managers working within such an organisation, it is argued, may display *satisficing* rather than maximising behaviour. That is, they will aspire to certain target levels of profitability, sales, market share, and so on. If these levels are not attained, managers will both revise downwards their aspirations and seek other ways of attaining them. In summary, the behavioural theories of the firm describe the *process* by which decisions are taken. Clearly, this process does not involve equating marginal cost and marginal revenue or anything remotely like it.

This brings us back to the second feature of firms in the real world that we mentioned in section 8.1: firms are (apparently) prevented from maximising profit by a lack of the requisite information on marginal cost and marginal revenue. Instead of attempting to maximise profit therefore, they may simply set prices according to some arbitrary mark-up principle – that is, they work out what their costs are, add on a bit for profit, and that is the price they charge. This is known as 'cost-plus' pricing and is the subject of the next section.

8.3 Cost-plus pricing

Hall and Hitch,[7] two American economists working in the 1930s, set out to test the empirical validity of the profit-maximising model of the firm. They did so in a rather naive way by questioning businessmen about how they arrived at their price and output decisions. The businessmen questioned denied strenuously that they equated marginal cost with marginal revenue or that they maximised profit. One is tempted to quote Mandy Rice-Davis's remark when asked by the Press to comment on a denial made in somewhat different circumstances: 'Well, they would say that, wouldn't they?'[8] In other words, it was a naive question to ask. Businessmen will not use the same words to describe their actions as economists do. Thus phrases like 'profit maximisation', 'marginal cost' and 'marginal revenue' are not within the businessman's vocabulary. We have already noted that information on marginal cost and revenue is unlikely to be available, and profit maximisation, as an objective, is not something to which firms would readily admit. Somehow it does not fit in with the image of the company they would like to promote as a socially responsible and caring organisation. What Hall and Hitch's enquiries failed to take into account is the fact that the phrase 'profit-maximising objective' is merely a shorthand way of saying that profitability is the criterion by which firms judge success, and that they seek success. Put in this somewhat less stark way, many firms would agree that this is indeed their objective. However, very few, if any, would agree that the

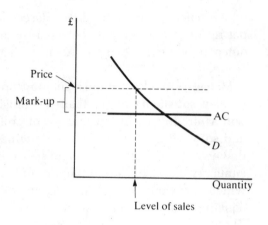

Figure 8.1

procedure they use to pursue it involves unmeasurable magnitudes like marginal cost and marginal revenue.

Most firms when questioned in fact described a process which has subsequently come to be called cost-plus, or full cost or mark-up pricing. They first work out their average cost which is reasonably constant over quite a wide range of output, as in Fig.8.1. They then add on a (possibly arbitrarily determined) mark-up of a certain percentage in order to arrive at the price to charge. They then sell what they can at this price. (Sales will, of course, be determined by the demand curve facing the firm, but firms will typically have no knowledge of this curve.)

The major deficiency with this explanation of how firms set prices is that it does not attempt to explain how the magnitude of the mark-up is determined. In practice it may be based on the average rate of return of similar firms in the industry or on some target rate of return. But the theory cannot explain how these average or target rates of return are set. What may well happen in practice is that the size of the mark-up is adjusted and its effect on sales and profitability noted, until by a trial-and-error process the firm arrives at the mark-up, and hence the price, which gives it most profit. In other words, the firm charges the profit-maximising price, but it arrives at that price via an iterative process rather than by a process which involves equating marginal cost and marginal revenue.

Thus, in common with many of the other behavioural models, full cost pricing is not necessarily inconsistent with the models of behaviour which take profit maximisation to be the objective. The purpose for which the two models are constructed is rather different, however. The cost-plus pricing model is a description of a process: its weakness is that it has little predictive or analytical power. The marginalist (profit-maximising) model is not meant to be a realistic description. Rather it is an analytical tool and to criticise it for its lack

8.4 Pricing and objectives: some evidence

of realism is to misunderstand the purpose behind its construction. There are two methods in principle of obtaining evidence about firms' objectives. The first is to ask firms (the Hall and Hitch method) but this is basically unsatisfactory because even if firms were disposed to give truthful answers, they are probably themselves unaware of precisely what criteria they use in setting prices or what ultimate objectives they pursue. The second method is to make inferences from published prices (that is 'hard data') about how those prices are arrived at and therefore the overall strategy on which they are based. This is the general technique we explore here. We shall look at the market for sailboards, a relatively straightforward market but nevertheless one which displays some interesting pricing behaviour from which it is possible to make inferences about firms' strategies.

The sport of boardsailing, or windsurfing, originated in the 1960s but it was not until the late 1970s that one could begin to talk in terms of a clearly defined industry. The market for sailboards is a maturing oligopoly, with a small number of major manufacturers – mostly German, French and Swiss – dominating the market worldwide, and a number of small manufacturing firms producing specialist boards, often restricting their activities to their home market. The market is international in the sense that the major manufacturers sell worldwide. Most boards sold in the UK are imported form Western Europe but there is now growing competition from the nascent UK producers. On the demand side the UK market is small and immature in comparison to that of Western Europe – the sport having been slower to develop here than in other Western European countries.

The aspect of the industry which concerns us here is the pricing behaviour of the firms within the industry. In particular, boards sold on the UK market are typically 20 to 30 per cent more expensive than identical boards sold on those European markets where sailboarding is a major recreational activity. The price differential cannot be explained in terms of transport costs (which are minimal anyway), nor can it be explained in terms of fluctuations in the exchange rate between the pound sterling and other European currencies. Table 8.1 illustrates the price differentials for a random selection of boards sold on the Dutch market and on the UK market.

Production costs are clearly the same irrespective of where the boards are sold and the variation in transport costs is small – perhaps smaller than one might imagine since many of the companies involved are merely design and marketing agencies, the actual manufacture of the boards being contracted out to major plastics companies and the manufacture of the sails to specialist companies in the Far East. Clearly, then, the price differentials reflect not a difference in costs but a difference in the mark-ups applied.

Table 8.1 Price differentials for sailboards sold on the Dutch and UK markets

Board model	Country of origin	Typical price in Holland (£)	Typical price in UK (£)	Price differential (per cent of UK price)
HiFly 300CS	W. Germany	318	399	20
HiFly 700CS	W. Germany	398	525	24
Wayler Breez Sailboard	Holland	305	499	39
Vario Mistral	W. Germany	374	498	25
Superlight	Switzerland	515	795	35
Bic Star 250	France	256	385	33
Mistral Maui	Switzerland	469	695	32

Source: research carried out by the author based on published prices in *De Telegraaf*, 2 June 1984, and *Board Magazine*, No. 15, July 1984. Guilder prices converted at 4.25 = £1.

A mark-up is applied in two stages: when the manufacturer sells boards to the retailer and when the retailer sells boards to the final consumer. The size of both of these mark-ups is in fact much smaller in Holland than in the UK. What inferences can be drawn from this? One possible interpretation is that manufacturers pursue different objectives in different markets – profit maximisation in the UK where prices are high, and some other objective in Holland where prices are lower. Such schizophrenic behaviour is extremely implausible, however. What is more likely is that the cost-plus pricing model (introduced in section 8.3) is flawed in arguing that firms base their prices on costs alone without any regard to demand conditions in the market for their product. The evidence of Table 8.1 suggests that firms do take account of demand conditions and that the mark-up they apply reflects this. Thus, although firms may not consciously set out to maximise profit and may not be aware of the elasticities of demand for their product, nevertheless they set prices which cannot be explained solely in terms of costs.

The differences between the market for sailboards in Holland and in the UK can only be fully appreciated after a rather lengthy study of the industry. A few key differences can be noted, however. Most importantly we could argue (by inference from the data of Table 8.1) that the elasticity of demand must be less in the UK than in Holland. The reason for this is related to the degree of maturity and the size of the market. In Holland sailboarding is a major sporting activity which has been popular for a number of years; in the UK it is much less popular. Hence in Holland low prices can be expected to persuade many people to buy a new board who would otherwise not have done so. In Britain the dedicated few are prepared to pay high prices for the board of their choice, but price cuts will not persuade others to take up sailboarding in preference to badminton or bowls. The large size of the Dutch market means that the retailer there can typically expect to sell perhaps ten times as many boards as his UK counterpart. This difference in sales volume in turn affects the extent to which the retailer's overheads can be spread. Thus higher sales volume implies lower unit selling costs, which, in turn, means that dealers can offer larger discounts thereby encouraging still higher sales volume. This therefore is a self-reinforcing process – higher sales volume makes possible lower unit selling costs, which in turn makes possible lower prices, which encourages still higher volume. Thus one could argue that the lower prices in Holland are partly due to lower selling costs; but note that such a strategy only works because demand is relatively elastic.

Even within the model range of a particular manufacturer, there exist price differentials which cannot be explained in terms of cost differences and which must therefore reflect differences in demand elasticities. For example, as Table 8.1 shows, the German HiFly manufacturer charges a higher price for the 700 model than the 300 model (regardless of where they are sold). However, the rigs (mast, sail and boom) on both boards are identical, and in all other respects the boards are almost identical save for the fact that the 700 is a smaller board and therefore, the 700 would be a cheaper board to manufacture. Why is it more expensive?

The reason is to do with the elasticity of demand. The 300 is a first-time-buyer's board, an all-purpose board, whereas the 700 is a board for the more experienced sailer 'who knows what he wants and is prepared to pay for it'. Demand for the 300 therefore is elastic and lower prices can be expected to result in substantially increased sales. Demand for the 700 is more inelastic so that the manufacturer charges higher prices (applies a higher mark-up) in this segment of the market.

Similar behaviour can be found in the market for cars, a market which has been extensively studied by economists. It is now quite well known that prices on the UK market are significantly higher than prices of identical models sold on the Continental European market. Again, this has nothing to do with differences in costs. Rather it reflects differences in the elasticity of demand between Britain and Europe. In Britain the demand for cars is relatively inelastic, partly because such a high percentage of cars are sold to companies rather than individuals. Thus mark-ups, and therefore prices, are high. Where demand is more elastic, as in Europe, prices tend to be lower. Moreover, within the model range of a particular manufacturer, mark-ups tend to be higher for larger cars. That is, manufacturers make more profit on large cars than small ones, since large cars are not much more expensive to produce than small ones. Price differentials within a model range owe much more to differing elasticities than to differences in the cost of production.

Notes

1. Baumol, W. T., *Business Behaviour, Value and Growth*. Harcourt, Brace and World Inc., 1967.
2. Marris, R. L., *The Economic Theory of Managerial Capitalism*. Macmillan, 1964.
3. Williamson, O., *The Economics of Discretionary Behaviour: Managerial Objectives in a Theory of the Firm*. Prentice-Hall, 1964.
4. Leibenstein H., 'Allocative-Efficiency versus X-Efficiency', *American Economic Review*, 1966.
5. Cyert, R. M. and March, J. G., *A Behavioural Theory of the Firm*. Prentice-Hall, 1963.
6. Simon, H. A., *On the Concept of Organisational Goal*, reprinted in Ansoff H. I. (ed.), *Business Strategy*. Penguin, 1969.
7. Hall, R. L. and Hitch, C. J., *Price Theory and Business Behaviour*, reprinted in Wilson. T. and Andrews, P. W. S. (eds), *Oxford Studies in the Price Mechanism*. OUP, 1951.
8. For those readers too young to remember or otherwise out of touch with British political scandal in the 1960s, Mandy Rice-Davis was a high-class call-girl who claimed to have had an affair with a cabinet minister, John Profumo. He initially denied the allegation. Miss Rice-Davis, when asked by the Press to comment on his denial, replied 'Well he would say that, wouldn't he?'

Questions

8.1   What do you understand by the following terms?
   (a)   divorce between ownership and control
   (b)   satisficing behaviour
   (c)   utility maximising behaviour
   (d)   managerial slack
   (e)   a 'mark-up' model of pricing behaviour
   (f)   marginalist theories of the firm

8.2   (a)   Why might the managers of a firm be more interested in growth of the firm than its profitability?
   (b)   What constrains these managers in their attempt to maximise growth?
   (c)   Why don't firms who base their prices on their full costs of production pay more attention to the demand conditions for their product?

8.3   Is the following statement true or false? Explain why. 'If a firm bases its price on full costs of production it will not be maximising its profits.'

8.4   Why do economists insist on using models of the firm which assume profit maximisation when it is so patently unrealistic?

9 Behaviour in oligopolistic markets

9.1 Concentration and the public interest

A long-standing debate in economics centres around the question of whether highly concentrated market structures (monopoly, oligopoly) are detrimental to the public interest. The idea that competition is good and monopoly is bad is founded on the proposition – based on rather shaky analysis – that price will be higher and output lower under monopoly than they would be under competition. The validity of this proposition can be easily demonstrated; but only if we make two crucial assumptions, one of which is clearly unrealistic. The assumptions are, firstly, that firms attempt to maximise profits irrespective of the market structure and secondly, that cost structures are the same whether the market for a particular good is supplied by one monopoly seller or by a large number of smaller competing firms. While the first assumption may be a reasonable approximation to reality (readers can judge for themselves having read Chapter 8), the second is clearly not, since large firms can almost always benefit from scale economies which will give them a cost advantage over smaller firms. If we do make these two assumptions however, then we can see from Fig. 9.1 the correctness of the proposition that monopoly price (P_m) is higher than the competitive price (P_c) and monopoly output (q_m) is lower than the competitive output (q_c).

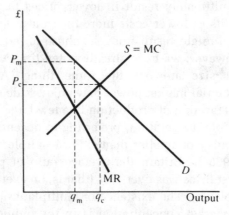

Figure 9.1

Note that in Fig. 9.1 the industry supply curve (S) is assumed to be equivalent to the monopolist's marginal cost curve (MC). This follows from the assumption we made that cost conditions are the same whether the industry is composed of one firm or is fragmented into a number of small competing firms. In competition, price is determined by the intersection of this supply curve and the demand curve, whereas the monopolist equates marginal cost to marginal revenue to arrive at an output level (q_m) and a price (P_m). In practice, of course, the monopolist would enjoy scale economies which would reduce his costs relative to those of smaller competing firms. If these scale economies were substantial the monopoly price would be less than the competitive price and the monopoly output level higher than the competitive output level. Figure 9.2 illustrates this possibility.

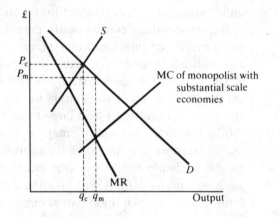

Figure 9.2

Thus the major justification for monopoly – or market concentration generally – rests on the proposition that large firms will enjoy cost advantages over smaller competing firms and that these lower costs will ultimately result in lower prices to the consumer. That is, the benefits of lower costs more than outweigh any possible dis-benefits which might result from the abuse of monopoly power.

However, we have already noted (in section 3.5) that firm size and plant size are not the same thing. Although large firms with substantial market power may enjoy scale economies as a result of the concentration of production in a few large plants, they often engage in *multiplant operation*, preferring to decentralise their production into a number of smaller plants. For example, it has been estimated[1] that in 1968 in Britain the average ratio of plants to firms for the five largest firms was over 10:1 (that is, on average each firm operated over ten plants). The existence of multiplant operation weakens the claim that market concentration is in the public interest. Concentration is only in the public interest if large firms enjoy technical cost advantages over smaller firms. Often, however, the advantages they have result from their market power rather than from technical economies of scale.

While bearing this point in mind it is nevertheless true that large firms do benefit from scale economies. This is borne out by the evidence of Chapter 5 and, in particular, Table 5.2 which gives engineering estimates of minimum efficient plant sizes (MEPS) for a number of industries. It would clearly be inefficient and against the public interest to insist that such industries operate below the MEPS merely to ensure a degree of competition in the industry, if significant cost penalties resulted from this.

In Britain the agency charged with the responsibility of investigating industries where firms have substantial market power is the Monopolies and Mergers Commission (MMC). In addition to the merger activity which it is required to investigate (discussed in section 9.7), the MMC is empowered to investigate market situations in which a single firm controls over 25 per cent of the market for a particular product (or where a group of firms, acting together so as to restrict competition, jointly controls over 25 per cent of the market). Thus the MMC's terms of reference are very much wider than might have been imagined from the definition of a monopoly as a single seller. In fact the expression 'a monopoly situation' used in this context is merely a convenient shorthand for some rather more cumbersome phrase about 'an oligopoly situation in which the dominant firm's market share exceeds 25 per cent.' The MMC's remit is to consider whether monopoly situations such as these are in the public interest, and in carrying out its remit the MMC has due regard to the evidence on scale economies it can obtain from the firm under investigation. In deciding whether a particular monopoly situation is in the public interest, however, this is only one aspect of such situations which is taken into account. Additionally the MMC investigates the firm's pricing behaviour, aspects of price and non-price competition and any alleged restrictions on competition. Further examples of this are given in sections 9.3, 9.4, and 9.11.

9.2 Traditional and modern views about monopoly

It is possible to discern a shift of emphasis (which some writers[2] have described as a revolution) in the way that economists view the whole question of monopoly and the public interest. The traditional view outlined in section 9.1 has two aspects:

1. A monopoly situation is a market structure which is defined purely in terms of the degree of concentration.
2. Monopolies, so defined, may or may not act against the public interest. This depends on the objectives of the firm, its ability to reap scale economies, and so on.

In contrast, the modern view can be characterised as follows:

1. A monopoly situation is a market structure which cannot be defined purely in terms of the degree of concentration. Rather, the ease with which new firms can enter the market (and leave it) should be taken into account.

2. A monopoly situation therefore can be defined as a situation in which a firm has a dominant position and is protected against the entry of new firms by effective barriers.

3. It is highly probable that monopolies, so defined, will act against the public interest so that it is appropriate that anti-monopoly investigations concentrate on the alleged anti-competitive devices employed by a firm (that is, devices designed to bolster the firm's monopolistic position by erection of entry barriers).

4. In addition, the modern view emphasises that ease of exit is also important. New firms will not commit themselves to high levels of capital expenditure (that is, they will not enter) if that capital equipment cannot subsequently be turned to an alternative use (that is, if they are unable to leave if they wish to do so).

To express these modern views in a slightly different way we can say that if (real) monopoly power exists it will probably be abused, that is, prices and profits will be higher. The existence of these profits will, however, invariably attract other firms into the market to secure some of the profits for themselves, provided that there are no barriers to entry. The threat posed by the potential entry of new firms will cause the existing firms to react in one of two ways. They may moderate their pricing behaviour, limiting themselves to the sort of prices and profits that would be found in a competitive market, thus eliminating the incentive for other firms to enter. Such firms therefore are not true monopolists because any attempt to exercise market power results in its eventual erosion. Alternatively, the threat of new entrants may cause the monopolist to react by indulging in tactics the sole purpose of which is to restrict competition. The erection of entry barriers, which take many different forms, is the most important of these anti-competitive tactics. Only if such anti-competitive tactics are successful in excluding new entrants does a true monopoly situation exist which requires some government intervention to limit its power and prevent it acting against the public interest.

In summary, we can say that the degree of concentration is not the only criterion by which to define monopoly situations. Of equal importance is the degree to which the firm enjoys a position protected from the threat of new entrants. This approach, sometimes labelled the 'contestable markets' approach, is thus more dynamic as opposed to the more static traditional approach. It draws attention to the likely

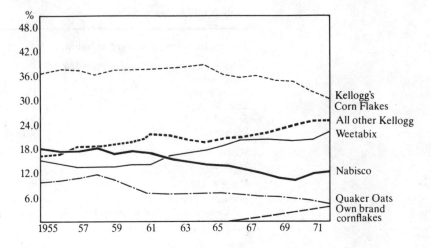

Figure 9.3 Market share (by weight) of RTE breakfast cereals (Source: as for Table 9.1)

9.3 The Kellogg's Corn Flakes case

future developments which may occur when and if new firms enter the market.

To illustrate the ideas outlined above we shall in this section study the way in which the MMC approaches the question of the abuse of monopoly power. The example we shall look at is the case of the market for ready-to-eat breakfast cereals – the Kellogg's Corn Flakes case – which was the subject of an MMC report[3] in 1973. Quotations in the following text are from this report.

As can be seen from Fig. 9.3, Kellogg had a dominant position in the market for breakfast cereals. During the period from 1955 to 1971 Kellogg's Corn Flakes had an average market share of over 36 per cent and all Kellogg cereals taken together had a market share of 57 per cent. In addition, the three-firm concentration ratio (Kellogg, Weetabix, Nabisco) was about 90 per cent. Clearly a monopoly situation existed according to the criterion then in operation. Kellogg was the dominant firm and thus determined prices in the industry generally. The question which the MMC set out to investigate, however, was whether Kellogg was guilty of the abuse of its monopoly position.

After investigation the Commission concluded that there was no price competition as such in the market. Rather, manufacturers preferred to compete by extending their product ranges, a strategy which Kellogg seems to have taken to extravagant proportions (see the list of products in Table 9.1). This strategy could be considered as an attempt to erect entry barriers through brand proliferation (see section 3.6). Kellogg's expenditure on advertising, though high, was not however considered excessive. The ratio of expenditure on advertising to sales fluctuated around 12 per cent during the late 1960s and early 1970s, somewhat less pro rata than two of the other major suppliers and about equal to that of the third. The Commission did,

Table 9.1 Breakfast cereals

The products supplied were as follows:

Kellogg Company of Great Britain Ltd

Corn Flakes	Rice Krispies	30% Bran Flakes
Raisin Bran	Coco Krispies	Sugar Smacks
Bran Buds	All-Bran	Frosties
Special K	Ricicles	Puffa Puffa Rice
Variety	Wheatamins	

Weetabix Ltd
Weetabix

Nabisco Ltd

Shredded Wheat	Shreddies	Golden Nuggets
Cubs spoon-size shredded wheat		

Quaker Oats Ltd

Sugar Puffs	Oat Crunchies	Puffed Wheat

Viota Foods Ltd

Corn Flakes	Wheat Bisk	

Source: Monopolies Commission Report 1973, *Breakfast Cereals: A Report on the Supply of Ready Cooked Breakfast Cereal Foods*, HMSO, App. 4.

however, state that 'advertising and promotion have helped to create and tend to maintain the kind of market in which it is possible for manufacturers to have substantial freedom to determine their prices as they wish' (para. 88).

The Commission noted the introduction of own-brand cornflakes, which occurred in 1966 when Viota Ltd acquired a cornflakes factory and started producing an own-label product for Tesco. In their submission Kellogg said that 'the advent of own-brand cornflakes had substantially sharpened price competition in relation to Corn Flakes' and Viota saw the market for cornflakes as very price competitive (para. 97). The Commission also noted the growing bargaining strength of the major retailers and their ability to exert influence on Viota's prices and thus on cornflake prices generally. Somewhat surprisingly, however, the Commission took the view that this was unlikely to exert a significant restraining influence on Kellogg's prices in the future, a judgement which with the benefit of hindsight appears somewhat questionable. The Commission considered that for most of the period under review, Kellogg's profits had been excessive when compared with manufacturing industry and the food industry generally. However, in the years immediately preceding the Report, Kellogg's profits had suffered a decline (as can be seen from Fig. 9.4).

The Commission assumed that this was likely to continue and it was this which, it seems, persuaded the Commission to state that 'We are not prepared to conclude that Kellogg's profits are excessive at

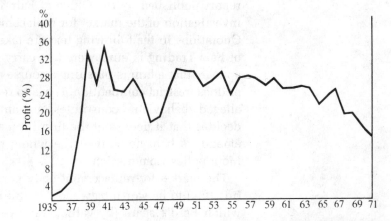

Figure 9.4 Kellogg's ratio of operating profit to sales on domestic business (Source: as for Table 9.1)

present' (para. 96). In a report full of contradictions and hedged around with ifs and buts, the Commission finally came down firmly on the fence, stating 'Our conclusion is that the determination by Kellogg of the level of prices at which breakfast cereals are supplied does not operate against the public interest but that it may be expected to operate against the public interest' (para. 101).

What is apparent, however, is that the Commission was unhappy about the lack of price competition in the industry and the dominant and protected position of Kellogg, bolstered by what the Commission saw as anti-competitive tactics (that is, non-price competition). Although Kellogg contended that many of the major food manufacturers had the technical and marketing expertise to break into the market if they so wished, the Commission took the view that new firms were unlikely to risk the heavy expenditure necessary to launch into the market dominated by Kellogg, particularly with a copy of an existing product. Thus, effectively, barriers to the entry of new firms existed.

In addition, the Commission clearly felt that there was 'no practical means of changing the structure of the industry or the nature of competition in the industry in such a way as to ensure the maintenance of price restraint on Kellogg' (para. 102), a conclusion which did little to satisfy the critics of excesses within the industry.

9.4 Anti-competitive tactics: replacement body panels for Ford

Section 9.3 was based on an investigation by the Monopolies Commission whose remit was to decide whether the behaviour of Kellogg acted against the public interest. That is, to condemn Kellogg it was not sufficient to demonstrate merely that they were indulging in anti-competitive tactics. Rather the Commission had to decide, taking into consideration all the relevant information, whether the situation as a whole was or was not in the public interest. In contrast, the case studied in this section is more modest in its scope. It is based on a report published by the Office of Fair Trading in 1984[4] following its investigation of the market for replacement body panels for Ford cars. Quotations in the following text are taken from this report. The Office of Fair Trading is empowered to carry out an investigation where it appears that a firm is pursuing a course of action which is designed to, or does, restrict competition. It has to reach a decision on whether the alleged behaviour constitutes an anti-competitive practice. If it decides that it does, and the firm in question gives no undertaking to amend its behaviour, then the whole matter may be referred to the Monopolies Commission.

The market for replacement body parts for Ford cars was estimated (in 1984) to be worth between £35 million and £45 million a year, of which Ford's share (by value) was over 85 per cent. The remaining market share was filled by independent manufacturers. The OFT investigation was prompted by the legal action taken by Ford against these independent suppliers who, Ford claimed, were in breach of the laws relating to artistic and design copyright. Ford claimed, with some justification under the relevant statutes relating to copyright and registered designs, that the independent suppliers were in breach of the copyright laws, and served notice on them that Ford intended to prosecute if they continued with their action. The independent suppliers in reply offered to pay Ford a royalty on the parts manufactured, an offer which Ford refused.

The market for replacement panels arises from two main sources. Firstly, panels are required for the repair of vehicles subject to accident damage. Secondly, panels are required to replace sections damaged through corrosion, this obviously being more important for older cars which need to be repaired to bring them up to the standard required for the DoT test. The price differential between panels manufactured by Ford and those manufactured by independent suppliers was considerable. This differential was particularly marked for those panels used to repair corrosion damage where the independent suppliers sold 'part panels' particularly suitable for repairing this type of damage cheaply. Ford, up to the time of the OFT investigation, did not supply 'part panels' and repairers were therefore compelled to purchase 'full panels' even though only part of the panel might be used in a repair, the rest being cut away and discarded. Table 9.2 shows the price comparison between the independent suppliers' part panels and the equivalent full panels supplied by Ford. Although not as marked, a sizeable price differential ranging between 6 and 400 per cent also existed for panels commonly used for crash repairs.

The most cogent arguments adduced by Ford in defending its policy are reproduced below verbatim from Ford's submission:

Table 9.2 Prices of corrosion part panels

Model	Independent supplier Part panel name	Price (£)	Ford Full panel of which corrosion panel forms part	Price (£)
Escort Mk1	Rear lower corner	2.61	Rear quarter panel (4-door)	41.98
	Rear wheel arch	1.75	Rear quarter (2-door)	73.40
	Front footwell	2.40	Floor pan	78.39
	Sill with extension (2-door)	2.25	Full sill (2-door)	12.66
Escort Mk2	Rear lower corner	4.45	Rear quarter panel (4-door)	62.35
	Rear wheel arch	3.25	Rear quarter panel (2-door)	69.75
	Sill (2-door)	2.50	Sill (2-door)	10.32
	Rear valance	2.90	Lower back panel	19.77
	Full sill (4-door)	4.04	Front and rear sill (2 parts)	15.69
Cortina Mk3	Front wing repair panel	3.73	Front wing	25.00
	Rear lower corner	2.66	Rear quarter panel (4-door)	31.43
	Rear wheel arch to door shut	1.64	Rear quarter panel (2-door)	41.55
	Rear wheel arch to door shut (section only)	0.70	Rear quarter panel (2-door)	41.55
Granada	Rear wheel arch	3.58	Rear quarter panel	53.08
	Rear lower corner	3.93	Rear quarter panel	53.08
Fiesta	Rear wheel arch	3.73	Rear quarter panel −1981 / 1981−	44.40 / 46.84
	Rear lower corner	2.10	Quarter panel rear section	34.20
Transit	Rear door skin (part)	2.10	Full rear door skin	13.42
	Rear wheel arch	3.80	Body side panel	64.97
	Door sill	1.60	Rocker step	10.35
	Skin sill lower	3.00	Body rocker panel extension	5.19

Source: report by the Office of Fair Trading, *Ford Motor Co. Ltd: Licensing for the manufacture or sale of replacement parts*, 21 March 1984.

1. The design of Ford's body panels enjoys protection under the law of copyright. As the legal owner of the copyright in its designs, Ford is entitled to utilise the designs itself, or to license others to do so, or to do both. Any of these courses would be an entirely normal exercise by Ford of the right granted by the law of copyright. (section 5.13)

2. To produce a new model Ford makes massive investments in design, engineering and tooling. (For example, the total design costs for the Sierra model were about £90 million and the total costs of developing the model and putting it into production about £560 million.) Those who manufacture infringing panels are able, without any investment in original design work, to copy the Ford part and to produce sufficiently close dimensional replicas for an expenditure of some tens of thousands of pounds. Thus the copier, who contributes nothing to the design of the panel, is able to benefit from all the design and development undertaken by the manufacturer of the original panel. (section 5.37 para. 2 and section 5.10)

3. Suppliers of infringing panels are concerned only to supply the fast moving, high volume panels. The typical supplier of infringing panels offers 25 panels for each Ford vehicle, making a total for all Ford vehicles of 150 panels, of which some 80% – 90% are corrosion part panels which are not offered by Ford. By contrast Ford has a responsibility to purchasers of its vehicles to make available a comprehensive range of spare parts including panels. In consequence Ford stocks around 150 panels for each of its models, and a total for all models of 4000 panels. Ford's responsibility for the supply of a full range of parts for all its vehicles entails maintenance by Ford of a massive warehousing and distribution system. (section 5.37 paras 3 and 4)

4. If a manufacturer's prices for its body panels and other parts are not competitive with those of other vehicle manufacturers, its sales of new vehicles will be affected. Over 40 per cent of Ford's car sales in the UK are to fleet purchasers and Ford's success in selling to such operators is of particular relevance. The managers of fleet purchasers are professionals with expert knowledge of the cost of car ownership, including the competitive costs of spare parts. (section 5.35)

In considering Ford's submission the OFT acknowledged that Ford was acting legally. This was not the point at issue, however. The point at issue was whether the exercise of this right produced a situation in which a firm was able to wield monopoly power. In a well-argued case the OFT concluded:

The effects on competition arising from the exercise of copyright depend on the market in which the particular good is supplied. Where there are reasonable substitutes for a particular good, the exclusive rights of supply do not confer monopoly rights in the market and the exercise of copyright is unlikely to have an anti-competitive effect.

For example, in the new vehicle market Ford's rights prevent others from manufacturing and supplying copies of its vehicles but other manufacturers are free to, and do, design alternatives to Ford vehicles. (paras 8.5 and 8.6)

In other words, although the law of copyright applies to the new vehicle market this does not confer monopoly power on Ford since there are substitutes available.

In contrast, the market for replacement body panels is different in competitive terms from the new vehicle market because there are no adequate substitutes. For example, the only part which is suitable for replacing a Cortina bonnet is a part which is identical in design to the original. It follows that a law which confers on Ford the exclusive right to supply such parts in the replacement body parts market confers monopoly powers on Ford in that market. Thus the OFT concluded that Ford's behaviour did constitute an anti-competitive practice. Shortly before the publication of the OFT report Ford announced that it had reviewed its policy and had recently decided to sell a range of corrosion part panels, comprising some 50 individual panels, and planned to extend the range. However, this development was insufficient to persuade the OFT not to refer the case to the Monopolies Commission and it was duly referred in May 1984. The Commission reported in February 1985. Recall however that the Monopolies Commission considered a different and a wider question to that considered by the OFT – namely whether Ford's behaviour was against the public interest. As such the Commission paid more attention to Ford's arguments summarised in the preceding quotations in paragraphs 2, 3, and 4 than the OFT did.

To summarise this case, there are three questions at issue. Was Ford's behaviour legal? Did it constitute an anti-competitive tactic? And was it against the public interest? The first question, though of interest to lawyers, is of no relevance for our present purposes (remember that there was no suggestion that Kellogg was at any time acting illegally). The second question has definitely been answered in the affirmative by the OFT and this was confirmed by the Commission. On the third question the Commission ruled that Ford's behaviour was against the public interest, but it concluded that no suitable remedy existed under the present law. It took the view that while it was feasible for the Commission to compel Ford to grant licences to independent suppliers to supply body panels, it was not part of its function to adjudicate between the parties in deciding what constituted a reasonable royalty. It was likely, it decided, that what Ford would consider a reasonable royalty would not be considered reasonable by the independent suppliers. The Commission therefore advocated detailed changes in the law of patent which would have the effect of limiting the period of copyright on body panels to a maximum of five years. It noted however that changes in the law would take time to implement and that in the interim – which might be very extended – the preservation of competition in the supply of body parts would 'depend upon Ford's readiness to respect the public interest.' If Ford were not willing to do this 'competition . . . might be impossible'[5].

9.5 Pricing strategies in oligopolistic markets

The pricing behaviour exhibited by the firms in the market for cornflakes which we looked at in section 9.3 was relatively straightforward to analyse because there was one firm (Kellogg) which was clearly the market leader. Kellogg's pricing behaviour was not designed to oust the smaller companies, nor did the smaller firms engage in the sort of price competition designed to steal market share. Rather the firms competed through non-price competition in ways which had the effect of reinforcing the status quo. Generally, however, pricing behaviour in oligopolistic markets can be a very complex phenomenon. Before we go on to investigate some further examples of oligopolistic pricing behaviour it will be useful in this section to examine the range of behaviour which could be found in such markets.

In a monopoly situation, as the reader is now aware, there is an incentive for the monopolist to raise prices above the competitive level and thus earn monopoly (super-normal) profits. In an oligopoly, particularly a tight-knit oligopoly in which the number of firms with a significant market share is very small, there will be an incentive for the firms to act in concert as if they were a single monopolist, jointly maintaining prices in the industry above the competitive level in an attempt to maximise industry profits. Such behaviour is known as *joint profit-maximising* behaviour. It involves *collusion* since prices in the industry are set and maintained by a tacit agreement among the major suppliers not to indulge in competitive price cutting. Although the incentive to collude is strong there will be an opposing tendency: to compete actively by cutting prices in an attempt to steal market share away from the other firms in the industry. Unfortunately for the firm instigating the price competition however, it is likely to provoke a response from its rivals within the industry. If the rivals match the price cuts of the instigator then the net result will be that prices in the industry will fall. The consumer benefits as prices fall below the joint profit-maximising level.

Short-term considerations must also be tempered by the desire to maximise profits in the longer run. High super-normal profits will provide an incentive for new firms to enter the industry. The entry of these new firms will weaken the monopolistic position of the existing firms and reduce their ability to earn super-normal profits in the long run. To prevent the possibility of this happening, existing firms may forgo some of the super-normal profits they could earn in the short run, opting instead for lower prices as a way of deterring new entrants. Such a policy is known as *limit pricing* since the prices set are just low enough to discourage other firms from entering the market.

With an eye to the longer term the firm may even attempt to drive its existing rivals out of business by engaging in *predatory pricing*. As the name implies, a market leader whose costs, by virtue of its size, are lower than its rivals, may prey on its rivals by forcing prices down. Faced with such an attack, the firm which is being preyed upon has only two defences. It can try to match the market leader's price cuts which it will probably be unable to do since its costs (including marketing costs) per unit are higher. Alternatively, it can stick to a higher price, in which case it will lose customers to the aggressive market leader. Whichever of these two options is pursued, it may fall victim to the aggressive competition of the market leader and be forced out of the market. This leaves the surviving market leader in a stronger monopolistic position where it can raise prices and reap the monopoly profits which are its reward.

Such actively aggressive behaviour is, however, rare, particularly in oligopolies where no clear market leader exists. Even where one firm does have a dominant position in the market, it is likely to tolerate the existence of its smaller rivals. In such situations the dominant firm often assumes the role of a *price leader*, dictating the price in the market, while the smaller firms assume the role of *price followers*. This brings considerable benefits to the firms in the market. If each of them 'knows its place' and acts in accordance with its allotted role then much of the uncertainty can be removed. Firms in oligopolistic markets live in a very uncertain world since the outcome of any particular action depends on the reaction of rivals. A *modus vivendi* which allows the uncertainty to be reduced brings benefits to all the firms concerned. Such an arrangement is, of course, a form of collusive behaviour.

9.6 Oligopolistic behaviour: game theory

All the world's a game and all the men and women merely players. Shakespeare could have said this but didn't. He was unfamiliar with the work of Von Neumann and Morgenstern who developed the analytical apparatus called Game Theory. It has widespread applications, not the least of which is in analysing oligopolistic market situations.

First we outline the main features of a Game. This is best illustrated by the Prisoner's Dilemma. Two prisoners, Smith and Brown, are held in custody, accused of committing a serious robbery together. The evidence against them is not particularly strong and the prisoners know that without some sort of confession by one of them the case against them is unlikely to succeed. They are also aware however that if they are found guilty their sentence will be considerably less if they pleaded guilty in the first place. They are held incommunicado – that is, they cannot talk to each other.

Brown's actions

		Plead guilty	Plead innocent
Smith's strategies	Plead guilty	10	7
	Plead innocent	15	0

Figure 9.5 The Prisoner's Dilemma

The elements of the matrix show the payoffs to Smith (in terms of years of imprisonment)

Figure 9.5 illustrates the dilemma facing Smith. He has two strategies, to plead guilty or to plead innocent. The outcomes will depend not just on the strategy he adopts but also what Brown does. The elements of the matrix in Fig. 9.5 show the *payoffs* to Smith – the number of years of imprisonment. Obviously the best outcome is for both men to plead innocent. Then the prosecution case fails and Smith goes free (as does Brown). But this is a high risk strategy because if Smith pleads innocent and Brown pleads guilty, Brown's evidence will be enough to convict Smith who will then receive the maximum 15 year sentence. It may be better for Smith to plead guilty. Then he will certainly be convicted but the maximum sentence he will receive is only ten years and he may get as little as seven years if his evidence helps to convict Brown. What should Smith do? Remember the two men cannot communicate (feminists please note: they are almost certain to be men, since over 96 per cent of the prison population in Britain is male. See *Social Trends*.).

In this situation there is no best strategy because the payoffs depend on Brown's action. Pleading guilty is the strategy involving least risk. We call this the *minimax* strategy. It minimises the maximum sentence Smith could receive. Pleading innocent could be called the *minimin* strategy (minimising the minimum sentence).

The strategy chosen will depend, among other things, on a player's attitude towards risk. Risk lovers will take a chance and opt for the minimin strategy (Smith pleads innocent). But Game Theory suggests that risk averse behaviour may be more common and more sensible. A risk averse player, known as a conservative gamesman, will choose the minimax strategy (Smith pleads guilty). This example demonstrates why it may be difficult to achieve the best outcome, which is for both men to plead innocent and therefore go free. If only they could have agreed between themselves before they were caught that they would both plead innocent this could be achieved. But even if they had come to such an agreement there is no guarantee that they would stick to it. As is well known, there is no honour amongst thieves.

Note, finally that this particular game is symmetric. That is, although the matrix in Fig. 9.5 shows the payoffs to Smith we could draw a similar matrix from Brown's point of view, showing his payoffs. This will not always be the case. Some Games are non-symmetric.

The Prisoner's Dilemma is the classic game. It is easy to imagine how the principles illustrated here could be extended to many other situations, including pricing behaviour in oligopolistic markets.

Figure 9.6 illustrates a situation in which firm A has three possible strategies – to lower prices, leave prices unchanged, or to raise prices. Firm A is a duopolist – there is only one other major player in the market, firm B. The payoffs to firm A depend not just on the strategy A adopts but also on the response of firm B. The payoffs shown in the matrix are the changes in A's sales revenue resulting from the adoption of a particular strategy.

Consider strategy S_1 (raising prices). Provided B responds by also

		Firm B's response		
		Raise prices	Leave unchanged	Lower prices
	S_1 (raise prices)	+30	+5	−15
Firm A's strategies	S_2 (leave unchanged)	+8	0	−4
	S_3 (lower prices)	+7	−1	−30

Figure 9.6 Pricing strategies: a game

The elements of the matrix show the payoffs to firm A (in terms of the change in sales revenue)

raising prices this produces the best possible outcome, an increase in revenue of 30. But it carries great risk, because if B responds by cutting prices, then many of A's former customers will switch to firm B and A's revenue will fall by 15. In short S_1 is a high risk strategy. It is the maximax strategy and it is unlikely to be adopted by a conservative player.

Now consider strategies S_2 and S_3. Careful study of the payoffs in the matrix shows that S_3 is always inferior to S_2. That is, no matter what B does the payoffs from S_2 are always better than those from S_3. We say that S_2 *dominates* S_3. Therefore strategy S_3 will not be pursued by any rational player, whatever his attitude towards risk.

In the Prisoner's Dilemma we identified a minimax strategy. To find the minimax strategy it is necessary to look at each *row* in Fig. 9.6 and identify the worst outcome. Then choose the row with the smallest worst outcome. Here the minimax strategy is S_2. It minimises the maximum loss of sales revenue that could be suffered by A. This is the strategy that will be pursued by a risk averse oligopolist.

The payoffs shown in Fig. 9.6 are merely illustrative, but they do make sense. The game theory approach to the analysis of oligopolistic behaviour illustrates two key features of oligopolistic markets. Firstly such markets are likely to be characterised by price stability. Aggressive price cuts or price increases are risky strategies likely to be shunned by risk averse players. Such strategies are not unknown however. The reader may wish to construct a matrix in which the rewards from price cutting make it a tempting, if risky, strategy.

Secondly the payoffs shown in Fig. 9.6 illustrate that the potential benefits of collusion between players are very great. If they could agree among themselves the players could jointly raise prices, and both firms' profits would increase substantially. However, there is no honour among oligopolists either, so this behaviour will be uncommon, though not unknown. It would of course be construed as an anti-competitive tactic, and hence deemed illegal by the Monopolies and Mergers Commission.

9.7 The kinked demand curve in oligopoly

In the previous section we saw that in an oligopolistic market the outcome of a particular pricing strategy would depend upon the reactions of rivals. The analysis developed by Sweezy, known as the kinked demand curve, focuses upon the response of rivals to price changes. He assumes that rivals will match any price cuts but will not respond at all to price rises on the part of the initiating firm. The demand curve facing such a firm will therefore be kinked as in Fig. 9.7

The existing price is P_1. Below this price the demand curve is rather inelastic since any price cut will be matched by rival firms. Market shares remain unchanged therefore. But if the firm raises its price above P_1 then rival firms will not match its price rise. This leaves the

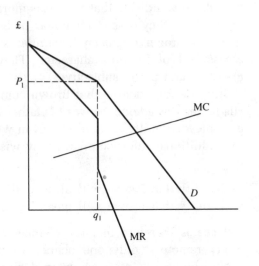

Figure 9.7

firm exposed. Customers switch to rival suppliers, and the firm loses market share. The demand curve is therefore rather elastic.

As we saw earlier (in section 6.1) there is a technical relationship between the demand curve and its associated marginal revenue curve. Marginal revenue is related to the slope of the demand curve. At P_1 the slope suddenly changes. The associated MR curve therefore has a discontinuity at this point. The profit-maximising firm will of course equate marginal cost with marginal revenue and produce an output level q_1.

As can be seen from Fig. 9.7 small changes in costs will not change the profit-maximising price and output levels. Thus the theory is quite consistent with the price stability which is characteristic of oligo-polistic markets.

9.8 A game with probabilities

As is so often the case in economics, the analytical techniques have an applicability which extends beyond strictly economic situations. Game Theory is one such technique. Decisions are almost always associated with risk and uncertainty. Identifying and adopting the minimax strategy is one decision rule which can be applied to such situations. But it is by no means the only rule.

Some writers distinguish between the terms risk and uncertainty, defining the former as a situation in which *probabilities* can be assigned and the latter as a situation in which it is not possible to assign probabilities. What is the nature of these probabilities? Suppose, for example that we are in the Prisoner's Dilemma illustrated earlier, where the payoff to Smith depended on whether Brown pleaded guilty or not. Suppose we said that the probability of Brown pleading guilty was 0.3 and the probability of him pleading innocent was 0.7 (the probabilities must sum to 1.0). These probabilities indicate that Brown is more likely to plead innocent but on what are they based? They may be based partly on past behaviour (perhaps Brown has been in similar situations before) or on some assessment of Brown's character. They are in other words partly objective and partly subjective.

Suppose for example that Brown comes from a long line of felons. His father was a felon, as was his father before him, and none of them ever pleaded guilty to anything, even when caught red-handed. With this additional information we may wish to amend the probabilities to:

probability that Brown will plead guilty = 0.05
probability that Brown will plead innocent = 0.95

It seems therefore that the chances of Brown pleading guilty are pretty remote – only one chance in twenty. If Smith knows this should he take it into account in deciding upon his plea?

Recall the possible payoffs to Smith from a strategy of pleading innocent. If Brown also pleads innocent then both men go free. There is only a 5 per cent chance that Brown will plead guilty, in which case an innocent plea by Smith would lead to the full 15 year sentence. A guilty plea by Smith will result in a 7 to 10 year sentence. In this situation it seems silly to ignore the extra information provided by these probabilities. The chances of the worst possible outcome occurring (a 15 year sentence) are only one in twenty and many people in Smith's predicament would surely take a chance and plead innocent.

Whether this is wise depends on whether the estimated probabilities do in some sense reflect the likelihood of the different states of the world occurring (that is, of Brown pleading guilty or innocent). The game theory approach implicitly assumes that we have no information on the likelihood of different states of the world occurring or treats them as equally likely.

Paradoxically it is the severity of a particular outcome, rather than its probability, which is likely to influence our choice of strategy. Consider the following game where the world community has two choices – to ignore the warnings of scientists about the threat of global warming or to take action now to limit its effects. Figure 9.8 presents the game in a schematic form. In our example note that the warnings of scientists are in all probability false. But there is a small probability – five per cent – that they are true. If they are true the costs to humankind are incalculably high. What is the correct strategy?

States of the world

	Warnings false prob. = 0.95	Warnings true prob. = 0.05
Take action	$50 bn per annum	$50 bn per annum
Ignore warnings	Zero	Incalculably high

Figure 9.8 Global warming: a game

The elements of the matrix show the payoffs – the future costs to the world community

9.9 Security and growth: diversification and integration

Firms are in business to do business, and it makes but little difference what business they do. There is no reason therefore why they should limit the range of their activities to those currently undertaken. Firms, particularly large firms, can move into new markets or withdraw from existing ones; they can move into or out of areas connected in some way with their main trading activities; they can even develop interests in areas which are totally alien to their existing activities. Normally, however, firms expand by developing in areas in which they already have some expertise. For example, the DIY market, a rapidly expanding sector, was entered by two firms – Sainsbury and W. H. Smith – who previously had no knowledge of DIY but did have plenty of expertise in retailing other products – food in the case of Sainsbury and books in the case of W. H. Smith. Both firms tackled the market in a similar way, by building very large supermarkets (hypermarkets) devoted to DIY products. When firms grow by expanding into new areas in this way it is known as *diversification*. The reason for choosing this development strategy is twofold. Firstly, it increases security since the overall risk is lessened by being spread: the old adage about not putting all your eggs in one basket (clearly relevant in the case of Sainsbury). Secondly, it allows the firm to grow as fast as its internal finances and its borrowing ability allow, rather than being constrained to grow at the same speed as the market in which it is currently operating (which may, of course, be stagnant or even declining).

Growth and security can also be achieved by a different form of expansion: *integration* (often known as *vertical integration*). Integration is a special form of diversification where the firm expands either backwards towards its source of raw materials or forwards towards its retail outlets. For example, if Sainsbury acquires a pork pie factory (and sells the pork pies in its supermarkets) this is an example of backwards integration. Similar examples of backwards integration are the chocolate manufacturers, many of whom own cocoa plantations, and the major rubber manufacturers who own rubber plantations. Forwards integration occurs when the brewers acquire public houses – the 'tied houses' – in which to sell their beer. British Airtours, a wholly owned subsidiary of British Airways, provides a further example of forwards integration. British Airways' main business is running a scheduled airline service but the establishment of British Airtours, a company which sells package holidays by air, provides a useful (captive) retail outlet for its services.

Note that integration, both forward and backward, can often serve to provide the firm with barriers to the entry of new firms into its existing markets. As such, these developments could be viewed as forming part of an anti-competitive strategy.

Both diversification and integration are examples of expansion into areas related in some way to the firm's existing activities. Some firms, however, are what is known as *conglomerates*; that is, they have interests in a number of unrelated areas. Lonrho, for example, is a major international company with interests in mining, newspapers (*The Observer*) and retailing. Similarly, Trafalgar House has interests in shipbuilding, publishing, property and mining. The archetypal conglomerate, however, was a fictitious company invented by the economist J. K. Galbraith. His company – Universal Global Enterprises or UGE for short (to emphasise its size) – was an amalgam of several real American corporations. UGE had subsidiary companies operating in every conceivable sphere of human activity, from cola to computers and from detergents to defence. The activities of conglomerates like UGE will be discussed in greater detail in Chapter 11 when we consider multinational corporations.

It should be clear that the three avenues of expansion we have identified – diversification, integration and conglomeration – are different ways in which the firm attempts to achieve both a more secure future for itself and faster growth of sales and profits. What is also clear is that the three types of expansion normally result from merger activity between two companies or takeover activity. Since mergers and acquisitions are such an important aspect of the growth of firms, they are considered in greater detail in the following section.

9.10 Mergers

An important element in the growth of firms is merger activity. Mergers may be motivated by the desire to diversify the firm's activities – so-called conglomerate mergers. They may involve the firms in vertical links (forward or backward vertical integration). Finally, they may take the form of the acquisition of former competitors.

Merger activity involving the acquisition of competitors will clearly result in increased concentration in the industry in question, together with a concomitant rise in the market power of the newly merged companies. Vertical integration by merger will often also result in an increase in market power even though it does not increase concentration *per se*. Of course, mergers may also result in improved efficiency through rationalisation and through an improved ability to reap the benefits of economies of scale. Indeed, this is the major justification which is put forward for merger activity.

Part of the remit of the Monopolies and Mergers Commission is to decide whether a proposed merger is 'in the public interest.' Its remit allows it to investigate any proposed merger where:

1. The merger would lead to an increase in market concentration.
2. The merger would increase the ability of firms to engage in anti-competitive tactics (as a result of increased concentration or through vertical links).
3. The value of assets taken over exceeds a certain sum, set at £30 m in 1984. This condition allows the MMC to investigate conglomerate mergers.

In recent years public policy towards mergers as carried out by the MMC has tended to evolve, albeit slowly, in two ways. Firstly, the 1980 Competition Act (which concerned itself with competition rather than with mergers) encouraged the MMC to pay more attention to anti-competitive behaviour, both actual and potential, rather than to market concentration *per se*.

The second shift in emphasis in public policy towards mergers has been away from a presumption that mergers are in the public interest (unless the MMC can prove otherwise) and towards a more neutral attitude towards mergers. This results partly from accumulated evidence which shows that the claim that mergers increase efficiency is non-proven. Some of the evidence is contained in the 1978 Green Paper, *A Review of Monopolies and Mergers Policy*. Table 9.3, reproduced from the Green Paper, summarises the results of a study by Meeks of the post-merger profitability of 213 larger quoted companies which merged in the period 1964–72. Meek's method was to compare the profits of the combined company in the six years following the merger with the profits of the acquiring and acquired firms in the three years prior to the merger. As Table 9.3 shows, average profits declined after the merger. Only in the year of acquisition did recorded profits rise and too much weight should not be attached to that finding since measurement problems are particularly acute in that year. Although Meek's findings may seem surprising they are in fact in accord with the weight of evidence (in the Green Paper and subsequently), both for the UK and internationally.

Notwithstanding these findings, merger activity continues unabated.

Table 9.3 Post-merger profitability and the proportion of firms showing a decline in profits

Year after merger	Number of firms	Change in profitability	% of firms with lower profits
0	213	+0.15	34
1	192	−0.02	54
2	174	−0.01	52
3	146	−0.06	53
4	103	−0.10	66
5	67	−0.11	64
6	44	−0.07	52
7	21	−0.07	62

Column three shows the change – relative to the average of the three pre-merger years – in the ratio of the profitability of the merged companies to the profitability of the industries to which they belonged.

Source: G. Meeks, *Disappointing Marriage: a study of the gains from merger*, CUP, 1977 (quoted in 1978 Green Paper).

Acquiring companies often claim that the proposed merger will lead to synergy – the profits of the merged company will be more than the sum of its parts. This may occur (although the evidence does not support this) but even if it does, one may question whether the increased profitability results from higher prices made possible by market power, or from lower costs stemming from increased efficiency. It is on this basis that the MMC has to decide whether a proposed merger is 'in the public interest'.

9.11 Mergers: cross-Channel ferries

To illustrate the issues involved when the MMC considers merger proposals we shall look at the market for cross-Channel ferry services. During the 1980s this market was the subject of a considerable amount of merger activity and there were several references to the MMC.

In 1981 a company then known as European Ferries operated nine routes (trading under the name of Townsend Thoresen) and owned a number of ports. The other major operator was Sealink (then a subsidiary of British Rail) who also owned ports. There were a few other operators the largest of which was P & O Ferries.

There existed a considerable amount of excess capacity on most routes as is illustrated in Table 9.4 and this had led to cut-throat price competition in order to attract passengers. As a result European Ferries' profits had been depressed and Sealink had made losses. European Ferries stated that they wished to acquire Sealink in order to rationalise the services and eliminate excess capacity. Failure to do so they argued might result in the withdrawal of services as a result of losses or continued low returns on investment. European Ferries were so keen to acquire Sealink that they even offered to give an

Table 9.4 Vehicle deck load factors

	Routes	Load factors[a]	
		1979	1980
short routes			
Sealink	Dover/Folkestone–Calais/Boulogne	36	29
EFL	Dover–Calais	45	36
P & O	Dover–Boulogne	45	38
longer routes			
Sealink	Dover/Folkestone–Ostend	72	66
Sealink	Newhaven–Dieppe	72	72
Sealink	Harwich–Hook of Holland	66	65
EFL	Dover–Zeebrugge	62	53
P & O	Southampton–LeHavre	73	60
P & O/NSF	Hull–Europort	75	70
Unweighted average of short routes		42	34
Unweighted average of longer routes		70	64

[a]Percentage of total space available for vehicles which is actually occupied.

Source: *The Monopolies and Mergers Commission Report on European Ferries/ Sealink Proposed Merger*, HMSO, 1981.

undertaking on price restraint.

The proposed merger was referred to the MMC in 1981. Earlier in the year the MMC had allowed a merger to go ahead between the only two hovercraft operators on the cross-Channel route. The Swedish owned HoverLloyd took over British Rail's Seaspeed. Although this gave the newly merged company, Hoverspeed, a 100 per cent monopoly of cross-Channel hovercraft services, the merger had been allowed because the MMC accepted the submission that without a rationalisation of capacity, hovercraft services might be withdrawn completely.

The MMC took a different view of the European Ferries' bid for Sealink however. The merger would have produced a monopoly (using the MMC's criteria). The merged company would have had over 50 per cent of the whole cross-Channel market and an even larger market share on other routes. In addition their ownership of many of the Channel and North Sea ports might have been used to discriminate against existing competitors and new entrants into the market.

In the event the MMC concluded that the proposed merger was against the public interest. The reduction in competition, they argued, might lead to higher prices and a reduction in consumer choice. Increased vertical integration (the ownership of many of the relevant ports) would also have conferred a disturbing amount of market power on the new company. In coming to this decision the MMC clearly took the view that any benefit resulting from rationalisation and increased efficiency would be outweighed by the costs to consumers of increased market power.

Some writers have pointed to the inconsistency in allowing the Hoverspeed/HoverLloyd merger to go through while blocking the European Ferries/Sealink merger. The reason for the MMC's decision is partly to do with the way in which a market can reasonably be defined. The hovercraft merger produced a 100 per cent concentration in hovercraft services, but hovercraft accounted for a relatively small proportion of cross-Channel traffic, and there were good substitutes available. The European Ferries/Sealink merger would have increased concentration (but to much less than 100 per cent) and increased market power (because of the ownership of ports) in a much more important and clearly defined market for which there was no substitute at all (apart from air transport).

Mergers and acquisitions 1984–90

In 1984 Sealink UK was officially put up for sale as part of the Government's privatisation programme. European Ferries asked to be allowed to bid, promising to cut cross-Channel ferry prices by 15–20 per cent if it were allowed to buy Sealink. However both European Ferries and P & O were barred from bidding for Sealink, which was eventually purchased by Sea Containers, a consortium registered in Bermuda.

In 1985 European Ferries bought the Anglo-French services of P & O increasing its market share of the cross-Channel route. In 1987 further rationalisation took place when P & O acquired the whole of European Ferries, the new company being known as P & O/European Ferries. Sealink was acquired by the Swedish owned Stena Line to become Sealink Stena. By the early 1990s the market was more or less evenly divided between these two principal operators with around 80–90 per cent of the market.

Enter the Tunnel

The prospect of a major competitor in the shape of Eurotunnel (scheduled to open in May 1993) changes the competitive environment. There will be a substantial increase in capacity and probably fierce competition in terms of price and quality of service.

In anticipation of this the two principal operators P & O/EF and Sealink applied to the MMC in late 1989 to be allowed to combine their operation. The MMC turned down the application clearly believing that in the four year run up to the opening of the Tunnel some competition was desirable.

It seems highly probable however that before 1994 the MMC will allow P & O/EF and Sealink to rationalise and combine their activities to compete more effectively against Eurotunnel, whose marginal costs have been estimated to be only 20 per cent of the ferries' costs. All the ferries invested heavily in the late 1980s and early 1990s in larger, more luxurious ferries designed to promote the pleasurable aspect of crossing by sea. The 1990s are likely to see a large growth in demand so that even if the ferries lose market share to the Tunnel their business may still grow. In the short term however they face reduced revenues as a result of the loss of duty free sales, and increased capital costs needed to bring their older ferries up to the more stringent saftey requirements introduced after the 'Herald of Free Enterprise' disaster.

9.12 Petrol: a case of oligopoly pricing

At the wholesale level the market for petrol in the UK is an oligopoly. Unlike the market for breakfast cereals, however, which exhibited a reasonably stable structure over the period studied, the market for petrol has witnessed a reduction in seller concentration over the last 30 years. Moreover, in the market for petrol no firm is now the undisputed price leader, a role comparable to that played by Kellogg in the breakfast cereal market. Table 9.5 shows changes in the degree of seller concentration in the market for petrol since 1953, a convenient starting point since this date marks the abolition of

Table 9.5 Reduction in concentration (shares of the UK retail market for petrol (%))

	1953	1960	1970	1975	1976	1980	1985	1991
Shell	51.4	49.4	41.9	40.8	22.9	16.9	14.6	13.6
BP					17.4	11.6	12.1	10.2
Esso	28.4	29.8	22.5	21.8	22.0	20.0	8.4	12.9
Texaco	14.0	12.5	8.9	8.0	7.7	8.0	8.0	6.5
Mobil	1.1	4.2	4.0	4.3	4.4	4.8	4.4	4.6
Petrofina	2.2	2.5	3.6	3.8	3.7	3.8	4.2	4.3
Others	2.9	1.6	19.1	21.3	21.9	34.9	48.3	47.9

The figures are the percentage share of total retail outlets, an approximate indication of sales.

Notes: Shell and BP shared a joint retailing organisation, Shell Mex and BP Ltd. until 1976, after which their respective market shares are shown separately

In 1991 the 'others' comprised Burmah (7.0%), Conoco (5.7%), Kuwait (4.5%), UK, Elf, Total, Anglo, Gulf, Murco and others not listed separately.

Source: early years figures quoted in R. W. Shaw and C. J. Sutton, *Industry and Competition*, Macmillan, 1976 and from R. M. Grant, 'Pricing behaviour in the UK wholesale market for petrol 1970-80: a structure-conduct analysis', *Journal of Industrial Economics*, Vol. XXX, March 1982. Later years figures from *Retail Marketing Survey*, 1991, *Petroleum Review* and *Institute of Petroleum*.

wartime price controls and the reintroduction of branding.

Market share in Table 9.5 is measured by the percentage of the total retail outlets supplied by each firm. As can be seen in 1953 five firms supplied virtually the whole market. One firm, Shell-Mex and BP Ltd, who at that time shared a joint retailing organisation had over 50 per cent of the market. The top three firms – Shell-BP, Esso and Texaco – had a combined market share of almost 94 per cent.

Since 1953 however concentration in the market has declined continuously, a milestone in this process being the splitting up of Shell-Mex and BP into separate companies in 1976. By 1991 the top four firms had less than 45 per cent of the market and there were numerous smaller players.

The figures in Table 9.5 measure market share rather imperfectly, since they may tend to overestimate the share of firms with a large number of small sites and underestimate the share of firms who concentrate sales into a smaller number of high-volume sites in prime locations. Data on gallonage are a more satisfactory measure of market share and this is shown for selected years in Table 9.6. As we would expect the picture which emerges is one of declining concentration.

The reduction in concentration was a key aspect of the change in the structure of the industry, which in turn brought with it a change in the conduct of the firms operating there. Note the wording of the previous sentence. It says that the change in structure *brought with it* a change in conduct. We could have said that the change in structure *led to* a change in conduct which implies a definite causal link, but this would have been too strong since the causal link, though hypothesised, is by no means firmly established. We could, alternatively, have said that the change in structure *was accompanied by* a change in conduct but this would have missed the whole point, which

Table 9.6 Wholesalers' shares of the retail market for petrol (by gallonage)

Company	Market share (%)					
	1964	1970	1975	1976	1980	1988
Shell-Mex and BP Ltd	45.0	39.6	35.0	—	—	—
Munster Sims						
Shell UK	—	— —	19.3	22.6	16.5	
Esso	27.4	23.4	19.2	18.7	19.6	19.3
BP Oil	—	—	—	14.7	15.1	12.7
Texaco/*Regent*	11.1	8.0	9.4	9.1	8.2	9.6
Mobil	6.0	7.1	6.6	7.0	7.1	7.7
Conoco/Jet	3.5	3.8	4.1	4.2	5.4	6.1
Total Oil	1.5	3.1	4.8	4.5	2.8	3.9
Elf/VIP/*Isherwoods*	0.8	2.1	2.3	2.8	2.8	3.0
Petrofina UK Ltd	2.5	2.4	2.8	2.9	2.2	3.9
Burmah/*Lobitos/Major*	—	2.6	2.9	3.1	1.6	4.6
I.C.I.	—	0.9	2.6	2.7	2.7	0.0
Gulf Oil	0.2	1.0	1.9	2.5	2.3	3.0
Amoco	—	1.2	1.8	1.8	2.5	1.8
Kuwait	—	—	—	—	2.5	2.3
Others	0.8	4.8	6.7	5.9	5.1	5.5

Companies whose names are shown in *italic* type were taken over during the period.
Source: as for Table 9.5 and for later years from MMC Survey Report.

is that the conduct (and performance) of an industry is influenced, if not determined, by its structure, the most important, but not the only aspect of which is the degree of concentration.

As we saw earlier the behaviour of firms in oligopolistic markets is uncertain because they are torn between the desire to compete and the opposing desire to collude. At any one time a firm's decision as to which of these two strategies to pursue will be influenced by the following considerations.

1. Seller concentration

Other things being equal, the smaller the number of firms in an industry the easier it will be for them to collude if they wish to do so. The recognition of mutual interdependence will be that much greater and communication, both direct and implied, between the firms will be easier. The extent to which firms recognize their mutual interdependence will depend on the degree of cross-price elasticity of demand for their products. In other words, if the output of one firm is a very close substitute for the output of another, the cross-price elasticity, and therefore the recognition of interdependence, will be high. This condition is clearly satisfied in the market for petrol, since petrol is viewed by the consumer as a more or less homogeneous commodity. The introduction in 1969 of the star-rating of petrol by octane level reinforced this.

2. Demand conditions

At the firm level the price elasticity of demand is likely to be high because of the perceived homogeneity of the suppliers' petrol. At the industry level, however, the price elasticity of demand will be an important influence on the extent to which monopoly profits can be earned. If demand is inelastic, price increases will not reduce demand significantly, so that revenue and profits will increase. The demand for petrol appears to be highly price inelastic in the short run – the price of petrol rose by 75 per cent between the beginning of 1974 and the end of 1975 yet consumption fell by only 0.6 per cent. Thus, to the extent that the demand for petrol is inelastic, the incentive for firms to collude in raising prices and reaping monopoly profits is that much higher.

3. Entry barriers

Entry barriers are a way of protecting in the long term the monopoly profits discussed above. In the market for petrol, barriers to the entry of new firms existed by virtue of the fact that at the beginning of the period under consideration existing firms – the 'majors' – were vertically integrated backwards towards the source of their raw materials. The majors were of course active in oil exploration and production and they also had, and still have, a virtual monopoly on UK refinery capacity. This was not an insurmountable barrier to potential entrants, however, since there was an alternative source of supply, the Rotterdam spot market (and in fact many of the smaller independent firms secured supplies through contracts with the majors, though at prices which allowed little scope for price cutting). During the period under review the existing firms also sought to strengthen their position by forward integration. This was achieved by buying up existing retail outlets, particularly those in prime positions, and by exclusive supply contracts with retailers (so-called 'solus site' arrangements).

Thus, the existence of these entry barriers discouraged new firms from entering the market but did not, as it turned out, prevent it. The inability of the existing firms to prevent this entry led to the reduction in concentration we have already noted. This reduced both the incentive for firms to collude and the ease with which they could do so, and was a significant factor in changing the observed pricing behaviour in the industry.

4.   Cost conditions

If one company had enjoyed a clear cost advantage it might have been tempted to compete actively with the others in an attempt to oust them from the market. This was not the case, however, since they all used similar technologies for producing oil and refining it into petrol, so that their costs were similar. This therefore tended to reduce the likelihood of competition and increased the likelihood of collusion.

5.   Supply conditions

Over the period studied supply conditions fluctuated between periods of shortage and periods of abundance. During periods when supplies were short the Rotterdam spot market dried up as a source of supply for the independent wholesalers, severely curtailing their ability to penetrate the retail market. However, in the period of abundant supplies between late 1974 and 1977 there was a substantial increase in market penetration by independents.

All the foregoing considerations are relevant to the change in the structure of the industry which took place. The most dramatic evidence of this changed structure is the observed reduction in concentration, but as we have seen there are other aspects which were important. The change in structure brought about a breakdown of the pricing discipline which had been a feature of the industry in the 1960s. During that period the major suppliers (principally Shell-Mex and BP but occasionally Esso) had acted as the price leader with the

Table 9.7 Inner zone scheduled wholesale prices for 4-star motor spirit

Date	Shell	Esso	Texaco	Mobil
16. 1.70	6/0	6/0	6/0	6/0
31. 7.70	6/0½	6/0½	6/0½	6/0½
6.11.70	6/1½	6/1½	6/1½	6/1½
21. 2.71	31.75	—	—	—
22. 2.71	—	31.75	31.75	31.75
28. 4.72	—	—	—	31.15
29. 4.72	32.15	—	—	—
1. 5.72	—	32.15	32.15	—
9. 9.72	32.65	—	—	—
11. 9.72	—	32.65	32.65	32.65
29. 4.73	33.65	33.65	—	33.65
15. 5.73	—	—	33.65	—
4.10.73	34.65	34.65	34.65	34.65
15.12.73	37.35	37.35	37.35	37.35
12. 2.74	45.25	45.30	45.25	45.27
18.12.74	52.20	52.15	52.20	52.20
2.12.75	55.00	—	—	—
3.12.75	—	55.00	—	55.02
8.12.75	—	—	55.00	—
9. 4.76*	13.74	13.745	13.74	13.75
29.10.76	14.51	—	—	—
30.10.76	—	—	14.63	—
3.11.76	—	—	—	14.52
6.11.76	—	14.51	—	—
21.12.76	—	—	—	14.74
1. 1.77	—	0	14.76	—
10. 1.77	—	14.73	—	—
29. 3.77*	15.61	14.83	15.86	15.84
26. 4.77	16.08	—	—	—
27. 4.77	—	—	16.08	—
29. 4.77	—	16.08	—	16.08
8. 7.77	15.49	—	—	—
8. 8.77*	14.39	14.95	14.98	14.98
27.10.77	—	—	—	14.65
1.12.77	—	14.14	—	—
8. 2.79	14.97	—	—	—
12. 2.79	—	—	—	15.21
16. 2.79	15.08	15.17	15.08	—
6. 4.79	—	15.82	16.08	15.82
9. 4.79	15.73	—	—	—
26. 5.79	—	—	18.58	18.42
12. 6.79	18.45	—	—	—
18. 6.79	—	18.43	—	—
2. 7.79	—	19.60	—	—
3. 7.79	19.81	—	—	—
4. 7.79	—	—	20.08	—
5. 7.79	—	—	—	20.41
29.11.79	20.20	—	—	—
28.12.79	—	20.30	—	—
29.12.79	—	—	20.50	—
1. 1.80	—	—	—	20.41
17. 1.80	21.08	—	21.20	21.20

Table 9.7 contd.

Date	Shell	Esso	Texaco	Mobil
18. 1.80	—	21.07	—	—
19. 2.80	21.08	21.64	—	—
20. 2.80	—	—	21.84	21.85
26. 3.80*	23.75	23.54	23.74	23.75
17. 5.80	—	—	—	24.35
21. 5.80	—	—	24.29	—
23. 5.80	24.13	—	—	—
24. 5.80	—	23.92	—	—
3. 6.80	24.66	—	—	—
7. 6.80	—	24.61	24.63	24.66
5. 7.80	24.28	24.23	—	—
9. 7.80	—	—	24.28	—
13. 8.80	—	—	—	23.90

Notes: 1970 prices in shillings and old pence per gallon: 1971–5 prices per gallon: 1976–80 prices in pence per litre.
Asterisks show changes in excise tax.
Prices include duty, exclude VAT.
Source: R. M. Grant, 'Pricing behaviour in the UK wholesale market for petrol 1970-80: a "structure-conduct" analysis', *Journal of Industrial Economics*, Vol. XXX, March 1982.

other firms dutifully following any change in prices. As can be seen from Table 9.7, this behaviour continued until the end of 1973.

Between 1970 and 1973, as Table 9.7 shows, firms charged identical prices and changed prices by the same amount. The response to a price change in most cases occurred either the same day or the following day. This 'well-orchestrated parallelism' was a clear example of collusion. Any price competition that did occur during this period took place by way of the discounts which wholesalers granted to retailers rather than through the posted wholesale prices shown in Table 9.7. Since the magnitude of these discounts was confidential, any competition between the wholesalers was thus furtive rather than open.

The Arab-Israeli war of late 1973 brought a brief period of shortage of supplies of petrol and a rapid increase in prices which was followed by a period of plentiful supplies. With supplies obtained from the Rotterdam spot market, where prices had dropped dramatically because of the glut, the independents were able to undercut the existing firms and increase their market share. This increased the pressure on the major suppliers to defend their position by price competition and, as can be seen from Table 9.7, the collusive pricing behaviour degenerated into more open competition.

9.13 Predatory pricing? Big boys attack Virgin

In oligopolistic markets outbreaks of price competition are relatively uncommon – so uncommon in fact that they are newsworthy. In September 1984, under headlines which talked about 'price wars', *The Times* reported the allegation that new entrants into the transatlantic airline business were being subjected to 'unfair competition' from the established firms. The new entrants, Virgin Atlantic and People Express, had commenced operations earlier in 1984, undercutting the existing operators. The President of Virgin Atlantic complained vociferously when the existing airlines announced that they too would be lowering their fares. 'It is a bit of a coincidence,' he said, 'that British Airways, Pan Am and TWA are all announcing this low fare on the same day. I would just like to point out that when Laker Airways was around they did a similar thing at a similar time. And after he had gone out of business fares went right up again. This is the first time fares have gone down like this since that time.' British Airways defended their new low fares, however, saying that it was economic and covered costs (the new fare of £259 was some £19 less than the pre-existing one and only £1 more than Virgin's). Virgin complained that British Airways' high profits from safe routes would enable it to crush smaller but more efficient competitors. For a small airline, competing with BA was 'like getting into a bleeding competition with a blood bank'.[6]

9.14 An entry-forestalling price: *TV Times* attacks *TV Plus*

For many years television viewers in the UK got their programme information from one of three sources. BBC programmes (Channels 1 and 2) were listed in the anachronistically entitled *Radio Times*, on sale each week priced at 50p. Programmes on the independent channels (ITV and Channel 4) were listed in the *TV Times*, also on sale at 50p. This rather cosy arrangement existed only because the television companies held copyright on their listings and refused to allow other companies to publish them, apart from the daily newspapers (the third source) which were only allowed to publish listings of the current day's programmes. Viewers requiring advance information therefore had to purchase both the *Radio Times* and the *TV Times*.

It was decided that this restrictive practice should be abandoned with effect from 1 March 1991. In the run-up to the due date *Radio Times* advertised heavily, hoping to persuade viewers, who henceforth would only buy one magazine, that the one to buy should be *Radio Times* rather than *TV Times*. Habit, the publishers knew, persists. Once captured, readers are comparatively easy to retain. Once lost, they are difficult to regain. *TV Times* responded by advertising of its own, thinking along similar lines.

With the impending removal of restrictions a third publisher entered the market with a magazine called *TV Plus* which also carried listings for all four channels. The price was 45p, five pence cheaper than the established rivals. The response of *TV Times* was immediate. It announced that for the first three weeks the price of the new *TV Times* would be just 25p – half the price it had been originally and substantially cheaper than the price charged by the new entrant.

9.15 Buyer power: the rise of the retailers

In all of the markets considered so far in this chapter the consumer has been faced with an oligopolistic market structure of varying degrees of concentration. However, the demand side of these markets has been atomistic – there have been lots of buyers, none of whom is large enough to influence the prices set by sellers. Most of the products which consumers buy are bought through retailers however and some parts of the retail sector are characterised by a high degree of concentration. In this section we examine one of the most important parts of the retail sector – the grocery trade.

In grocery retailing the most significant development in the last 30 years has been the rise of the multiples selling through supermarkets, and latterly through very large supermarkets. The corollary of this has been the decline of the small independent retailer. Table 9.8 illustrates this trend.

Table 9.8 Market shares in grocery retailing 1961–96 (%)

	Multiples	Co-ops	Independents
1961	29.2	10.9	59.9
1971	46.5	7.1	54.4
1981	62.7	13.7	23.6
1989	74.5	10.9	14.6
1996	77.6	13.3	9.1

Source: from various sources brought together in S. Jenkins, Grocery Retailing, unpublished undergraduate dissertation. The primary sources include IGD (Institute of Grocery Distribution) and AGB (Audits of Great Britain) data made available through industry sources. The 1996 figure is a forecast.

Among the multiples themselves the degree of concentration is large and becoming larger as Table 9.9 illustrates. The C5 ratio shows that in 1990 the top five firms accounted for 65 per cent of total sales. Even this figure tends to underestimate the true degree of concentration since, for reasons of distributional efficiency the multiples tend to concentrate their activities in particular geographical areas. Sainsbury for example does most of its business in London and the South East but has few stores in Scotland, whereas Argyll and Gateway are strongly represented there.

The 1980s saw an increase in concentration associated partly with

Table 9.9 Percentage market share of the multiples

	1986	1990
Sainsbury	12.8	19.1
Tesco	12.5	16.4
Argyll	9.3	10.1
Asda	7.5	9.8
Gateway	12.2	9.7
C5 ratio	54.3	65.1
Kwik Save	2.8	7.8

Argyll comprises Lo-cost (discount supermarket), Cordon Bleu (freezer centre), Presto, Liptons, Templetons, Galbraith and Safeway.

The Gateway Corporation (formerly the Dee Corporation) comprises Lennon's, Key Markets, International, Fine Fare and Carrefour. In 1989 Gateway was acquired by Isosceles Plc.

Source: as for Table 9.8.

takeover activity. For example, Gateway (formerly the Dee Corporation) acquired Lennon's, Key Markets, International, Fine Fare and Carrefour before itself being taken over by Isosceles Plc. The two largest firms however grew organically – that is, without acquiring other firms. Some commentators have argued that in the 1990s the Big Five shown in Table 9.9 will give way to the Big Four or perhaps even the Big Three. Other commentators have seen the top two firms – Sainsbury and Tesco – as an emerging duopoly. An opposing view sees the trend towards higher concentration slowing down in the 1990s and niche markets developing with smaller operators satisfying the requirements of the top-up shopper, the less mobile, and the convenience shopper. Whatever evolves in the 1990s the degree of concentration is unlikely to fall however.

Among the multiples there is intense competition for market share. A key element of this competition, though by no means the only one, is price. Clearly therefore each of the multiples will wish to secure supplies of a particular product as cheaply as possible so that they can undercut their rival retailers while still maintaining an acceptable mark-up to cover the overheads of the store. The market power of the multiples enables them to impose considerable pressure on their suppliers. Where these suppliers are individual farmers supplying fresh produce the balance of advantage is clearly with the retailer – a real David and Goliath situation, except that here of course, Goliath wins. Where the suppliers are food manufacturers the balance of advantage is not so heavily weighted in the supermarkets' favour, for the food manufacturers themselves form an oligopolistic grouping with a few large firms dominating the market. However the food manufacturers have complained that the multiples use their market power to great effect to squeeze manufacturers' profit margins. The threat to 'de-list' a product (that is, not to stock it on the supermarket shelves) is normally sufficient to persuade a manufacturer to accept the terms which the multiple dictates.

It would be wrong to suppose however that the supermarkets have it all their own way in the bargaining situations with their suppliers. If the good in question is more or less homogeneous – that is, if the products of rival suppliers are more or less indistinguishable or at least acceptable substitutes – then the supplier will be in a weak bargaining position. He will have no market power. If, on the other hand the supplier can successfully differentiate his brand from that of his rivals, and establish loyalty with consumers, he will be in a strong bargaining position, that is, he will enjoy an element of monopoly power. The extent to which suppliers of manufactured food products are able to do this is refered to by marketing people as 'the strength of the brand'. For example Nescafe instant coffee and Heinz tomato ketchup are both strong brands. They enjoy a privileged position in their respective markets since they are acknowledged as the market leaders. Since they are perceived by the consumer as being superior to rival brands they can be sold at a premium (that is, at a higher price than rival brands). The extra profit which this makes possible can be 're-invested' in advertising, further reinforcing the strength of the brand. The stronger the brand the more that can be spent on advertising. The more that can be spent on advertising, the stronger the brand – a process of circular causation which protects the privileged position of the market leader and creates barriers to the entry of new firms.

A strong brand then is one for which there are no close substitutes. The extent to which the brand is perceived as being superior to rivals is due partly to real differences in the product and partly to imaginary differences created by advertising. The most effective form of advertising is that which seeks to convince the consumer not just that the brand in question is superior but that no acceptable substitute exists – slogans such as 'Beanz means Heinz'. That is, baked beans are identified exclusively with that particular brand. The elasticity of demand for Heinz beans is therefore lower so that higher prices for Heinz beans do not cause consumers to switch to rival brands.

Own-brands

One of the most significant effects of the increase in buyer concentration in retailing has been the development of own-label products, sold under the brand name not of the food manufacturer but of the supermarket that sells them. Own-label now accounts for over

Table 9.10 Own-brand turnover of retailers (1985) (%)

Marks and Spencer	100
Sainsbury	60
Co-op	33
Tesco	40
Waitrose	55
Argyll	40
Dee Corporation (Gateway)	10

Source: P. J. McGoldrick, *Retail Marketing*, McGraw-Hill, 1990.

Between 1980 and 1990 the average own-brand share amongst the multiples increased from 22.2 to 31.5 per cent (source: IGD).

60 per cent of Sainsbury's sales. Figures for other retailers are shown in Table 9.10.

Own-label products are sometimes manufactured by the brand leaders themselves, or more often by rival manufacturers (for example, General Foods, the manufacturer of Maxwell House instant coffee, also manufactures own-label instant coffee for Sainsbury). The own-label product undercuts the manufacturer's brand by a considerable margin.

From the retailer's point of view the attraction of own-label is threefold. Firstly, by charging lower prices they hope to steal market share from their rivals. Secondly, the mark-up (for the retailer) on own-label may be more than on branded goods. Thirdly, the fact that the own-label becomes the brand means that the retailer can begin to enjoy the sort of brand loyalty previously enjoyed by the manufacturer. This carries with it all the advantages of a differentiated product and consequent barriers to the entry of new firms which typify the aspirations of oligopolistic firms. The own-label supplier *par excellence* is Marks and Spencer who sell exclusively own-brand products.

The manufacturers themselves would probably prefer not to supply own-label since the profit margin which they receive on own-label is less than on branded products. However the strength of the retailers, coupled with the need to fill some manufacturing overcapacity, has compelled the manufacturers to enter into long term contracts to supply own-label to the retailers.

Countervailing power

The economist J. K. Galbraith has argued that there is a natural tendency in market economies for the existence of monopoly power to give birth to countervailing groups seeking to win some of those monopoly profits for themselves. He calls this *countervailing power*. The growth of concentration among retailers, pitted against the oligopolistic power of the food manufacturers can perhaps be seen as an example of countervailing power. However, most economists – including perhaps Galbraith himself in later works – would stop short of seeing the growth of retail concentration as evidence for the existence of a natural law of countervailing power. If there were such a natural tendency in market economies this would be regarded by supporters of the market system (that is, capitalism) as one of the strengths of the system. A dynamic system of checks and balances which ensures that no one group gets too much power, and ensures that the abuse of a monopoly position carries with it the seeds of its own destruction, would indeed be a powerful justification for the market mechanism as an equitable way of allocating resources. What is more likely however is that the increase in concentration among retailers is nothing more than an historical accident brought about by changes in social patterns (for example, the increase in car ownership, and the change in shopping habits brought about by the increased ownership of fridges and freezers).

The profit motive is a powerful incentive however. In the 1980s the multiples extended the range of activities in their superstores to include non-food items such as clothes, banking and petrol, hoping to capture for themselves some of the profits to be made in those areas. At the same time, ironically, the petrol retailers were attempting to exploit the niche market for convenience shopping by opening up shops selling a limited range of grocery products at their petrol stations. In April 1990 for example, Shell announced plans to incorporate 'corner shops' into its portfolio of 2850 petrol stations.

9.16 The UK motor-cycle market

The UK motor-cycle market is an oligopoly. Textbooks tell us that in oligopolistic markets we should expect certain types of behaviour. This section analyses the conduct of firms within the market in the last ten years and provides some interesting real world examples of the behaviour of oligopolistic firms.

The problem with most industry studies – for both the student and researcher alike – is their extreme complexity. In contrast, the UK motor-cycle market comprises a compact and well-defined market. Almost all the bikes sold are imported. There are no domestic producers of any significance. We can therefore legitimately argue that there is no UK motor-cycle industry as such. This leaves us free to concentrate on the demand side of the market without having to worry about cost structures, scale economies and all the other complexities of the supply side of the industry.

An oligopoly is a market dominated by a few large firms. Table 9.11 shows that the UK motor-cycle market fits this description very neatly. Four large producers – all Japanese – dominate the market. In addition there are some smaller players. BMW have a specialist niche

Table 9.11 Shares in the UK motor cycle market (% by volume)

	1983	1986	1988	1990
Honda	43	41	32	24
Yamaha	20	17	22	23
Kawasaki	12	14	19	22
Suzuki	19	11	12	15
BMW	1	4	3	4
Others	5	13	11	13

Source: SMMT and MCI.

within the market supplying a high quality and highly priced product, many of the machines being sold to police forces. The Eastern European manufacturers – who make up most of the 'others' – produce a technically rather backward but low priced machine – the motor-cycling equivalent of a Skoda perhaps.

In any industry study one of the first questions to ask is: what is the market? What is the product being sold? Here we obviously have to ask: what is a motor-cycle? Although the question seems trivial, it is in fact fundamental. A product is defined by its *characteristics*, and characteristics relate to the sort of people that consume the product and the circumstances in which they use it. For example a 1000 cc 150 mph multi-cylinder racing bike costing in excess of £5000 is really quite a different product from a cheap 100 cc machine used mainly for short commuting and shopping trips. These are both motor-cycles, in the sense that they have two wheels and an engine but in marketing terms they are clearly very different products. We could think of a spectrum of products, the two ends of the spectrum being the archetypical machines illustrated above. It is simpler however, and probably more satisfactory to think in terms of market *segments*. In this case just two are sufficient – a small, cheap commuter bike, say under 125 cc, and the large expensive enthusiast's machine. For brevity we shall label these the 'commuter-bike' and 'superbike' segments respectively.

In the commuter-bike segment the motivation which prompts consumers to purchase a motor-cycle is very different from that in the superbike segment. For machines under 125 cc the primary considera-tion is (usually) economy. They are a cheap form of personal transportation – cheaper than public transport or the private motor car. This suggests that purchase price will be an important factor in influencing demand. As in so many areas of microeconomics the concept of elasticity is of prime importance. Here we could say that demand will be elastic – that is, consumers will be very price sensitive.

In the superbike segment of the market consumers will not be so deterred by high prices because the motivation for purchase is not overwhelmingly the desire for an economical form of transportation. Purchasers are often young unmarried and unmortgaged males with a surprisingly high disposable income. They are often 'enthusiasts' for whom motor-cycling is a major recreational pursuit. In this respect 'motor-cycling' probably includes cleaning it, maintaining it and talking about it to their motor-cycling friends. Demand will therefore be relatively inelastic and in consequence one would expect to see some very highly priced machines.

Of course the above taxonomy is not perfect. Because of the licensing laws in the UK which restrict learner drivers to machines under 125 cc, manufacturers will produce some machines in this range which are 'sporting' in appearance and rather highly priced. Equally, there will be some larger capacity machines used for longer distance commuting or perhaps by professional motor-cycle couriers who require a reliable and economical workhorse. The styling of such bikes will be functional rather than sporting and compared to their more sporting counterparts they will be relatively cheap. The key to analysing all this however is the elasticity of demand. Because of this, it is sufficient to distinguish just two market segments – one in which demand is rather elastic (the commuter-bike) and the other in which demand is rather inelastic (the superbike). If you are still unconvinced of the importance of elasticity, just consider the highly priced BMW bought by the police. This is the motor-cycling equivalent of the company car. The demand for company cars is more inelastic than that for private cars. As we noted before people are always much more careful when they are spending their own money rather than somebody else's. In this case police forces are spending taxpayers' money and they are likely to demand the 'best' irrespective of price – that is, demand will be very inelastic, and hence prices will be high.

Any market in the real world is complex to analyse. Even the motor-cycle market which as we have seen is comparatively straightforward, does not readily lend itself to analysis unless we have a framework which we can use. As economists, our framework is that of structure–conduct–performance (SCP). That is, we identify what type of market structure we are dealing with – in this case, clearly an oligopoly. We then turn to a textbook to see what type of behaviour we might expect to see exhibited by such firms. You can only spot something if you are looking for it. Without some analytical framework to help you interpret the world the myriad pieces of data are just white noise.

Non-price competition is a feature of oligopolistic markets, advertising being perhaps the best known. Such advertising raises the minimum efficient scale (MES) of operations, favouring the large firms already in the market and deterring new entrants. Another particularly effective strategy in deterring new entrants is brand proliferation, seen most notably in the market for cigarettes where a duopoly produces a multiplicity of brands differentiated only by advertising. In the motorcycle market we should perhaps talk of 'model proliferation' rather than brand proliferation. With the possible important exception of Kawasaki (see below) each of the big four Japanese manufacturers produces a whole range of models covering every conceivable market niche. Each model in the range (particularly in the superbike segment) sells in comparatively small numbers. Any new entrant, producing perhaps one or two models, can therefore expect to pick up only a very small slice of the total motor-cycle market (but see below).

Oligopolies are fairly stable market structures. As Table 9.11 shows however there has been over the last ten years a discernible erosion in the market share of the Big Four. Eastern European bikes have captured a larger market share. What factors could have been responsible for this?

One important factor has been changes in exchange rates. Honda, Kawasaki, Suzuki and Yamaha all come from the Land of the Rising Yen. MZ, CZ and the other Eastern European machines come from countries whose currencies are in contrast distinctly 'soft'. That is, the external value of these Eastern European currencies has depreciated over the last ten years vis-à-vis the pound whereas the yen has appreciated. It is these exchange rate movements which have given the Eastern European manufacturers their competitive edge and enabled them to gain market share. The products they are producing are inferior to their Japanese rivals both in terms of technical specification and the all-important styling which produces the consumer appeal. But they are cheap to the UK consumer and this is entirely the result of the exchange rate.

Naturally the Eastern European manufacturers have attacked the price-sensitive end of the market – that is the commuter-bike segment where demand is elastic. Because of the favourable exchange rate they can undercut the Japanese producers.

How do our economic models predict that an oligopolist will react to the threat of new entrants? Entry barriers such as brand proliferation and advertising have already been mentioned. With consumer durables like motor-bikes a system of exclusive dealerships is a way of manipulating the retailing of such products in a way which favours existing large firms. New entrants find it difficult to sell their product because they cannot find a retail outlet. Honda has established exclusive dealerships with its 'Honda Five Star dealers'. In defence of such a practice they would of course argue the desirability of maintaining a comprehensive after-sales and spares service. This is legitimate. Controlling retail outlets does however give market power to existing larger firms.

Table 9.11 also shows that Honda, once the clear market leader, has experienced a dramatic fall in its market share. This is due to Honda's reliance on small bikes and mopeds where Honda is pre-eminent. In contrast, Kawasaki (and to a lesser extent Yamaha) have experienced an increase in market share. How can this be explained? Well, it is perhaps not coincidental that Kawasaki is the only member of the Big Four never to have had any substantial presence in the commuter-bike segment of the market. Kawasaki produce big bikes. The superbike segment of the market has not been subject to attack by the Eastern Europeans. As we have seen they have gone for the price-sensitive commuter-bike segment of the market.

This section has shown how a little bit of statistical information about market share and a basic understanding of the economic theories of oligopoly can be used to analyse a market in the real world. Economic theories are very powerful tools if applied with a bit of imagination and common sense.

Notes

1. See Hart, P. E. and Clarke, R. *Concentration in British Industry 1935–75.* NIESR Occasional Paper XXXII, Cambridge, 1980, p. 44.
2. See Davies, G. and Davies, J. 'The revolution in monopoly theory', in *Lloyds Bank Review*, July 1984, No. 153.
3. The Monopolies Commission, *Breakfast Cereals: A Report on the Supply of Ready-Cooked Breakfast Cereal Foods.* HMSO, 1973.
4. Report by the Office of Fair Trading, *Ford Motor Company Ltd: Licensing for the manufacture or sale of replacement parts,* 21 March 1984.
5. MMC Report on Ford Motor Company Ltd., *A report on the policy and practice of the Ford Motor Company Limited of not granting licences to manufacture body parts for Ford vehicles.* HMSO, February 1985, Section 6.73.
6. *The Times,* 20 September 1984.

Questions

9.1 If a competitive industry is replaced by a monopolistic one, which of the following statements are true? Correct the false ones.

(a) Prices in the industry will inevitably rise.

(b) The monopolist may choose not to maximise profits, so prices may not rise.

(c) The monopolist will have lower costs by virtue of his size so prices will fall.

(d) The monopolist may have lower costs by virtue of his size, but prices will rise if the monopolist exploits his market power.

(e) The MES in the industry may be quite small so that further concentration does not lead to significant cost reductions.

(f) Increased concentration at firm level will result in increased concentration at plant level. Unit costs will therefore fall.

9.2 Which of the following definitions of a 'monopoly situation' is used by the Monopolies Commission?

(a) one firm supplies the whole market

(b) one firm supplies over 50 per cent of the market for a particular good

(c) a single firm, or a group of firms acting together so as to restrict competition, controls over 25 per cent of the market

(d) the 3-firm concentration ratio exceeds 90 per cent

9.3 In addition to the current level of seller concentration, what other factors might be relevant in assessing whether a monopoly situation exists?

9.4 This question relates to section 9.3, on the Kellogg's Corn Flakes case.

(a) What form(s) of non-price competition were pursued by Kellogg? What was the principal purpose of such tactics?

(b) What was the impact of the introduction of own-brand cornflakes?

9.5 This question relates to section 9.4, on replacement body panels for Ford. The exercise by Ford of its artistic and design copyright constituted an anti-competitive tactic when applied to the replacement parts market but not when applied to the new vehicle market. Why?

9.6 If Boots the chemist took over a manufacturer of shampoo this would be an example of:

(a) vertical integration   (b) forward integration

(c) backward integration   (d) both (a) and (b)   (e) both (a) and (c)

9.7 If Boots the chemist started to sell package holidays in their retail outlets this would be:

(a) forward integration

(b) diversification

(c) 'a logical extension of their existing activity in retailing'

9.8 Suppose two former competitors merge and the subsequent profitability of the merged companies exceeds the profits that could have been expected if the two companies had remained separate. Consider whether the following statements are true.

(a) Since profits have increased the merger must have increased efficiency. Therefore the merger was in the public interest.

(b) If profits have increased it is evidence that market power has increased. Therefore the merger was against the public interest.

9.9 Of what relevance is the concept of MEPS in assessing the desirability of a proposed merger?

Questions 9.10, 9.11 and 9.12 relate to section 9.11 on European Ferries and Sealink.

9.10 The ownership by European Ferries of a number of cross-Channel ports is an example of:
    (a)   not putting all your eggs into one basket
    (b)   vertical integration
    (c)   innovation

9.11 The ownership by European Ferries of these ports constituted:
    (a)   a threat to national security
    (b)   a better service to consumers as a result of scale economies
    (c)   a potential barrier to the entry of new firms

9.12 Why did the MMC allow the merger between the two hovercraft companies but disallow the proposed merger between European Ferries and Sealink?
    (a)   the MMC accepted that without rationalisation hovercraft services would cease
    (b)   hovercraft were a British invention
    (c)   the relevant market (from the MMC's point of view) was seaborne cross-Channel services. Hovercraft services did not constitute a market in themselves, merely one type of service, for which adequate substitutes existed.

9.13 What motivated the oil companies to re-introduce the branding of petrol in 1953? What was the reason for the introduction in 1969 of the star-rating of petrol by octane level?

9.14 Firms in oligopolistic markets are torn between the desire to compete and the opposing desire to collude. Consider each of the following factors and state whether it will increase or decrease the likelihood of collusion:
    (a)   the degree of seller concentration is high
    (b)   demand for the industry product is inelastic
    (c)   there are no effective barriers to the entry of new firms
    (d)   one firm enjoys a significant cost advantage

9.15 This question relates to section 9.13 on the Virgin Airlines case. Comment on the validity of the following statement: 'The action by British Airways is an example of cut-throat competition. Competition is good because it leads to lower prices which must be in the consumer's interest.'

9.16 List the scale economies which you think large supermarket chains enjoy. Which of these are real and which are purely financial economies of scale?

9.17 The following advertising slogans are all designed to convince the consumer that no acceptable substitute exists for the brand in question:

'Once you've tasted Perrier nothing else will do.'

'Australians wouldn't give a XXXX for any other lager.' (slogan for Castlemaine Four X)

What implications does this have for the elasticity of demand for the product and for prices and profits? Give examples of other advertising slogans which have the same intention.

9.18 Why do you suppose that Marks and Spencer, a firm with an established reputation as a retailer of good quality clothes, entered the food retailing business with an almost exclusively own-label range of products?

10 Trade

10.1 Specialisation

In 1776 Adam Smith, a Scottish professor of moral philosophy published the book now regarded as the most important foundation of neo-classical economic analysis. This book was *An Inquiry into the Nature and Causes of the Wealth of Nations*. In 1776 long titles were very much in vogue. Nowadays we refer to it simply as *The Wealth of Nations*.

Smith was writing in Britain at a time when industrial processes had begun to make available a vastly increased amount and variety of goods. Articles which before the Industrial Revolution had been made by hand, and were hence expensive and in short supply, were now made by machines and were available cheaply to everyone. Smith's great achievement was to stand back and see in perspective the changes that were taking place in his society. In particular he was able to focus on the essential characteristics that made possible this flow of industrial goods.

Smith realised that the key to wealth creation lay in the *division of labour*. In other words products were no longer produced in their entirety by single craftsmen as they were in pre-industrial times. Rather separate *stages* of the production process were performed by individuals each one of whom specialised, and therefore became adept and efficient at producing only a small fraction of the item being manufactured.

Smith used the example of a pin factory to illustrate this. It seems that even in Glasgow in 1776 the manufacture of pins was a highly specialised business. It consisted of no less than 18 separate operations each one of which would have been performed by different individuals, using specialised machines. It was this specialisation which enabled mass production to take place enabling nations to increase the amount of goods (wealth) they created and enabling ordinary men and women to consume quantities and varieties of products which previously had only been available, if at all, to the very rich.

All of this may seem fairly obvious to twentieth-century man. Mass produced goods, which involve specialisation and the division of labour are now the norm, hand-crafted articles the highly-priced exception. Smith's great genius was in recognising that it was specialisation that made possible the wealth of nations. More than two centuries later in 1990 the Toshiba electronics company produced a television commercial which, inadvertently, makes the same point. A kimono-clad Japanese girl explains that she 'makes the chickambop for NICAM TV' for it is well known, at least in the advertising industry, that Japanese people cannot pronounce the word 'thingumy-bob'. The (English) voice then explains, singing a catchy little tune that:

> She's the girl that makes the thing
> That holds the oil
> That oils the ring
> That takes the shank
> That moves the crank;
> That works the thingumybob.
>
> It's a ticklish sort of job
> Making a thing for a thingumybob
> Especially when you find out what it's for . . .
>
> But she's the girl that makes the thing
> That fills the hole
> That holds the spring
> That works the thingumybob that **makes the engines roar** . . .
>
> And it's the girl that makes the thing
> That holds the oil
> That oils the ring
> That makes the thingumybob that's going to make some more.

The nature of specialisation is illustrated very effectively by this television commercial (Toshiba spent 2.5 m. on this campaign). Interestingly, the song is not original. Rather, it was a popular song in the Second World War, when of course lots of British women were engaged in making thingumybobs to use against the chickambops made by the Japanese.

The wartime version was of course slightly different. The last line for example 'that's going to make some more' originally read 'that's going to win the war.'

More importantly for our present purposes, the wartime version hinted that many female operatives working in factories may not have known the nature of the end product which they were helping to make. Sociologists have talked about the alienation in the workplace that results from this. The wartime song-writer expressed it rather differently for the second verse originally read:

It's a ticklish sort of job
Making a thingumybob
Especially when you *don't know what it's for* . . .

Notice that in the Toshiba advertisement 'don't know' is changed to 'find out', a subtle but essential change. Advertising is all about image. If someone spent £2.5 m. on promoting a company's image as Toshiba did in this campaign they would not want to suggest that the division of labour necessary to produce high-quality products cheaply may unfortunately involve workers in tedious repetitive tasks. Production line workers in electronics factories may be unaware – or may not care – whether they are producing television components, burglar alarms or weapons guidance systems. One printed-circuit board – PCB in the trade – looks much like another.

10.2 Specialisation and trade

The previous section explained how specialisation can enable a vastly increased flow of goods to be produced. The corollary of specialisation is *trade*. This is because the makers of thingumybobs will not of course want to consume all of their output themselves. Rather they will want to trade their thingumybobs with the thingumybobs made by someone else.

The word 'trade' as used here can mean either international trade or simply trade between people and firms in the same country. The only difference between the two types of 'trade' is that in the former (international trade) different currencies are involved, which at some stage have to be exchanged, one for another, on the foreign exchange market at some rate of exchange.

10.3 Comparative advantage

In the nineteenth century, the neo-classical economist David Ricardo considered the question of why countries choose to trade. His analysis extended Smith's ideas on the division of labour. He explained that in a bilateral trading situation *both* countries would gain from trade since the total amount of goods available would be greater than if each country chose to be self-sufficient. He enunciated what is known as the *theory of comparative advantage*. This theory has become a very important part of the economist's analytical apparatus. Ricardo first developed this theory in the context of specialisation and trade between countries with different currencies – that is, what we call 'international trade'. But it applies with equal force to specialisation and trade within a country, or between countries with the same currency (as will eventually be the case in the European Community). In fact, it applies to all questions of resource allocation, even those facing the individual, for example, as we shall shortly show.

First however let us develop the theory of comparative advantage in the context of an example in which two countries say France and Spain each produce only two commodities, say wine and cars. Suppose also for the moment that both countries share a common currency. This is of course a hypothetical example where we would have to assume that both wine and cars are homogeneous commodities, which is clearly unrealistic.

We also need to make a number of other simplifying assumptions. Firstly assume that the only factor of production which is important is labour, so that labour costs are the only relevant costs in the production of wine and cars. Secondly assume that in the production of both wine and cars there are constant returns to scale, which implies that production levels of wine and cars can be varied without altering unit costs. These unit costs – which of course consist only of labour costs will by definition be both average and marginal costs. It may also help if we assume perfect competition in the product markets where these goods are sold so that price is equal to these marginal costs. Finally, we shall also assume for simplicity that the wage rate is the same in France and Spain. Neither of these last two assumptions is strictly necessary however.

Table 10.1 shows the labour requirements in both France and Spain to produce one unit of each of the commodities – that is, it takes 20 man-hours in France to produce one unit of wine, 80 man-hours to

Table 10.1 Labour requirements in the production of wine and cars (hours per unit produced)

	France	Spain
Wine	20	30
Cars	80	90

produce one car and so on. Since we have assumed that the wage rate is the same in both countries, and that labour is the only relevant cost, the figures show that France is more efficient than Spain both in wine production and in car production, since it takes 30 man-hours to produce wine in Spain (and only 20 in France) and 90 man-hours to produce a car in Spain (and only 80 in France). Thus we say that France has an *absolute advantage* in the production of both wine and cars.

Despite this absolute advantage however it would benefit France to specialise in producing that commodity in which she has a comparative advantage. To get some feel for this, consider the concept of opportunity cost (introduced in section 6.5). We define the opportunity cost of a good to be the number of units of other goods which must be given up to make one unit of the good in question. Thus in France the opportunity cost of one car is four units of wine whereas in Spain the opportunity cost of one car is only three units of wine. In other words in France cars are expensive to produce because you have to give up more to produce one unit than you do in Spain.

Similarly wine is expensive to produce in Spain because there the opportunity cost of one unit of wine is a third of a car whereas in France it is only a quarter of a car. Thus it looks already as though France has a comparative advantage in the production of wine and Spain a comparative advantage in the production of cars.

10.4 The gains from trade

Since France and Spain each have a comparative advantage in different products we can show, following Ricardo, that total output will be increased if each country specialises in doing what it does best. That is, France should specialise in the production of wine, in which she has a comparative advantage, and Spain should specialise in cars in which she has a comparative advantage. To demonstrate this, consider the following, where we are continuing to assume that the unit labour requirements (ULRs) are those shown in Table 10.1. France could reduce her car production by one unit, freeing 80 man-hours. These resources could be transferred into wine production which would therefore increase by four units (since ULR in French wine production is 20 hours per unit produced). Spain for her part could give up three units of wine production, freeing a total of 90 man-hours (3 × 30) enabling her to produce an additional car (ULR = 90 man-hours for Spanish cars). The net effect of all this is to lead to an increase in 'world' wine production of one unit without any loss of world car output. The situation is summarised in Table 10.2.

Table 10.2 The gains from specialisation

France gives up one unit of car output	− 1 car
and gets 4 extra units of wine	+ 4 wine
Spain gives up 3 units of wine output	− 3 wine
and gets one extra car	+ 1 car
net increase in 'world' output	= 1 unit of wine

The net increase in world output of one unit of wine represents the gain from specialisation and trade. Car output can be increased in a similar way – though the numbers in our example would not work out so neatly. Clearly if we continue to assume constant returns to scale in the production of wine and cars our analysis suggests that world output could be increased further if further specialisation were to take place. If France switched 800 (rather than 80) man-hours from cars to wine the net increase in world output would be ten units of wine (rather than one). Switching 8000 would result in 100 extra units of wine and so on.

What this analysis demonstrates is that it is possible to have more of *both* wine and cars if countries specialise in producing those goods in which they have a comparative advantage. Note that France has lower ULRs in both wine and cars – she has an absolute advantage in both. This is not important however. It is the *relative* efficiency with which she produces one good in comparison to the other which is important.

To demonstrate this simple truth we had to assume away a number of complexities which would enter into our consideration were this a real-world rather a hypothetical example. A number of questions present themselves.

1. What determines whether the extra units of output accrue to France or to Spain? Or if they both benefit, do they benefit equally, or does one benefit more than the other?
2. What difference would it make if we assumed they used different currencies and what would determine the exchange rate between these two currencies?
3. How realistic is the assumption of constant returns to scale? If it is realistic, is it desirable that specialisation should continue until the whole of France is covered in vineyards and the whole of Spain in car factories?
4. What difference would it make if we dropped the assumption that labour was the only relevant factor and explicitly recognised that capital and land may be important too?
5. More fundamentally what determines the ULRs shown in Table 10.1? That is, *why* is France relatively more efficient at producing wine than producing cars? Do French people have large feet specially suited to treading grapes and is the Spanish national character ideally suited to work in car factories? Or are other factor endowments important?

If we did relax some of our simplifying assumptions we would find that our analysis became considerably more complex. The basic result would be the same, however. France should give up car production (or at least reduce car production) because she is comparatively disadvantaged there. She should concentrate on wine. Spain should concentrate on cars. If this happens total output will be greater than would otherwise have been the case – there will be gains from specialisation and trade.

This was Ricardo's message, developed as we have seen in the context of international specialisation and trade. But the theory of comparative advantage is a general principle which has much wider, indeed almost universal application in all questions of resource allocation.

Consider two individuals, Sam and Janet. Janet is better at

everything than Sam who is rather slow and clumsy. Janet is good at house-painting and she is also good at typing. When it comes to house-painting Sam is not as good as Janet but at typing Sam is very poor indeed.

Janet, of course, could try to do everything herself spending some time typing and some time painting her house. But she is *comparatively disadvantaged* at house-painting. Since she enjoys a comparative advantage in typing she should specialise in this. In so doing she will make enough money to pay someone else to paint her house (maybe even Sam) and still have enough money left over for something else.

The principle, of course, is that of comparative advantage. Suppose now that Sam and Janet get married to each other (though goodness knows what she could possibly see in him) and that they have children. Who should stay at home to look after the children? Janet is better at looking after the children (because she's better at everything) but she can also earn more money in her job than Sam can in his. Will Sam become a house-husband?

10.5 Trade flows: avocados, tomatoes and dry-cell batteries

The theory of comparative advantage explained in the previous section can by no means provide a complete explanation of all trade flows. In this section we consider the reasons behind trade flows in three products selected at random: a horticultural product (avocados); a horticultural product produced using intensive techniques (tomatoes); and a manufactured product (dry-cell batteries).

Avocados are pear-shaped fruit grown in tropical and sub-tropical climates. It is not surprising therefore that all avocados sold in the UK are imported (mostly from South America, California and South Africa). The UK has a comparative disadvantage in the production of avocados since it is not naturally endowed with a suitable climate, and it would be very expensive to produce artificially the conditions necessary to grow them.

The same holds true, ostensibly, for tomatoes but a moment's reflection reveals that the tomatoes that we purchase in our supermarkets are cultivated in glasshouses. Until recently a major supplier of tomatoes to the UK were the Channel Islands of Guernsey and Jersey. Situated off the French coast and enjoying an enviable amount of sunshine, these small islands had a comparative advantage in tomato production by virtue of their natural endowments. In recent years however the Channel Islands' horticultural industry has undergone a dramatic decline. At the same time the Dutch horticultural industry has grown in size. Much of the horticultural produce that the UK used to import from the Channel Islands is now imported from Holland.

If the theory of comparative advantage has any validity we would therefore have to investigate why the Channel Islands have lost their comparative advantage in tomato production while Holland has gained a comparative advantage. Clearly the answer does not lie in climatological change. We need to look at the abundance or scarcity of the other factors of production involved.

Horticultural products, even those grown intensively, require large amounts of land. Therein lies the problem for Jersey and Guernsey. These are small islands. They enjoy a good climate and being outside both French and British jurisdiction are a tax haven. Many people, particularly retired people, would like to go and live there. This therefore means that the demand for houses – and hence for land – is very high, driving up its price. Because the price of land has become so high in the Channel Islands the costs which growers face have risen. Therefore they can no longer compete with other producers – particularly the Dutch. At the same time the Dutch have been gaining comparative advantage as a result of low energy costs used to heat the greenhouses (the Dutch have large supplies of natural gas). Do not shed any tears for the inhabitants of the Channel Islands, however. Their comparative advantage now lies in offshore banking (as a result of their tax free status) and making Bergerac films.

In analysing some trade flows therefore, the theory of comparative advantage does have some explanatory power. In the market for many manufactured products however the UK both imports and exports a substantial fraction of the goods consumed and produced. A typical example is provided by the market for dry-cell batteries. As can be seen from Table 10.3 in 1988 approximately half the batteries consumed in the UK were imported (£74 m. out of a total of £146 m.). But the UK producers also exported a substantial proportion of their output – about one third (£41 m. out of a total of £113 m.). There was thus a substantial two-way flow in batteries. Table 10.3 also shows that the UK has now become a net importer of batteries whereas in 1984 imports and exports were approximately in balance. Two-way flows such as this are quite typical in the market for manufactured goods and the theory of comparative advantage is of little help in

Table 10.3 'Apparent consumption' of dry-cell batteries (£m)

	1984	1986	1988
Sales of batteries by			
UK manufacturers	98.3	98.6	112.8
minus exports of batteries	45.0	46.8	41.3
plus imports of batteries	49.6	59.2	74.5
equals apparent consumption	102.9	111.2	146.0

Source: *Retail Business*, No. 383, January 1990.

Table   10.4 Dry-cell   batteries
market   shares   1988   (%   of
volume)

Ever Ready	47
Duracell	24
Own-label	9
Vidor	7
Varta	4
Philips	2
Kodak	2
Others	5
	100

Source: *Retail   Business*,   No.
383, January 1990.

explaining them. Here more detailed knowledge of the battery market
is required.

Table 10.4 gives some information on market shares in 1988. As can
be seen 70 per cent of the market was supplied by just two firms, Ever
Ready and Duracell.

Dry-cell batteries can in fact be made of any two dissimilar metals.
Traditionally zinc and carbon have been used and this market was
dominated by Ever Ready. In the early 1980s however Duracell
entered the market with a higher performance alkaline manganese
battery and quickly became established as the major manufacturer of
this superior product, without any serious competition until the
launch of Ever Ready's Gold Seal alkaline battery in 1983. The market
for zinc carbon batteries has declined continuously over the 1980s
from 80 per cent by volume in 1983 to 50 per cent in 1990 as
consumers switch to the higher performance – and higher priced –
substitute. This reflects in part higher incomes (alkaline batteries are a
superior product) and also to some extent changes in the use of
batteries (a quarter of all batteries are now used in cassette players and
recorders which require higher performance alkaline batteries). Shares
in the two sectors of the market are shown in Table 10.5

Ever Ready is a UK producer (owned by Hanson plc). Duracell is
now an independent company supplying the UK Market from its plant
in Belgium. Most of the other manufacturers (except Crompton-Vidor)
import their batteries. Moreover, the refusal of Ever Ready to supply
own-label to supermarkets has meant that most of these have been
imported too. Thus the increasing 'openness' of the battery market in
the UK, and the increasing trade deficit in batteries, reflect changes
that have occurred within the market itself.

Table 10.5 Dry-cell batteries market shares by sector (1988) (% by volume)

	Zinc-carbon	Alkaline-manganese
Ever Ready	63	25
Duracell	—	55
Own-label	11	8
Varta	5	3
Vidor	10	3
Philips	2	1
Kodak	2	1
Others	7	4
	100	100

Source: *Retail Business*, No. 383, January 1990.

10.6 Trade flows: aggregates

In the previous section we looked at trade flows in three specific products. In the last of these, dry-cell batteries, we discovered that a two-way flow took place. The theory of comparative advantage was insufficient on its own to explain the relative magnitudes of the inward and outward flows. Additional factors were important in explaining these flows.

In this section we broaden the focus of our analysis. Previously we considered specific products in the context of the UK economy. We now consider broad groups of products in the context of the economy of the European Community as a whole.

Table 10.6 Extra-EC imports and exports (selected industries, 1987 (billion ECU))

	Imports	Exports	Intra.EC trade
EC net exporter			
Processed Foodstuffs	12.9	13.20	22.3
Chemicals	19.7	32.0	44.9
Plastics	8.3	14.1	29.6
Machinery	60.5	85.8	91.1
Transport Equipment	19.5	43.8	64.9
Glass, ceramics	2.3	6.5	9.3
Footwear	2.8	3.6	5.6
EC net importer			
Audio/video/photo equipment	18.2	14.6	16.7
Textiles	25.8	19.3	35.9
Paper and board	14.6	7.2	15.1
Leather	5.9	3.9	5.2

Source: derived from 'Panorama of EC Industry 1989', Commission of the European Communities 08.01/1336, p. 20.

Table 10.6 shows data for the EC (i.e. West Germany, France, the UK, Italy, Spain, the Netherlands, Belgium, Denmark, Portugal, Ireland, Greece and Luxembourg). Thus 'imports' means imports into the EC from non-EC countries; and 'intra-EC trade' means trade within the EC.

For each of the industries considered there is a two-way flow. For example, the EC imports 12.9 billion ecus of processed foodstuffs, but exports slightly more – 13.2 billion ecus – so that it is a net exporter of processed foodstuffs. In addition, as one would expect, there is a sizable amount of trade in processed foodstuffs between the individual Community countries (22.3 billion ecus).

As can be seen from Table 10.6 in some industrial sectors the EC is a net exporter, in others a net importer. In some instances it is easy to determine why this should be so. For example the EC is a net importer of paper and board and the reason for this is easily explained in terms of factor endowments and the theory of comparative advantage. Most of the EC imports of paper come from Norway and Sweden, non-EC countries sparsely populated with people but densely covered with trees. The climate in these regions makes them ideally suited to forestry but unsuited to other forms of agriculture.

10.7 Hecksher–Ohlin and the Leontief paradox

In other industrial sectors however it is not so easy to explain why the EC is a net importer or a net exporter. One might expect to find that the EC would be a net exporter of capital-intensive, high-technology products and a net importer of labour intensive, low-technology products. A development of the theory of comparative advantage by Hecksher and Ohlin suggests precisely this. The Hecksher–Ohlin theorem seeks to explain why some countries have a comparative advantage in the production of some products while other countries have comparative advantage in other products. The explanation they put forward focuses on initial factor endowments, and in particular endowments of labour and capital. They argue that developed economies such as those of the United States, the EC and Japan will tend to specialise in producing capital-intensive products and will therefore be net exporters of such products because they are comparatively well endowed with capital. In contrast poorer countries such as those of the Third World will tend to export labour-intensive products since they are comparatively well endowed with labour.

Empirically, however, this theorem is not always supported by the evidence, at least, not at first sight. The economist Wassily Leontief observed what he described as a paradox, namely, that the United States was an exporter of wheat, a product characterised ostensibly by labour-intensive production techniques. In fact the Leontief Paradox is easily resolved. Goods can be produced by a variety of techniques, some of which are more capital-intensive than others. In less developed countries labour intensive techniques are used to produce agricultural products. But in the United States and most of Western Europe agricultural products are produced using large amounts of capital and very little labour.

Thus it is probably too simplistic to characterise some products as intrinsically labour-intensive and others as instrinsically capital-intensive. Although some of the net trade flows shown in Table 10.6 accord with the naive version of the H-O Theorem others do not. For example, the EC is a net importer of textiles, as we would expect, since these are normally produced using labour-intensive production methods. Similarly it is a net importer of leather goods, for similar reasons. But it is a net exporter of footwear, a finding which is paradoxical since the manufacture of footwear, like that of leather goods, is labour-intensive.

Table 10.7 Share of world trade (% of total exports) 1989

United States	13
Japan	9
EC	39
Other OECD	12
Total OECD	73
Rest of world	27
	100

Definitions: EC (European Community) = Belgium, Denmark, France, Germany, Greece, Ireland, Italy, Luxembourg, the Netherlands, Portugal, Spain and the United Kingdom.

Other OECD = non-EC countries in Europe, i.e. Austria, Finland, Iceland, Norway, Sweden, Switzerland and Turkey, plus Canada, Australia and New Zealand.

Source: derived from *International Financial Statistics*, January 1991, IMF.

10.8 Trade shares

There is of course an additional dimension to all this. Most trade takes place not between developed countries and developing countries but between one developed country and another. The developed countries dominate world trade, particularly in manufactured goods. Table 10.7 shows that the developed market economies of the world account for about three-quarters of world trade.

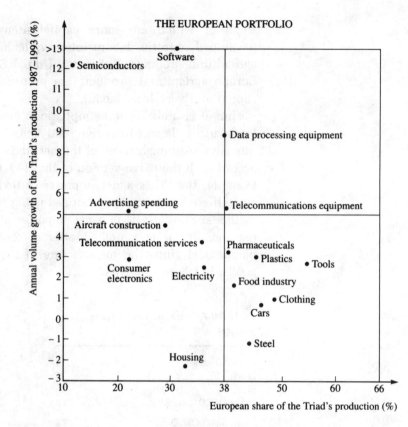

Figure 10.1

The term "Triad" refers to total activity in Japan, the United States of America and the European Community.

It is worth pausing for a moment to note our definition of 'developed market economies'. This is taken to be synonymous with the economies of the OECD (the Organisation for Economic Co-Operation and Development). This comprises:

1. North America (the US and Canada) and Japan
2. The EC (12 countries of which the most important are Germany, France, the UK and Italy)
3. Western European countries which are not members of the EC, such as Sweden and Switzerland, and
4. Australia and New Zealand.

A further definition is given in Table 10.7

It is also worth noting two more definitions. The term 'G7' countries refers to the group of seven countries whose economies are the largest in the world i.e. the United States, Canada, Japan, Germany, France, the UK and Italy. The term 'Triad' is used unofficially by some authors to refer to the United States, Japan and the EC. The G7 countries have about 54 per cent of world exports. The Triad

Industrial sectors in the EC

Inter-regional and international trade

10.9 Free trade versus protectionism

countries about 61 per cent.

It therefore follows that much of the extra-EC trade shown in Table 10.6 is trade with other developed countries – in particular with the other two members of the Triad – the United States and Japan. The question of whether the EC is a net importer or a net exporter will depend upon the circumstances of the industry in question. Figure 10.1 shows the EC's share of the Triad's production for specific industries, and also the rate of growth of production for each industry. As can be seen the EC is comparatively weak in some sectors, such as semiconductors, and comparatively strong in others.

Finally it is important to note that statisticians only record trade flows when goods or services pass from one nation state to another – for example, from France to Germany. They do not record trade flows when goods pass from one part of a nation state to another part of the same nation state – for example, from England to Wales, or from Texas to California. This means, therefore, that the statistics shown in Table 10.7 have to be interpreted with caution. Table 10.7 shows that the United States accounts for 13 per cent of world trade and the EC accounts for 39 per cent. This does not mean that the EC economy is three times as large as that of the United States (in fact the US economy is larger than that of the EC). Most of the 'trade' in the United States is from one state to another and hence is not recorded as international trade. Similarly if a 'United States of Europe' were ever achieved what was formerly international trade would be reclassified as inter-regional trade. The specialisation and exchange which formed the basis of that trade would not have been diminished however. Indeed, the removal of barriers to trade would almost certainly have led to greater specialisation within the EC.

We began this chapter by examining the benefits that could flow from specialisation and trade. The analysis relied heavily on the Theory of Comparative Advantage. The implications of the analysis for economic policy are quite clear, namely that free trade is to be encouraged and any restraints on trade between nations should be eliminated.

It should be borne in mind however that the Theory of Comparative Advantage was developed by a British economist at a time when Britain was the most powerful industrial nation, having been the first to industrialise. As such Britain was the country most likely to benefit from the free trade doctrines which she preached. Other countries, struggling to industrialise, did not share Britain's enthusiasm for free trade particularly where their infant industries were concerned. Rather they strove to protect these industries with tariff barriers until the day when they became sufficiently mature to compete on equal terms with the foreign competition.

The argument between the advocates of free trade and the advocates of protectionism lives on to this day. Those who call for protection are invariably those whose livelihoods are being threatened by exposure to low-cost foreign producers: thus French farmers demonstrate against agricultural policies by slaughtering British lambs on the dockside at Calais; American car workers demonstrate against the flood of Japanese imports; and Japanese farmers campaign to retain restrictions on the import of low-cost American rice. In contrast the advocates of free trade are those most likely to benefit from that freedom: they are the traders themselves, often transnational companies seeking to exploit the global market.

Although the Theory of Comparative Advantage provides a clear endorsement of free trade the analysis is static, ignoring dynamic considerations. That is, it takes the comparative advantage of one country over another in particular products as a given datum without considering how this arose or how it might change in the future as a result of policies undertaken now. Moreover it ignores the trauma associated with the decline of an industry exposed to lower-cost foreign competition. In the long term as the Theory of Comparative Advantage suggests there may indeed be a net increase in output as resources transfer from a declining sector to an expanding one. Many of these resources are people however, and the short term trauma of redundancy and unemployment is not inconsiderable, particularly when work is for many people the most important facet of lifestyle, as it is for farmers for example.

10.10 Should we retain controls on Japanese cars?

By the 1980s the Japanese car industry had become highly efficient in comparison to North American and particularly European producers. This was mostly as a result of a high level of automation and greater scale economies. As a result the European car makers sought to protect their industry by asking the Japanese manufacturers to limit the number of vehicles exported from Japan to Europe (to about 11 per cent of total EC sales). These Voluntary Export Restraints (VERs) are in effect self-imposed quotas.

One of the consequences of this policy however has been that Japanese cars sold on the European market and particularly in the UK are more expensive than the same vehicles sold in Japan (see Table 10.8). In effect if Japanese cars were sold in Europe at the same price as in Japan the demand would outstrip the supply available under the VER. Japanese manufacturers are able to choke off the excess demand by charging higher prices (and by not supplying the cheapest models in the range). The prices set by Japanese manufacturers are in line with those charged by European manufacturers who are less efficient and have higher costs.

European consumers would probably benefit – in the short run at

Table 10.8 Japanese car prices (in £) in UK, US and Japan

Small/medium cars (e.g. Mazda 323, Toyota Corolla, Honda Civic)

UK	7 642
US	5 620
Japan	5 227

UK/Japan differential 46.2%

Medium/large cars (e.g. Honda Accord, Nissan 300, Toyota Celica)

UK	14 282
US	11 577
Japan	10 775

UK/Japan differential 37.5%

Source: *The Independent*, 20 July 1990, 'UK motorists paying extra for Japanese cars'.

least – from the removal of VERs. Although it is by no means certain what the result of this would be it is probable that it would lead to a reduction in the price of Japanese cars in Europe and that to maintain market share the European producers would respond by cutting prices to the further benefit of consumers. Thereafter the dynamic of the situation becomes less clear and it is this lack of clarity which gives such scope for the arguments between the advocates of free trade and those of protectionism. One scenario is that competitive pressures would force European producers to become more efficient. Another is that competitive pressures would force them to close down, leaving Europe increasingly dependent on imported vehicles. This of course would worsen the trade deficit and lead to unemployment among car workers. In the longer term however these resources would flow to other sectors where Europe enjoyed a comparative advantage, at least in theory, though some resources might not find an alternative use.

An additional consideration of course is that Japanese firms may increasingly seek to overcome tariff barriers by establishing production facilities in Europe. This was already well under way by 1991 when Nissan UK became officially classified as a UK producer, the domestic content of its vehicles produced in Sunderland having risen above the minimum percentage required for such classification. Nissan, like Ford and General Motors before it, had become a multinational, which is the subject of the next chapter.

Questions

The following table shows the number of units of labour input required to produce one unit of output in the clothing and domestic appliance industries in two hypothetical countries Alphaland and Betaland.

	Alphaland	Betaland
clothing	5	7
domestic appliances	50	63

(a) Does either country have an absolute advantage in both clothing and domestic appliances?

(b) In Alphaland what is the opportunity cost of one unit of clothing? What is it in Betaland?

(c) Which country has a comparative advantage in appliance production?

(d) Which country has a comparative advantage in the production of clothing?

(e) What should Alphaland specialise in?

(f) Suppose a multinational conglomerate owns clothing factories and appliance factories in both countries. Assume that redundant appliance workers are always redeployed in the conglomerate's clothing factories, and vice versa. How much extra output could the conglomerate produce if it closed down its 1000 unit appliance factory in Alphaland and transferred appliance production to Betaland?

(g) Up to now we have implicitly assumed that wage rates are the same in Alphaland and Betaland. Now relax this assumption and assume that wage rates in Alphaland increase by 50 per cent. The input requirements in terms of the number of wage units (measured in £s) would then become:

	Alphaland	Betaland
clothing	7.5	7
appliances	75	63

Which country now has a comparative advantage in the production of appliances?

(h) What would a profit-seeking multinational company do as a result of the wage rise described above?

(i) Suppose the value of the alpha (Alphaland's currency) falls vis-à-vis the beta by 20 per cent. What would the input requirements then become, when measured in money terms (construct a table similar to those above). What then would the multinational company do?

11 Multinationals

In Chapter 9 we looked at the behaviour of firms operating in oligopolistic markets. A typical feature of such firms is their large size, but size in itself is not the only characteristic. A related feature of such firms is that they tend to be multinational. The word 'multinational' means something specific and is not merely a pseudonym for 'international'. A multinational firm (or MNE – multinational enterprise, or MNC – multinational company) is one that has production facilities in more than one country. Thus Ford, which has car plants all over the world, is by definition multinational. In contrast a company like Rover which produces in only one country and then exports part of its output is by definition not multinational. The difference, though seemingly trivial, is very important, as we shall see.

11.1 A brief history of the multinational company: the product life cycle

Multinational companies began to develop in a significant way in the inter-war period when companies based in America expanded their operations by establishing production facilities outside the United States. Initially most of this expansion was in Europe. There are several reasons why such companies adopted this strategy rather than choosing to export to Europe goods produced in America. Many of these reasons are illustrated by *Vernon's product life cycle theory*[1] (though there is no suggestion that a single rather simplistic theory can adequately explain the historical reasons for the growth and diversity of multinational activity). Vernon's theory suggests that all products go through a number of evolutionary phases during their life cycle. The cycle is initiated by the discovery or invention of a new product – for example, the telephone, the motor car, the microcomputer, and so on. The discovery is then refined to the stage where a product can be sold to the mass market. When Vernon first put forward his product life cycle theory, the United States economy had a position of pre-eminence such that most research and development work leading to the discovery of new products took place there. The American mass market was also by far the most important market because of its size and the level of income per capita. Hence new

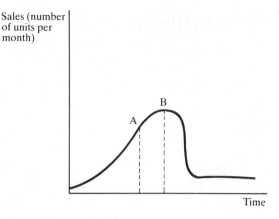

Figure 11.1

products were developed in America and the American market was the first to be exploited. The products which Vernon had in mind were consumer durable products. As the name implies, such products tend not to wear out very quickly so that the growth of sales of, say, vacuum cleaners would have a time profile rather like that in Fig. 11.1.

Sales increased more or less exponentially up to point A and then started to tail off as the market became satiated. At point B every household that wanted one would already own a vacuum cleaner, so that the potential for further sales was limited to replacing those that were worn out. Although with experience some manufacturers became more adept at making their products wear out more quickly, the scope for so doing was restricted since products which wore out too quickly would be perceived by consumers as being of low quality and sales of that brand would suffer as a result. 'Built-in obsolescence' could also be achieved by major technical advances which brought a significant improvement in the performance of new versions of the product, but there was little scope for this in vacuum cleaners or in many other consumer durables. 'Design improvements' were thus limited to cosmetic changes which failed to persuade even the most gullible of consumers that they should replace their old model with a new one.

With the domestic American market saturated, manufacturers sought new markets overseas – particularly in Britain and continental Europe. They could, of course, have exported to Europe products made in America. They preferred, however, to establish production facilities in those countries whose markets they wished to exploit. The advantages of so doing were many. Firstly, it overcame the problem of import restrictions which some governments had imposed. Secondly, it reduced transport costs. Thirdly, labour costs in Europe were generally lower than those in America so that products could be produced more cheaply. By establishing production facilities in Europe, American firms were able to compete not on equal terms with European rivals but on superior terms since the research and development expenditure associated with the new product had already been amortised (written off) in the American market. Because American firms in Europe had this significant advantage over their European competitors, they prospered. The age of the multinational had begun.

On the European market of course the growth of sales of a particular product had a time profile similar to that illustrated in Fig. 11.1. When the European market had been satiated therefore, the American multinationals had again to look around for new markets to exploit, and these they found in the Far East, in Africa, in South America and Australia – in short, in all corners of the globe.

Although Vernon's theory is introduced here as a (partial) explanation of the emergence of the multinational company, it has a much wider and more general application since many products seem to experience a life cycle which can be broken down into three phases: rapid growth of sales, satiation and then stagnation. Some products, of course, have an extremely short life cycle – the hula hoop, the skateboard and the Rubic Cube are three examples of products with a life cycle of less than one year. It could be argued that these are just 'crazes', playthings which have no useful function. The same could also be said, however, about the cheap home computer which appears to have had a life cycle of about three years. Other products of course have a life cycle extending over several decades – the motor car for example. It is suggested that the current worldwide overcapacity in the car industry is partly the result of the approaching satiation in the demand for cars. In products like cars, however, the replacement demand is still substantial since obsolescence is built into the car, both because it is designed to wear out and because technical improvements, though modest, are sufficient to convince consumers that the new model is an improvement on the old. Note that cars could be designed to wear out more slowly but that this would generally lead to lower performance and higher cost. Finally, it should be noted that although certain products do appear to have a life cycle like that illustrated in Fig. 11.1, some writers argue that there is no empirical support for the theory. Clearly for non-durable products, and even for durable products where significant scope for design improvement exists, there is no reason why saturation should ever by reached. In other words, one is always operating on the upward-sloping portion of the life-cycle curve.

11.2 The size of multinationals

The product life cycle helps to explain the reasons for the initial emergence of the multinational company. It is, of course, an over simplification and many of the most important multinationals do not fit into this model. Some are European-based multinationals like Unilever and Philips. Others are Japanese, like Mitsubishi, and many are oil companies whose activities naturally lend themselves to a multinational format. Multinationals have distinct advantages over purely national companies. These advantages (which are discussed in section 11.3) have resulted in the growth rate of such companies far exceeding that of companies which stick to national boundaries. A corollary of this is that companies which wish to grow rapidly are forced, sooner or later, to extend their activities beyond the frontiers of their native land. Initially they do this by exporting, but to secure the advantages of the truly multinational company they must eventually establish or take over subsidiary companies in other countries. Hence, when we look at the statistics we find that the growth rate of MNCs exceeds that of other companies both because existing MNCs have advantages over other companies, and because other companies are themselves forced to become multinational to secure these advantages.

There is therefore a resulting tendency for MNCs to become the dominant organisational form both in world trade and world economic activity generally. The world's largest multinationals are now very large indeed. Table 11.1 lists the top 50 industrial companies in 1990 which, with few exceptions, are multinational. The annual sales figures of these companies can be compared with the figures for Gross Domestic Product (that is, annual output) for a selection of countries shown in Table 11.2. As can be seen, the annual sales figures of the largest companies easily exceed the GDP of middle-ranking countries like Denmark and Greece.

Table 11.1 The world's top fifty industrial groupings

Rank	Company	Head-quarters	Main activity	Sales £bn
1	Sumitomo	Japan	conglomerate	80.5
2	C.Itoh	Japan	conglomerate	77.2
3	Mitsui	Japan	conglomerate	76.4
4	General Motors	USA	vehicles	71.6
5	Marubeni	Japan	conglomerate	68.6
6	Mitsubishi	Japan	conglomerate	62.5
7	Nissho Iwai	Japan	conglomerate	56.6
8	Ford Motor	USA	vehicles	54.2
9	Exxon	USA	oil	54.1
10	Royal Dutch Shell	Netherlands/UK	oil	44.0
11	BP	UK	oil	37.4
12	IBM	USA	computers	35.4
13	Mobil	USA	energy	31.9

Table 11.1 contd. ·

Rank	Company	Head-quarters	Main activity	Sales £bn
14	General Electric	USA	consumer products and power systems	30.8
15	Sears Roebuck	USA	retailing	30.3
16	Toyota	Japan	vehicles	27.0
17	Daimler-Benz	Germany	vehicles and engines	26.2
18	Philip Morris	USA	tobacco, beer and food products	25.2
19	Fiat	Italy	vehicles	24.4
20	Tomen	Japan	conglomerate	23.8
21	IRI	Italy	state holding company	23.1
22	Volkswagen	Germany	vehicles	22.4
23	Nichimen	Japan	conglomerate	22.1
24	Nippon Tel. & Tel.	Japan	telecommunications	21.7
25	Siemens	Germany	electrical and general engineering	21.0
26	Kanematsu	Japan	conglomerate	20.7
27	A. T. and T.	USA	telecommunications	20.3
28	Unilever	Netherlands/UK	food products, detergents, etc.	20.2
29	Du Pont	USA	diversified energy company	20.0
30	Chrysler	USA	vehicles	19.7
31	Nestlé	Switzerland	food products	19.4
32	Chevron	USA	oil	18.5
33	Texaco	USA	oil	18.3
34	Deutsche Bundespost	Germany	postal and telecommunications	18.0
35	Renault	France	vehicles	17.9
36	Philips	Netherlands	electrical and electronic	17.4
37	Veba	Germany	electricity, chemical, glass, transport	16.9
38	K Mart	USA	discount stores	16.6
39	BASF	Germany	chemicals, plastics	16.3
40	Matsushita	Japan	electrical and electronic	16.0
41	Hoechst	Germany	chemicals, plastics	15.8
42	Peugeot	France	vehicles	15.6
43	ENI	Italy	petroleum, chemicals	15.4
44	Tokyo Electric Power	Japan	electric utilty	15.4
45	Elf Aquitaine	France	oil	15.3
46	Nissan	Japan	vehicles	15.0
47	Electricité de France	France	utility	15.0
48	Bayer	Germany	chemicals	14.9
49	Wal Mart Stores	USA	discount stores	14.5
50	CGE	France	electrical engineers	14.7

Source: *The Times 1000*, 1990–91.

Sales figures relate to year end 31 March 1990 or 31 December 1991. Since sales are expressed in £bn the rate at which national currencies are converted into £s will affect the rankings. The exchange rates used are those at 29 June 1990.

Table 11.2 General Motors and GDP of some
'middle-ranking' countries billions of US dollars
1989

General Motors (sales revenue)	127
New Zealand	42
Denmark	106
Finland	115
Greece	54
Ireland	34
Luxembourg	6
Norway	91
Poland	82
Portugal	41
Turkey	71
for comparison:	
USA	5163
Japan	2849
France	956
Germany	1189
UK	832

Source: derived from *International Financial Statistics*, 1991, IMF. National currencies have been converted to dollars using market exchange rates. This tends to give an overestimate of the GDP of countries such as Finland and Norway and an underestimate for countries such as Greece and Portugal.

A more telling statistic perhaps is that in 1989 the combined annual sales revenue of the top eight companies in the world exceeded the entire annual output (GDP) of the UK. The large multinational companies therefore represent a concentration of economic power which, for many writers, is cause for concern and alarm.

The importance of the multinational enterprise in world trade is particularly striking. One author[2] has estimated that in 1981 just 72 firms accounted for half of Britain's exports, and only 18 per cent of Britain's exports were not accounted for by multinationals. In the following two sections we examine why MNCs have prospered. Section 11.3 considers some of the specific advantages they possess in comparison to national companies, and section 11.4 considers particular aspects of multinational activity.

11.3 The advantages of being a multinational

Some of the advantages enjoyed by MNCs exist simply by virtue of the size of such companies rather than as a result of any particular organisational form. Size in itself facilitates further growth for a number of reasons. For example, the cost of acquiring funds for investment may well be lower for the large firm than it is for the small firm. This is so because large firms have access to privileged sources of funds only available to large, financially secure firms. One such source of funds is the Eurodollar market where large sums are borrowed and lent by multinationals at interest rates which are generally lower than elsewhere. Furthermore, there is no exchange rate risk since the funds are borrowed and lent in dollars and are never converted into any other currency. Large firms are also able to finance much of their investment through internally generated funds, that is, through retained earnings. Such advantages are, of course, just one of the economies of scale enjoyed by the large firm. It is important to distinguish however between real economies of scale and pecuniary economies of scale. Real economies benefit both the firm and society at large because there is a real saving in the resources required to do a particular job. Pecuniary economies, on the other hand, benefit the firm but are irrelevant from a societal point of view because there is no saving in resources resulting from increased efficiency. Financial economies are the most obvious example of a pecuniary scale economy which results from the market power and bargaining strength of the large firm. This market power may enable it to negotiate more favourable credit terms on loans, or to purchase materials and other goods more cheaply than the small firm is able to do. These financial economies, then, are mostly pecuniary in nature rather than real. However, a not insignificant part of the financial economies results from the lower transactions costs per unit associated with the bulk purchase of materials or the negotiation of larger loans rather than small. These are real economies.

The decision as to whether a particular financial saving should be classified as 'real' or 'pecuniary' becomes more difficult when one recognises that lending to large firms is less risky than lending to small ones. Large firms are less likely to default. The lower risk explains in part the cheaper interest rates available to the large firm. However, on reflection it can be seen that the reason that lending to large firms is less risky than lending to small ones is that large firms are able to internalise the risk within the firm and thus bear the risk themselves rather than impose it on the lender. Thus in the two cases the risk is borne by different parties – by the lender when loans are made to small firms and by the firm itself when loans are made to large firms. The risk inherent in the investment to which the loan relates is the same, however, regardless of who is undertaking it. This inherent risk depends on the nature of the investment project itself.

Risk spreading   The ability to spread the risk inherent in business activity, and hence to reduce its overall impact on the company is, of course, one of the major advantages conferred by size. The multinational company, however, can add an extra dimension to this risk-spreading activity by diversifying its activities over several countries and continents as well as over several product ranges and types of business activity. Thus the Ford Motor Company, an American multinational, has subsidiary companies (Ford would probably call them 'affiliates') in many parts of the world. The early 1980s saw a period when Ford of America was making heavy losses but was being supported by the profits being repatriated to it from Ford of Europe who at that time were highly profitable. By spreading risk in this way the multinational is thus less susceptible to the effects of cyclical fluctuations in economic activity. These fluctuations – recessions and booms – tend of course to be a worldwide phenomenon affecting all those countries linked by trade. However, the timing of these fluctuations and their magnitude differ from country to country. Moreover, the impact which these fluctuations will have on the multinational and its affiliates will depend on a complex set of factors, one of the most important of which is the behaviour of exchange rates.

11.4 Aspects of multinational activity

The important point to note is that a multinational format allows a company to take advantage of movements in economic activity. Being footloose and fancy free, without any ties or allegiances, the multinational is able to turn to its own advantage those movements in economic activity which, for purely national companies, would present severe problems. These movements in economic activity may be cyclical, such as the short-term recessions mentioned above, or they may be secular – that is, part of a long-term trend.

Investment flows

The multinational will, for example, respond to secular movements in economic activity by adjusting its investment flows accordingly. That is, investment will flow to those areas where the rate of return is highest. If, for example, the American or the South African economy is growing faster and offering greater investment potential than the UK economy, then UK-owned multinationals will tend quite naturally to direct their investment flows out of the UK and towards the USA and South Africa. This investment in itself facilitates economic expansion, of course, and raises the growth rate of these other economies, thus confirming the multinational in its belief that the rate of return on investment overseas was greater than that in the UK. To the extent that this occurs, it clearly depresses the growth rate of the UK economy.

Sourcing

Multinational companies involved in manufacturing activity, such as the motor companies, frequently assemble their products utilising components manufactured by their subsidiaries in other countries. Table 11.3 shows the sources of the components used in assembling the Vauxhall Astra, a nominally British car built by Vauxhall Motors, the UK subsidiary of the US multinational General Motors. This car can validly be described as a British car in the sense that it is assembled in the UK, and if one includes the cost of the manpower

Table 11.3 Sources of components for Vauxhall Astra

Front doors	UK	Transmission	
Floor pan	UK	1.3 litre cars	Austria
Rear doors	WG	1.6 litre cars	Japan
Tailgate	WG	Automatics	France
Roof	WG	Electrical wiring	Eire/WG
Bonnet	UK	Wheels	UK
Glass	UK	Bumpers	WG
Radiator	France	Suspension	WG
Engine		Seat frames	WG
1.2 litre cars	WG	Upholstery	UK
1.3 litre cars	Austria/WG	Interior trim	UK
1.6 litre cars	Australia	Instruments	UK
1.8 litre cars	WG	Headlamps	WG
diesel	WG		

WG = West Germany.
  Source: *The Observer*, 21 October 1984.

involved in its assembly then the local (i.e. British) content is estimated to be 62 per cent.[2] The remainder is sourced from a variety of GM subsidiaries in Europe and elsewhere.

The procurement of components and materials from subsidiaries in other countries is a common feature of multinational activity. It is sometimes referred to simply as 'sourcing'. One implication of sourcing is that products which appear (for example) to be British made may contain a high proportion of foreign-made components. This has implications for the balance of trade since if, for example, Vauxhall Astras are sold on export markets, the net benefit to the balance of trade is much less than the gross benefit since each car contains a high import content.

Transfer pricing

Sourcing is, of course, a legitimate business practice. It has been alleged, however, that some multinationals source their products so as to maximise the profits of the group by engaging in *transfer pricing*. That is, the prices which are charged by one subsidiary to another for the transfer of components are such as to benefit the group, that is the multinational parent, possibly at the expense of one of the subsidiaries. To see how this could work out in practice, consider the following hypothetical example.

Suppose that, for example, two countries which we will label Hightax and Lowtax have different rates of corporation tax. Both countries are host to the subsidiaries of an American multinational car company. Both countries also assemble cars which are sourced both locally and abroad. The price at which components are transferred from one subsidiary to another will clearly affect the cost and therefore the profitability of the subsidiaries. Specifically, if components are transferred from the Lowtax subsidiary to the Hightax subsidiary at an inflated price, then this will increase the costs and reduce the profitability of the Hightax subsidiary. Similarly, the profits of the Lowtax subsidiary will be increased by an equivalent amount. Since the rate of corporation tax is lower in Lowtax than it is in Hightax, the overall tax liability of the group is therefore reduced.

It should be stressed that this is a hypothetical example and, for obvious reasons, few data exist to support the allegation that internal prices are deliberately distorted in this way by multinational companies. Given the informational requirement that needs to be satisfied for the practice to benefit the company, it seems unlikely that the practice is either widespread or carried out in a systematic way. Moreover, the discussion of costs in Chapter 5 illustrates the difficulty of defining how the cost of a particular component should be defined and therefore what constitutes a fair price to be used in internal transactions within the company. Having said this, however, it is clear that companies (and individuals) do take advantage of such things as differences in tax rates, investment incentives and the like, and that such behaviour will influence, to a lesser or greater extent, key macroeconomic variables like investment flows, growth rates and the balance of trade. However, it has been estimated[3] that 30 per cent of Britain's exports are to related concerns – that is, to subsidiaries of UK parents or to other subsidiaries of foreign-based MNCs. The scope for engaging in transfer pricing is therefore considerable.

Notes

1. A survey of product-cycle theories is provided in Vernon, R. (ed.) 'Technological and International Trade', *National Bureau Committee for Economic Research*, 1970.
2. *The Observer*, 21 October 1984.
3. Locksley, G. and Minns, R., 'Multi-nationals and the failure of economic management', *Guardian*, 3 April 1985.

Questions

11.1 'All multinationals operate on an international scale but not all international companies are multinationals.' Explain.

11.2 Assess the extent to which the product life cycle hypotheses can be applied to:
(a) video recorders   (b) home computers   (c) colour televisions   (d) washing machines   (e) coffee-making machines
To what extent have design improvements been able to stave off the day when the market for these products becomes satiated?

11.3 In 1986 the Nissan car company established a major production facility in the UK. Why did it do this rather than continue to export vehicles assembled in Japan?

11.4 What are the main advantages a company like Ford has over a company such as British Leyland?

11.5 A multinational sells cars in two national markets, Alphaland and Betaland. All cars are assembled by the Alphaland subsidiary using gearboxes produced by the Betaland subsidiary. Corporation tax is 40 per cent in Alphaland but only 30 per cent in Betaland. The following are the national prices which could be charged for internal transactions within the company:

price for gearboxes transferred from Beta to Alpha	300	250
price for cars transferred from Alpha to Beta	4000	5000

If the company wishes to maximise the post-tax profits of the group, which prices will it charge?

12 The consumer

12.1 Diminishing marginal utility

In the last few chapters we have been concentrating on the supply side of the market. In this chapter we shall focus our attention on the demand side by considering in greater depth some of the points introduced in Chapter 2. Specifically, we shall be investigating the factors which influence consumption behaviour.

The concept of *utility* is central to the economic analysis of consumer behaviour. Utility, in an economic sense, means the satisfaction or pleasure which results from some act of consumption. Goods and services are therefore said to possess utility. Consumers, if they are rational, will spend their income in such a way as to maximise the utility they get from the goods and services they purchase. This statement is a very general proposition, so general in fact that it is axiomatic. Nevertheless, it deserves some comment. Different people derive utility from different things and the statement is by no means inconsistent with the observation that while some crave a lifestyle of glamour, excitement and extravagance, others derive utility from solitude and contemplation – one man's meat is another man's poison. Nor is the assumption of rationality in any way inconsistent with the observation that some individuals engage in activities which to others appear to be acts of sheer lunacy. Rationality in this context simply means that when faced with a choice, the consumer will follow that course of action which will give him more utility rather than less.

Utility of course is not capable of being measured on a scale like temperature or barometric pressure. The Utilitarian school under John Stuart Mill, who introduced this concept, argued however that it was not in principle impossible to do so. A device for measuring utility – a 'hedonometer' or 'pleasure-meter' – has even been talked about. If it were possible to measure it on a scale, that is to measure it cardinally, the units of measurement would, of course, be *utils*. More realistically, utility could be measured ordinally; that is, one could rank consumption bundles in order of preference – first, second, third, and so on. Note that the distinction between cardinal and ordinal utility is

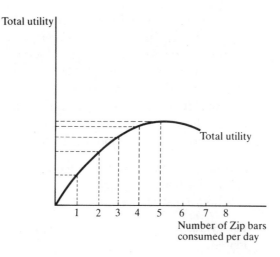

Figure 12.1

the same as that between the cardinal numbers (one, two, three, etc.) and the ordinal numbers (first, second, third, etc.).

Goods generally are said to possess *diminishing marginal utility*, which means that the increments to utility provided by additional units of consumption become less and less as consumption increases. Consider Fig. 12.1, noting carefully the axes. The horizontal axis shows the total number of chocolate bars ('Zip bars') eaten per day, and the vertical axis the satisfaction or utility derived from them, measured of course in utils. Note that the curve shows the total utility derived, whereas the slope of the curve shows how much extra utility is derived from eating an additional chocolate bar. That is, the slope of the curve shows the *marginal utility*. (The relationship between total and marginal utility is of course the same as that between total cost and marginal cost, and total revenue and marginal revenue. It may be helpful to re-read section 5.3 if you are unsure about this.) It is easy to see from Fig. 12.1 that the extra satisfaction – the marginal utility – derived from the first bar is greater than that derived from the second. Similarly, the third and fourth bars yield less extra utility than those which came before. The marginal utility of the fifth bar is very small and beyond this point satiation is reached and additional units of consumption reduce rather than increase total utility – that is, marginal utility has become negative (the slope of the curve is negative): too much chocolate makes you sick.

It seems not unreasonable to accept that all goods and services possess this property of diminishing marginal utility. It is perhaps a little more difficult to accept that income has diminishing marginal utility since additional large increments to income may make possible consumption experiences which were impossible previously and from which the individual may derive considerable satisfaction. This is not a proposition which can be refuted, of course, since utility in practice cannot be measured; at least, it cannot be measured cardinally. In passing it is worth noting what Shakespeare had to say on the subject of diminishing marginal utility. He of course pre-dated the Utilitarians by some two centuries so would not have been able to use the same terminology but, in *Antony and Cleopatra* he explains Antony's infatuation with the Goddess of the Nile with these words:

> Other women cloy the appetites they feed,
> But she makes hungry
> Where most she satisfies. (II.ii.241)

For Antony then, Cleopatra had increasing rather than diminishing marginal utility.

12.2 Utility maximisation

As we saw in section 12.1, the consumer is assumed to be a utility maximiser and as we argued there, the assumption that the consumer attempts to maximise his utility is axiomatic. It is another way of saying that people act rationally, not necessarily in a coldly calculating way, weighing up the amount of satisfaction derived from each pound's worth of expenditure, but rather they are rational in the sense that they do what they like doing. They buy those things, and engage in those pursuits, which give them satisfaction. In this section we shall derive the formal condition which needs to be satisfied in order that utility is maximised.

Consider an individual who spends all his income on just two commodities, cakes and ale, which are the only two things which give him satisfaction. Suppose the price of cakes, P_C, is 10p per cake and the price of ale, P_A, is 20p per pint. Both these goods of course possess diminishing marginal utility. At current consumption levels, however, suppose that the last cake yields an increase in total satisfaction of 5 utils and the last pint of ale yields an increase in total satisfaction of 8 utils. That is, at current consumption levels the marginal utility of cakes is 5 utils and the marginal utility of ale is 8 utils. In summary: $P_C = 10$, $P_A = 20$, $MU_C = 5$, $MU_A = 8$.

Has the consumer arranged his consumption spending in such a way that he is maximising his utility? Clearly not, for if he reduces his ale consumption by one pint he can afford two more cakes. As a result of the drop in ale consumption his total utility will fall by 8 utils but the additional cakes he buys will increase his satisfaction by $2 \times 5 = 10$ utils, thus giving him a net increase in total utility of 2 utils. By transferring expenditure from ale to cakes he will therefore increase his total utility.

However, since both cakes and ale have diminishing marginal utility, the increase in cake consumption will reduce the marginal utility of the last cake consumed (to somewhat less than 5 utils) and the reduction in ale consumption will increase the marginal utility of the last pint of ale consumed (to somewhat more than 8 utils). The increase in the marginal utility of ale and the reduction in the marginal utility of cakes thus sets a limit to the extent to which total satisfaction can be increased by substituting cakes for ale in consumption. If this were not the case of course, that is, if the goods in question did not possess diminishing marginal utility, then the rational consumer should give up ale altogether and spend all his income on cakes.

A few moments' reflection will show that the consumer maximises his total utility when he arranges his consumption set in such a way that the ratio of marginal utility to price is the same for all goods. That is, the following condition must be satisfied:

$$\frac{MU_A}{P_A} = \frac{MU_C}{P_C} \qquad\qquad [12.1]$$

In other words, total utility is maximised when the last penny spent on cakes yields the same increase in total satisfaction as does the last penny spent on ale. If this condition is not satisfied, the consumer can increase his total satisfaction by substituting cakes for ale in the way described above, and this process of substitution should be continued until eqn [12.1] is satisfied. Clearly eqn [12.1] can be extended to any number of goods, not just cakes and ale. In a more general form it can be rewritten as:

$$\frac{MU_A}{P_A} = \frac{MU_B}{P_B} = \ldots = \frac{MU_n}{P_n} \qquad\qquad [12.2]$$

where A, B, . . ., n are all the goods and services in the economy.

12.3 Income and substitution effects: the choice of family size

The previous section showed how the rational consumer could maximise his utility when faced with a choice between cakes and ale. In the real world of course, consumers have to make choices between an enormously wide range of goods and services, all of which make some claim on their income and have the potential for yielding utility. The consumer, in short, is faced with what in the jargon is called a *choice problem*; and economics is about making choices.

An area of application of economic analysis recently explored is that of fertility rates. Underlying this analysis is the notion that family size is the result of a choice process, or in other words, couples (or individuals) choose whether or not to have children, when to have them and how many to have.

The question of family size may seem an improbable area of application of economic analysis. Can the cold logic of the economic calculus really be applied to this most fundamental of human desires? What about unplanned pregnancies? Should one really analyse reproductive behaviour as if people acted in a rational and considered manner? If one considers the question more deeply, however, it is clear that these objections are not valid. In a biological sense, birth follows conception, which follows intercourse in a natural sequence. In a social or a statistical sense, however, they are not linked in this strict sequence. Most acts of intercourse are not followed by conception – the birth rate would be very much higher if they were. This is not to deny of course that there are some unplanned pregnancies. However, the dividing line between planned and unplanned pregnancies is not easy to draw. Some pregnancies are planned but do not occur due to infertility. Some pregnancies are planned by one partner but not by the other. But all pregnancies occur because effective contraceptive measures are not taken, and herein lies the choice. If you choose not to take a raincoat when going out you run the risk of getting wet, not normally a serious risk. If you choose not to take a waterproof clothing with you when going hill-walking you run the risk of getting wet and chilled, a more serious risk which may even prove fatal. Since most people would be more likely to take seriously the consequences of getting wet when hill-walking than when walking down a city street, they are more likely to guard against that eventuality. The perceived seriousness of the consequences will determine how carefully you plan against those consequences occurring. Similarly, women for whom conception is seen as extremely undesirable will take effective contraceptive measures, even to the extent of sterilisation in certain circumstances.

Of course, in individual cases the best-laid plans often go awry. Some pregnancies do occur which were not 'planned' and other pregnancies which were 'planned' do not occur. That is why the economic analysis of choice behaviour cannot predict or explain the size of any one particular family. It can however attempt to explain the size of families on average or, if you like, it can be applied to the study of fertility rates.

Children as a consumption good

Children, at least in developed Western societies, can to some extent be regarded as a consumption good. That is, parents derive utility or satisfaction from the rearing of children in much the same way as they derive utility from their material possessions such as their house, car, TV and from the services which they consume such as holidays or going to the zoo. The amount of satisfaction derived from child-rearing depends of course on personal tastes and circumstances. Some people like children, others do not. Other things being equal, therefore, those individuals that like children will tend to have larger families. Other individuals will prefer to spend their time and income in different ways. In formal terms of course this implies that the utility-maximising consumer will arrange his consumption set such that:

$$\frac{MU_A}{P_A} = \frac{MU_B}{P_B} = \ldots = \frac{MU_K}{P_K} = \ldots = \frac{MU_n}{P_n} \qquad [12.3]$$

where A and B are any two other goods from the n goods available and good K is the consumption good, children. In words, the last pound devoted to children will yield exactly the same increase in total satisfaction as does the last pound devoted to consumer good A, good B, and so on for all n goods. In reality, of course, the utility-maximising consumer will have a much more difficult task than if he were simply choosing between cakes and ale. Children are more akin to a consumer-durable good like a house which yields a stream of services through time, as opposed to goods which yield immediate satisfaction, like cakes and ale, and are then used up. Moreover, the consumer will have to base his decision on very imperfect information – he will probably already have tasted cakes and ale and be contemplating repeat purchases. He (or she) may never have experienced parenthood and the complete experience takes a lifetime to acquire. Nevertheless, even though our rational individual will not achieve the condition set out in eqn [12.3] we could argue that if she is rational she will strive towards it.

The price of children   Children of course do not have a purchase price but child rearing does involve a cost. Certain complementary goods have to be acquired – a cot, a pram, nappies, toys – but the cost of these items is normally fairly insignificant in comparison to the main item in the cost of having a child, which is the *income forgone* by the parent who stays at home to look after the child rather than engage in paid employment. Thus the main cost of having a child is the *opportunity cost* of not working during the child's pre-school years (and possibly the difficulty of re-entering the labour market thereafter). This realisation immediately leads to two interesting and possibly testable predictions. Firstly, following the birth of one child the cost of producing a second child is low. The necessary capital equipment has already been acquired (pram, cot, etc.) and this can be used for more than one 'unit', thus lowering the unit cost. Moreover, if the parent is already staying at home to look after one child the further loss of earnings involved in rearing a second child is comparatively small – perhaps six years' lost earnings instead of four. There are, in short, economies of scale in child-rearing. Thus we might expect to find that very large families were commonplace were it not for the fact that, along with other consumption goods, children possess diminishing marginal utility – the more you have of them the less you want more of them. Secondly, we might expect to find that family size is related to socio-economic variables but in a rather complicated way. For example, as income increases would we expect couples to have more children or less? The answer, it turns out, depends on the strengths of the *income and substitution effects*. Assuming that children are not an inferior good (that is, assuming that their income elasticity is positive – a reasonable assumption) then as income rises we would expect couples to have more children, other things being equal. Other things are not equal, however, because the cost of children also tends to rise as income rises, since the major element in the cost of having children is the income forgone by the parent. Thus children become more expensive relative to other consumer goods as one rises up the socio-economic scale and hence we would expect the rational consumer to 'consume' less children and to consume more of the substitutes whose price is falling relative to the price of children.

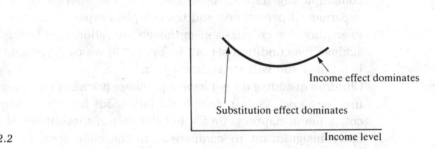

Figure 12.2

This may produce the result that both low-income and high-income families tend to be somewhat larger than those families in the middle of the income range. This is illustrated in Fig. 12.2. The distribution shown in Fig. 12.2 results from the fact that initially as income rises the substitution effect dominates – children become more expensive relative to other goods and therefore the utility-maximising individual chooses to consume fewer children and more of the cheaper substitutes. As income continues to rise beyond a certain level, however , the income effect begins to dominate and families, by virtue of their high income, can afford more of everything, including children. Very high-income families may even be able to afford to employ a nanny to look after them.

The reason for illustrating the income and substitution effect in the context of the analysis of fertility rates is to show that the analysis of choice behaviour can be applied to many situations which initially appear to be beyond the scope of economics. Note the important (but rather disappointing) result we derived, which was that the substitution effect and income effect potentially working in opposite directions produced a result that was indeterminate.

Questions

12.1 Which of the following statements illustrates the concept of diminishing marginal utility?
(a) 'When I've eaten one Choc-o-Crunch bar I don't like the second one as much as I did the first. But I still like it.'
(b) 'Once you get the taste for Choc-o-Crunch bars it's difficult to stop eating them.'
(c) 'When I've had one Choc-o-Crunch bar I go right off them.'

12.2 A consumer buys only two commodities, Seven-up and crisps, both of which have diminishing marginal utility. At current consumption levels the marginal utility of crisps is 12 and the marginal utility of Seven-up is 14. The price of crisps is 20p and the price of Seven-up is 28p. Which of the following are true?
(a) The consumer is maximising his utility.
(b) The consumer would probably increase his utility by buying more Seven-up and less crisps.
(c) The consumer should buy more crisps and less Seven-up to increase his total utility.
(d) If the consumer eats more crisps he will get even more thirsty so the utility of Seven-up will rise.

12.3 An electrical retailer records the prices and sales·volumes of both colour and black-and-white television sets for 1986 and 1989.

	Price		Sales	
	Black & White	Colour	Black & White	Colour
1986	£70	£250	100	400
1989	£60	£250	80	500

Consider whether the drop in sales of black-and-white sets (despite a drop in price) could be explained in terms of income and substitution effects (incomes rose between 1986 and 1989).

13 Factor markets

13.1 How to build a swimming pool

The study of economics gives the student a transferable skill. It provides her or him with an analytical apparatus which can be applied not just to the specific area of economics from which it springs but more generally to a whole panoply of issues. Here we introduce some powerful tools from the economist's tool kit.

Imagine that you have decided to build a swimming pool in your back garden. The basic technology to be employed is straightforward: you dig a big hole and line it with concrete. There are a variety of ways in which this can be accomplished however. You could go out and buy a shovel and start digging or hire labourers with shovels. Digging is a very labour-intensive activity however and you may decide that it would be better to employ a more capital-intensive method of digging the hole, perhaps by hiring a small mechanical digger from your local hire shop. You may even decide, if you are planning a large pool, to contract out the earth-moving operation by hiring a large mechanical digger such as a JCB together with its driver.

The choice of production technique can be characterised as either *labour-intensive* or *capital intensive*. Your choice of technique will depend *inter alia* on the cost of hiring labour and the cost of hiring capital.

Having dug your hole you then have to line it with concrete. Again you have a choice of techniques available, some more capital intensive than others. The most labour intensive technique would be to drive to your local DIY store, buy bags of cement and sand, load them in the boot of your car, drive home, unload them and then proceed to mix the cement using the shovel purchased previously. Alternatively you may decide to use a bit more capital and a bit less labour, by hiring or buying a cement mixer. You may even decide to use a lot more capital and a lot less labour by arranging to have a load of ready-mixed concrete delivered to your house.

The choice of production techniques available is illustrated in Fig. 13.1 where labour inputs are measured on the vertical axis and capital inputs on the horizontal. Each point represents a feasible way of building a pool of a given size.

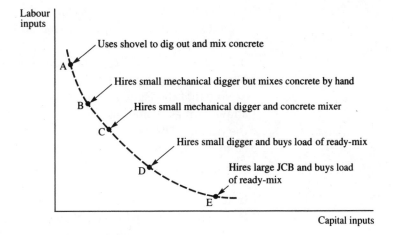

Figure 13.1

The general point is that there is a choice of production techniques available some of which use lots of labour and not much capital, and some which use lots of capital but not much labour. Where a choice of techniques exists it is possible to substitute capital for labour (that is, use more capital and less labour) and vice versa.

Imagine a situation in which labour and capital were *continuously substitutable* that is, at the margin you could use a little bit more of one factor and a little bit less of the other. Clearly this is not the case when building our swimming pool because in that example there are *indivisibilities* – if you decide to order a lorry load of ready mix you have to take the whole load. Nevertheless, conceptually it is feasible to think in terms of continuous substitutability, and it is convenient for the moment to do so. Thus we have joined together the points in Fig. 13.1 with a dotted line. This line is called an *isoquant* (literally, 'equal quantity') because combinations of capital and labour along this line are capable of producing the same output (in this case, a

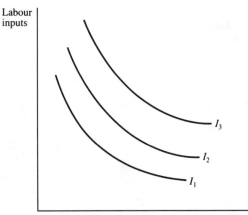

Figure 13.2

swimming pool of a given size). In Fig. 13.2 we generalise this idea by drawing a series of isoquants. Isoquants I_2 and I_3 correspond perhaps to larger pools, or to more pools of the same size. As we move in a north-easterly direction the isoquants we encounter correspond to larger and larger outputs.

Note that the isoquants are bent towards the origin rather than being straight lines (some textbooks describe this as being convex towards the origin). Thus in Fig. 13.1 the isoquant is steeper as we move from A to B, than it is from D to E. This illustrates what is called a *diminishing marginal rate of technical substitution*. At point A the addition of a small amount of extra capital allows substantial savings in labour inputs (while maintaining the output level intact). At point D, in contrast, it takes a lot more capital to produce comparatively small savings in labour input. The assumption of diminishing marginal rates of technical substitution is one which is normally made. However, it is not necessarily always a realistic description of the technical possibilities, nor indeed may it be valid in the example we are using here. It is a convenient assumption to make, however, since as we shall see it allows us to identify a unique optimal combination of factor inputs.

It is important to emphasise that we are assuming a single objective, namely to minimise the cost of building a swimming pool of a given size. With this in mind what then is the optimal combination of factor inputs? Clearly the answer to this question will depend upon the price of one factor relative to another.

Suppose you had £1000 to spend on building your swimming pool. If the price of one unit of labour is P_L the number of units you could afford to purchase is $1000/P_L$. Similarly if the price of one unit of capital is P_K the number of units of capital you could afford to purchase is $1000/P_K$ (note that, following convention, we are using the symbol K to denote capital). This is illustrated in Fig. 13.3 by the

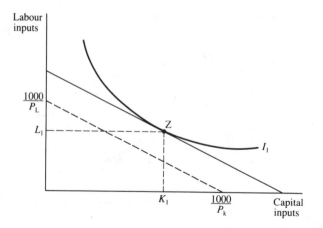

Figure 13.3

dotted line, which some authors refer to as an *iso-cost* line since it shows different combinations of labour and capital which cost the same in total. It is worth emphasising that $1000/P_L$ and $1000/P_K$ are the maximum *amounts* of labour and capital that can be purchased for a budget of £1000.

However the *slope* of this line also reflects relative prices. The slope is P_K/P_L. This is because we measure the slope by the vertical distance divided by the horizontal, which in this case is

$$\frac{\dfrac{1000}{P_L}}{\dfrac{1000}{P_K}} = \frac{1000}{P_L} \times \frac{P_K}{1000} = \frac{P_K}{P_L}$$

In our particular example this also tells us that £1000 is insufficient to build a pool because our £1000 budget line (or iso-cost line) does not touch the isoquant at any point. We need to spend more. That is, we need to shift our budget line north-east, indicating increasing expenditure but keeping the new budget line parallel to the original one reflecting the same relative prices. The new budget line – the solid line – represents the minimum expenditure that must be undertaken to build a pool. As can be seen it is tangent to the isoquant at point Z which represents the least-cost method of building the pool. This corresponds to labour inputs of L_1 and capital inputs of K_1. The slope of the isoquant is of course equal to the slope of the budget line at point Z. Since the slope of the isoquant measures the marginal rate of technical substitution, and the slope of the budget line measures relative prices, we can conclude that to produce a given output at minimum cost the marginal rate of technical substitution between capital and labour must be equal to the relative prices of the two factors.

13.2 What if factor prices change?

Once the basic analysis has been understood – and that may require a re-reading of the previous section – it is comparatively easy to see that a change in the price of one of the factors will result in a change in the slope of the budget line. This in turn leads to a change in the least-cost combination of capital and labour required to produce a given output. Consider the effect of a rise in the price of labour. Since we assume that the price of capital is unchanged this rise in the price of labour represents a change in *relative prices* – capital has become relatively cheaper compared to labour. We would expect to find therefore that there is a switch to more capital-intensive techniques as these are now relatively cheaper and hence more cost-effective.

However the rise in the price of labour means that any technique involving even a small amount of this factor will cost more than it did previously. Hence, even though we economise on the use of labour which is now relatively expensive, it will still cost more in absolute terms to produce a given output than it did previously. To build a swimming pool of a given size we need to spend more. That is, we need a larger budget.

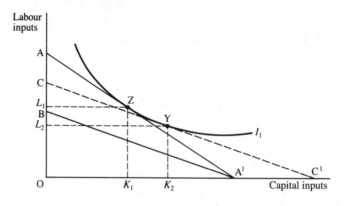

Figure 13.4

Figure 13.4 illustrates how the 'relative price effect' and the 'budget effect' can be combined. The isoquant shows, as before, the minimum amounts of capital and labour necessary to produce a given output – a pool of a given size. At the old set of relative factor prices indicated by the budget line AA^1 the least cost method was one which required K_1 units of capital and L_1 units of labour. When the price of labour rises the maximum amount which can be purchased with our pre-existing budget falls from 0A to 0B. Hence our new budget line is BA^1. This new budget line does not touch the isoquant. Hence we need to spend more to build the pool. This is illustrated by an outward shift of the budget line from BA^1 to CC^1, the two lines being parallel reflecting the new set of relative prices. CC^1 is tangent to the isoquant at Y where the least-cost combination of factor inputs is K_2 units of capital and L_2 units of labour. As expected we are now using more of the factor which has become relatively cheaper (capital) and less of the factor which has become relatively more expensive (labour).

The relative price effect (or substitution effect) will always result in the increased use of the factor which has become relatively cheaper. However, it is possible that, as a result of the increase in factor prices, you decide to build a smaller swimming pool than the one you had originally planned. This will give rise to an *output effect* illustrated in Fig. 13.5 by the isoquant I_0 which represents a smaller pool than I_1. The labelling of the iso-cost lines in Fig. 13.5 corresponds to those in the previous figure. The increase in capital usage from K_1 to K_2 is the substitution effect which we noted earlier. However the reduction in the size of pool being constructed, indicated by the lower isoquant I_0,

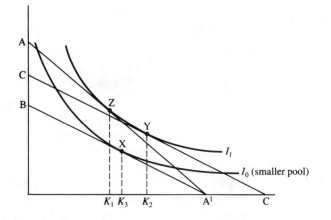

Figure 13.5

may result in the total amount of capital employed being only K_3. Although more than the K_1 units originally employed this is less than the K_2 units that would have been employed if the output level had been maintained.

> The increase in the price of labour rotates the budget line from AA^1 to BA^1. If you decide to keep expenditures unchanged you will have to build a smaller pool (I_0). If you had built the pool originally planned you would have used K_2 units of capital now that relative prices have changed. However the reduction in pool size results in only K_3 units being used.
>
> Z is the least-cost combination of factor inputs at the original set of relative prices. Y is the combination you would use following an increase in the price of labour if you were prepared to spend more in total to build the pool originally planned. X is the combination which results when you reduce the size of the pool to fit within your original budget.

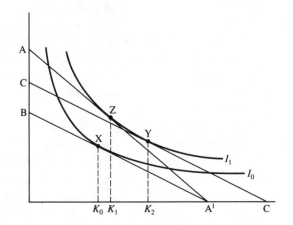

Figure 13.6

It is even possible as Fig. 13.6 illustrates for the output effect to outweigh the substitution effect such that the total amount of capital employed falls to K_0 which is *less* than the K_1 units originally employed. For example, because you are now building a smaller pool you may decide not to hire a JCB but to dig it out using shovels.

> This is similar to the previous figure except that here the output effect outweighs the substitution effect resulting in a net reduction in capital usage.
>
> The difference between the two figures lies in the technical possibilities for substitution between labour and capital as represented by the shape of the isoquants. The shape of I_0 in Fig. 13.6 is different from that in Fig. 13.5.

13.3 The production function

The preceding analysis implies the existence of what economists call a *production function*. Used in a mathematical sense the word 'function' means a relationship between two (or more) variables. If those variables are y and x then

$$y = f(x)$$

means y is a function of x, or depends on x. If you tell me what x is, then I can tell you what y will be, provided I know what the functional relationship between the variables is.

A production function relates inputs to outputs

$$output = f(inputs)$$

In the previous section we identified two sorts of factor inputs which we called capital and labour. Hence we could write

$$q = f(K,L)$$

where q stands for output, K for the number of units of capital, and L for the number of units of labour.

The *concept* of a production function is very important in economics though its practical application is beset by difficulties.

A production function implies a transformation process whereby inputs are converted into outputs. Firms are a specific example of economic units which transform factor inputs into output. However the concept of a production function relates more generally to any transformation process, in which inputs – not necessarily capital and labour – are converted into output.

The concept of *efficiency* is an integral part of the concept of the production function. An increase in output not attributable to an increase in factor inputs must by definition be attributable to an increase in the efficiency with which these inputs are transformed.

While the last point may seem painfully obvious, non-economists often fail to distinguish between inputs and output or worse still confuse the two. 'Mr Busy works very hard. He's always in his office by 8 o'clock in the morning and never leaves until 8 o'clock in the evening. All the effort he puts in makes him a real asset to the organisation.' No. This is a *non sequitur*. A classic case of equating inputs with output. Mr Busy's output may be very high, but it does not follow from the fact that his input is high. He may, in fact, be the most inefficient worker in the organisation so that his output is actually less than Mr Clever who comes in at 10 a.m. and leaves at 4 p.m. but uses his time to better effect in the interim.

There are a large number of specific functional forms relating inputs to output. The analysis of the preceding section assumed substitutability between capital and labour – there was more than one way of building a swimming pool, some techniques being more capital intensive than others.

In contrast we could assume *fixed factor proportions*. That is, we could assume that there is only one technically efficient way of producing any given output. There is only one combination of factors which is feasible. Equation [13.1] is an example of a production function characterised by fixed factor proportions

$$q = 4K + 30L \qquad [13.1]$$

It takes four units of capital and 30 units of labour to produce one unit of output. The factors must always be combined in this ratio.

Such a production function would not give rise to the smooth, convex to the origin isoquants we encountered earlier. Rather the isoquants would be single points or L-shaped as in Fig. 13.7. In the previous section we saw that the optimal factor combination will vary as factor prices vary. This will not happen with the L-shaped isoquants in Fig. 13.7 however. Factors must be combined in fixed proportions. Hence if the firm has only four capital inputs available, having 60 or 90 labour inputs adds nothing extra to production.

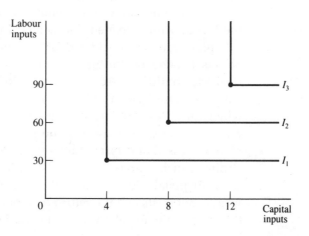

Figure 13.7

Which type of isoquant is the more realistic description of production relations in the real world – continuous substitutability or fixed factor proportions? Well, transnational car companies seem to use approximately the same production methods in labour-rich countries (such as Taiwan) as they do in capital-rich countries (such as the USA). So do MacDonald's fast food restaurants. Launching a space satellite is not noticeably more labour-intensive in the USSR, a country where labour is comparatively abundant, than it is in the USA, where capital is relatively abundant.

On the other hand there is quite clearly more than one way of building a swimming pool and it would be very surprising to find labour-rich countries using capital-intensive techniques when the same output could be achieved more cheaply using labour-intensive techniques. Normally some substitutability is possible.

13.4 What is capital, exactly?

The production function technique described in the previous section can be interpreted in two ways. Firstly it can be interpreted as an analytical concept relating output to two types of input, which could be labelled A and B but which here we have labelled 'capital' and 'labour'. Alternatively it can be taken literally to refer to capital and labour. This then raises the question: what exactly is this stuff which economists call 'capital'? How would one recognise it? In what units is it measured? Is it a homogeneous sort of substance? Similar questions can of course be posed about the other factor, labour.

These fundamental questions about the nature of capital and labour have occupied economists since the beginnings of the discipline. For Marx, capital was 'embodied' labour. It represented the efforts of previous workers, distilled into a tangible form. Thus a machine such as a tractor represented the physical embodiment of many hours of labour time expended in the past by workers in the tractor factory, the oil refinery, the paint factory and so on. Labour, and only labour, was capable of producing value – the so-called Labour Theory of Value. Returns which accrued to capital should rightfully have accrued to the labour which created that capital in the first place.

Capital can be considered as consisting of the durable physical objects created by the production process – for example machines, roads and buildings. Additionally it can be considered as consisting of *claims*. These claims are pieces of paper, or some other medium, which give the holder the right to own or acquire these durable physical objects. The most liquid form in which these claims exist is money. Less liquid forms include bonds and shares.

Stocks and flows

Capital can be thought of as a stock of assets – some physical and some financial. To this stock there corresponds a flow. This flow is what economists call the *return to capital* – if you like, the earnings of this factor. Financial capital (money, bonds and shares) will earn a financial return (interest, dividends). Physical capital will produce a stream of factor services – a car will provide transportation services, tractors will plough fields, provided of course that they are combined with suitable other factors, such as tractor drivers.

Land is sometimes treated as a type of capital 'provided by nature'. As such it yields a return in the form of rental income (if rented out to another person) or in the form of a stream of services (you can walk on it, grow things on it, build things on it or simply contemplate the beauty of it).

In market economies capital earns a return which in some equilibrium sense approximates to the rate of interest. This is easiest to understand when one considers financial assets. Interest is the reward you receive by lending financial capital (such as money) to others. But this financial capital is merely claims which can be exchanged for real capital, and vice versa. You can use your money to buy a tractor; and you can reverse the decision by selling the tractor for money.

In the long run we would expect those people holding assets which produce a lower than average return to dispose of them. Others will buy these assets, but at a lower price than that paid originally. A price in fact which reflects the relatively low returns to be expected from that particular asset so that when we calculate the percentage return it is no lower than that which can be earned elsewhere. This explains why in equilibrium the rate of interest can be described as the *opportunity cost of capital*. It also explains why the rate of return from all assets tends to be equalised. Thus we can talk about *the* rate of return to capital – in practice rates of return will vary but over time competitive forces will tend to make them equal, one to another.

13.5 ... and what is labour?

Defining what is meant by the word 'labour' is perhaps not quite as difficult as defining capital. However there are operational difficulties, not the least of which is that labour is clearly non-homogeneous – an hour of an accountant's time is not a perfect substitute for an hour of a telephone engineer's time. In this sort of analysis however we tend to simplify the real world by assuming that labour is homogeneous, so that we can talk about *the return* to labour. This return is of course the price of labour – or the wage rate.

13.6 Marginal productivity theory[1]

Consider the following example, where a shop manager whose objective is to maximise the profit he gets from his shop, can hire as many sales assistants as he wishes at the going rate. Generally speaking, the more staff he has, the greater will be his sales, but the more staff he hires, the smaller will be the extra contribution of each additional assistant. There will come a point when additional staff will actually reduce sales, not because the extra staff are less efficient or more surly, but simply because the size of the shop is fixed and the number of potential customers they could serve is limited. In other words, the staff get in each other's way and put off the customers by their excessive zeal. Clearly, there are too many staff in this situation, but what is the optimal number to hire?

Suppose that the shopkeeper knows the relationship between the number of staff and the net revenue from sales (that is, total sales revenue minus the bought-in prices of the goods he sells) as in Table 13.1 cols. 1 and 2. He can, therefore, calculate the extra net revenue attributable to each additional assistant. This is the value of the marginal product of each extra assistant (col. 3). The number of staff which the manager wishes to hire will depend upon the wage he has to pay. Suppose the going rate is £60 per week. The first assistant will be worth hiring because he adds £100 to net revenue but only £60 to costs, thus increasing profits by £40. Similarly, the second and third

Table 13.1 Shop assistants

Number of assistants	Net revenue from sales £ per week	Value of marginal product £ per week
1	100	100
2	180	80
3	245	65
4	300	55
5	320	20
6	320	0
7	310	−10

assistants add more to net revenue than they do to cost, so that they will be hired. But the fourth assistant adds only £55 to net revenue and a further £60 to costs, so that by employing him the manager will be reducing the shop's profits. Hence, he will not be employed. When the wage is £60, the manager will hire three assistants; that is, the demand for labour is three.

If wages rise to say £70 per week but the productivity of the assistants remains unchanged then we can easily check that the third assistant will no longer be employed because the wage that he has to be paid exceeds the value of his marginal product. At the higher wage of £70, the demand for labour drops to two.

In fact, the value of marginal product curve is the manager's demand curve for labour, since it shows how many assistants will be hired at each wage level, as in Fig. 13.8. If the four points in Fig. 13.8 were joined up, they would constitute a demand curve for labour. In our particular example, this is a step function rather than a smooth curve, but one can readily appreciate that what Fig. 13.8 illustrates is

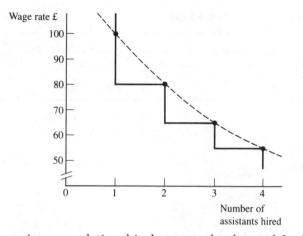

Figure 13.8

an inverse relationship between the demand for labour and the wage rate.

This example also illustrates a fundamental conclusion, namely that at the margin the wage rate is equal to the marginal product of labour. For example at a wage of £80 (well, £79.99 I suppose) two assistants will be hired and the wage rate – the price of labour – will be equal to the extra output generated by the second worker. Thus in symbols we could write that in equilibrium

$$MP_L = w = P_L$$

that is, the marginal product of labour equals the wage rate (which is the price of labour).

The same will be true of all factors so that we could also write that in equilibrium

$$MP_K = r = P_K$$

that is, the marginal product of capital equals the interest rate (the rate of return on capital) which is also the price of capital. In general, then, factors earn a return which reflects the value of their output. Factors which are more productive earn a higher return.

13.7 Investment in human capital

We have already noted that labour is a non-homogeneous factor. Marginal productivity theory suggests that factors earn a reward related to their productivity – more productive factors earn higher rewards. Hence we would expect to find that skilled labour earns more than unskilled labour. The question remains however as to why some units of labour are more skilled than others. One possible explanation is to do with the influence of education. Educated individuals, so the argument runs, possess *human capital*, so that part of the return which they receive is in fact a return to the capital vested in them rather than a return to labour. Education makes people more productive. Hence they receive higher rewards – that is, earn higher incomes.

Table 13.2 Gross weekly earnings by highest educational qualification attained; and by sex (Great Britain 1985)

	Degree or equivalent	Below degree higher education	GCE A-level or equivalent	GCE O-level/ CSE grade 1	CSE other grades/ commercial apprenticeship	No qualifications	Total
index (total = 100)							
Men	145	121	107	101	91	86	100
Women	156	134	106	99	90	81	100
Median weekly earnings (£)							
Men	240	200	176	167	151	141	165
Women	174	150	119	110	100	91	112

Source: *General Household Survey,* 1985 HMSO Table 7.13.

Table 13.2 shows that earnings rise with education. The higher the level of educational attainment the higher will be the average earnings of the individual in question, other things being equal. Of course earnings are also affected by sex (men earn more than women) and by age (earnings tend to rise with age). To assess the separate influences of education, sex, and age on earnings we can consult the age-earnings profiles shown in Fig. 13.9.

The figure relates to males only so that we have excluded any gender influences on earnings. Note that earnings tend to rise with age, more steeply in the early years, but to tail off slightly above the age of 50 for all groups except graduates. Similar age earnings profiles exist for women though average earnings are lower. The story told by age-earnings profiles is very clear: earnings are related (positively) to education.

The question remains however as to why educated people earn more than less educated people. The analysis of the preceding section suggests that the answer is straightforward. The higher rewards they receive reflect the fact that they are more productive. They are more productive because education has made them so. Part of the reward they receive is a reward to the human capital vested in them.

This may be true but an alternative possible explanation suggests that the reason why some individuals earn more than others is that they are *innately* more able than others – more intelligent and with a greater capacity for work. Because they have this innate advantage they succeed in the educational process whereas their less able classmates fail. Able pupils overcome the initial hurdle of GCSEs and go on to take 'A' levels. From this group the more able overcome

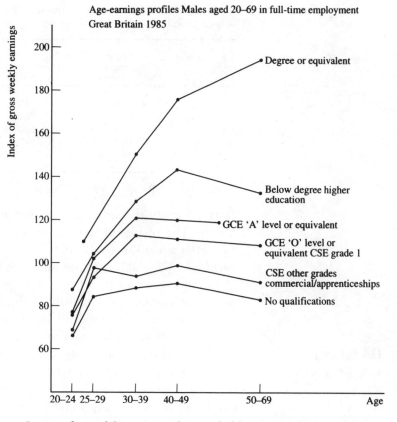

Age-earnings profiles Males aged 20–69 in full-time employment Great Britain 1985

Figure 13.9

Source: derived from General Household Survey 1985 Table 7.13.

the 'A' level hurdle and go on to higher education where again only the more able succeed in getting good degrees. This view sees the educational process as a *filter*. At each stage it filters out the less able, allowing only the more able to proceed. It also indicates to potential employers which candidates are the ones with more intelligence, ambition, capacity for work – and perhaps willingness to conform. These people secure highly paid jobs because they possess these qualities. So, in this explanation, education identifies them as such but does not confer these qualities upon them.

So, does education make people more productive or does it simply act as a filter? The answer, probably, is that it does both these things to some extent. But to what extent? The only way of answering this question would be to see how much earnings rise with educational attainment when we hold all other factors constant – factors such as age, sex, social class – and innate ability. A small number of longitudinal studies have followed cohorts of individuals over a number of years. The performance of these individuals in intelligence

Table 13.3 Swedish study (mean incomes before tax of males at age 35 by years of schooling and I.Q. at age ten; thousands of Kroner (City of Malmo, Sweden 1964))

| I.Q. | Years of schooling | | | |
	Under 8	8–10	11–14	14 or more
−85	14.6	14.9	17.7	35.5
86–92	17.7	17.5	20.5	—
93–107	15.3	18.2	21.7	31.4
108–114	16.6	19.5	19.4	41.0
115+	17.4	21.9	33.7	43.1

Source: Husen (1968) quoted in Blaug, M., *Economics of Education*, Penguin.

tests taken at an early age is used as a (crude) measure of innate ability. The results of the Swedish study shown in Table 13.3 show that even when innate ability is held constant education still increases earnings by a significant amount. For example, if we take the group with the lowest IQ (top row) those who received the most years of schooling earned more than twice as much as those who received the least. This therefore provides strong evidence to suggest that education is indeed an investment in human capital and is not just a filter.

13.8 Do labour markets work?

Some economists would argue that the foregoing analysis of investment in human capital contains a major flaw. A flaw so profound in fact that it renders the whole analysis invalid. And this it is, namely, that factor markets – and in particular the market for labour – may not in practice ensure that factors are paid a reward which reflects the value of the extra output they produce. In other words marginal productivity theory may simply be an unrealistic account of what happens to labour in the real world.

The first reason for suspecting such a flaw is that it is extremely difficult to measure the value of the extra output – the marginal product – attributable to most individuals in the workplace. It is difficult for economists trying to analyse the situation, but also for that amorphous mass known as 'the market' which according to its supporters is supposed to possess the ability to know what individuals find it impossible to know. The managing directors of large companies receive very large salaries – for example, in 1991 Ian Maclaurin, boss of Tesco, is said to have received £1.48 m. Who is to say that such salaries do not reflect the contribution of such individuals? It is a mistake however to argue that *because* these individuals receive such high salaries this therefore is an indication of the value of the contribution that they make to the organisation. In other words high salaries do not 'prove' that the individual is worth what he is paid by the organisation, particularly if the individual in question has some influence in the process which determines his salary, as is often the case.

Table 13.4 Men earn more than women (gross weekly earnings of full-time employees 1987 (and 1971), Great Britain)

	Males	Females	Female as % of male	Female as % of male (1971)
Manual employees	185.5	115.3	62.1	52.7
Non-manual employees	265.9	157.2	59.1	51.9
All employees	224.0	148.1	66.1	56.8

The figures relate to the mean earnings in £. Figures for median earnings produce a lower figure but the ratio of male:female earnings is similar.

Source: *Social Trends* 19, 1989, from *New Earnings Survey*, HMSO.

A second piece of evidence adds weight to the suspicion that labour markets do not in practice work perfectly, in the sense of ensuring that individuals are paid a wage in accordance with the value of their marginal product. This evidence relates to the existence of *discrimination* in labour markets. This discrimination may be on the basis of race or sex. Here we concentrate on the latter.

13.9 Discrimination in the labour market

On average men earn more than women. Table 13.4 shows that female earnings are only about two-thirds of male earnings on average, though the gap has narrowed somewhat since 1971, mostly perhaps as a result of the implementation of the Equal Pay Act in the early 1970s.

Earnings differentials are not in themselves proof of discrimination however since all of the other factors which affect earnings have not been held constant – factors such as the number of hours worked in a week, age, the number of years of experience and, of course, education. Table 13.5 gives an indication of the influence of each of these factors. The table shows the same educational attainment levels as those in Table 13.2 but now the table has been extended to show the average number of hours worked and the average age. Not surprisingly perhaps men tend to work somewhat longer hours than women – about 8 per cent higher on average. This in itself could be responsible for an 8 per cent difference in earnings all other things being equal, but as we have seen the male/female differential is of the order of 30 rather than 8 per cent.

A more surprising statistical finding, at first sight, is that the average age of men in the workforce is more than three years greater than that of women. This curious statistical fact is presumably because women tend to retire at 60 whereas the retiring age for men in the UK is still 65. This will tend to pull up the average age of men in each group. Since we know that earnings increase with age, especially for graduates, this in itself explains in part the higher earnings of males relative to females. Again, however, it cannot explain all of the differential that exists.

Table 13.5 Gross weekly earnings, hours worked, and age by highest educational level attained and sex (persons aged 20–69 in full time employment. Great Britain, 1985)

	Highest qualification level attained						Total
	Degree or equivalent	Below degree higher education	GCE A-level or equivalent	GCE O-level/ CSE grade 1	CSE other grades/ commercial apprenticeship	No qualifications	
Median weekly earnings £							
men	240	200	176	167	151	141	165
women	174	150	119	110	100	91	112
Earnings of women relative to those of men (%)	73	75	67	66	67	64	68
Hours **Mean hours worked per week**							
men	42.6	41.4	41.5	42.7	42.4	43.4	42.6
women	39.5	39.0	38.4	38.3	39.0	39.8	39.1
Mean hours of women relative to those of men (%)	93	94	92	90	92	92	92
Age **Mean age (years)**							
men	38.7	37.0	34.0	35.4	41.7	44.4	39.8
women	32.4	36.4	29.1	30.7	38.0	43.6	36.5

Source: as for Table 13.2.

What the table does not record is the average number of years participation in the labour force. Most women leave the workforce at some time to bear and rear children and this reduces the number of years of accumulated experience which again partly explains their lower earnings. It is interesting to note however that in some countries the business of child-rearing does not preclude women from participating in the workforce. Figure 13.10 shows the difference in the female participation rates between countries. At the one extreme in Denmark about 85 per cent of women work and there is no noticeable decline during the child-bearing years (though there was 20 years ago). At the other extreme in Ireland participation in the workforce slumps with the onset of pregnancy – and most women

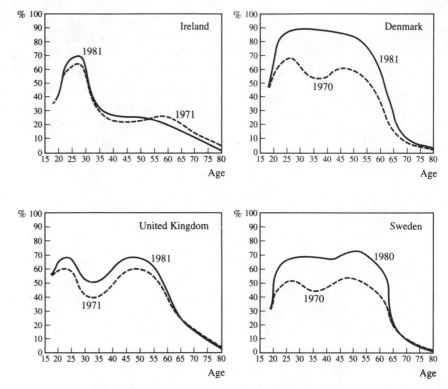

Figure 13.10 Female
participation rates in selected
European countries.
(Source: *UK Economic Studies,*
Winter 1990)

never return to the workforce.

All of the factors we have mentioned contributed partly to the differentials we have observed. Estimating the independent effect of each of them is of course a difficult statistical task. It is interesting to note from Table 13.5 however that earnings differentials between men and women seem to narrow as educational attainment increases.

Questions

13.1 Consider the extent to which the following are characterised by:
   (a) fixed factor proportions
   (b) opportunities for labour/capital substitution.
      i car manufacture
     ii teaching
    iii osteopathy
    iv growing daffodils
     v farming
    vi banking

13.2 Whatever happened to Renaissance Man?

13.3 Say whether the following statements are true or false. If false correct them:

(a) All graduates earn more than non-graduates.
(b) The higher the level of educational attainment the higher the lifetime earnings, *ceteris paribus*.
(c) Earnings and educational attainment are positively correlated but so are earnings and age.
(d) Earnings and gender are correlated.
(e) IQ influences educational attainment which in turn influences earnings. Therefore IQ determines earnings.

14 The price system as an allocative mechanism

14.1 Markets and the allocation of resources

Economics, as the reader should now be aware, is about how resources are allocated. One way in which resources can be allocated is by a system of state planning such as that used in the countries of the Eastern bloc for most of the post-war period. In what is basically a capitalist or free enterprise economy such as that of Britain, however, most resources tend to be allocated by the market mechanism or what we call the *price system*. The purpose of this chapter is to examine how the market mechanism does this in theory and to consider whether the theory is a reasonable description of reality. The analysis which we will present forms the basis of what is known as *welfare economics* and it provides a theoretical underpinning to many microeconomic policy decisions. The analysis was formulated originally by the Italian economist Vilfredo Pareto.

We saw in Chapter 12 how a rational economic man will divide his consumption spending such that the following condition will be satisfied:

$$\frac{MU_A}{P_A} = \frac{MU_B}{P_B} = \ldots = \frac{MU_n}{P_n} \qquad [14.1]$$

That is, he will allocate his spending in such a way that the last penny spent on purchasing good A yields exactly the same increase in total satisfaction as does the last penny spent on good B. If this were not the case, we argued, he could always reallocate his spending so as to produce a net increase in his overall level of satisfaction.

Assume now that the goods which our rational consumer buys are sold on markets in which prices reflect production costs. Specifically, assume that in each market, price is equal to marginal cost. This condition will of course be satisfied in perfectly competitive markets but may not be satisfied in markets where elements of monopoly are present. If price is equal to marginal cost in all markets, however, then we can rewrite eqn [14.1] as

$$\frac{MU_A}{MC_A} = \frac{MU_B}{MC_B} = \ldots = \frac{MU_n}{MC_n}$$

[14.2]

simply by replacing P_A by MC_A, and so on. This equation represents a very fundamental statement about the way in which resources are allocated or should be allocated. If this condition is satisfied for all consumers then we can make the following statement: such a system produces an allocation in which the extra resources devoted to producing the last unit of good A (that is, MC_A) yields exactly the same increase in total satisfaction as do the extra resources devoted to producing the last unit of good B (MC_B), and that the same is true for all goods.

It is not easy for the reader coming to eqn [14.2] for the first time to understand exactly what is being said. It is impossible however to underestimate its importance since it is a statement to the effect that the price system will produce an allocation of society's resources which is the 'best' that is attainable. 'Best' in this sense means *Pareto Optimal*. What this means is that with any non-Pareto Optimal allocation of resources it is possible to imagine a reallocation which will produce a net improvement in society's welfare. Such an improvement would be called a Pareto improvement. Of course, a reallocation which shifts resources towards one particular individual at the expense of others will be seen from the point of view of that individual as a preferred or improved allocation of resources. The term 'Pareto improvement', however, refers to a reallocation in which one individual is made better off and no one else is made worse off. A Pareto optimal allocation of resources therefore is a situation in which nobody can be made better off without at the same time making someone else worse off. The key conclusion is that the market mechanism, that is, the unfettered operation of the laws of demand and supply, ultimately produces an allocation of society's scarce resources which is optimal in the restricted sense of the term employed here. The allocation cannot be bettered. As such this analysis represents a strong case for private enterprise.

Before we go on to consider the validity of the analysis presented above, it is worth elaborating on its main points.

Firstly, the role which prices play in the resource allocation process is central. Prices act as signals to which both producers and consumers respond. We saw in the previous chapter how the utility-maximising consumer would respond to a change in relative prices by modifying his consumption pattern. For example, if the price of cakes rose relative to the price of ale, the rational consumer would then buy fewer cakes and more ale. In a similar way, producers respond to changes in the prices of the factors of production which they use. For example, if the price of steel rises relative to the price of plastic then producers will tend to replace steel components by plastic ones where it is technically feasible to do so. In this way they minimise their production costs in an attempt to maximise profits, in the same way that the consumer attempts to maximise utility.

Prices, then, convey information about relative scarcity. Goods which are in scarce supply and for which there is a high demand, will command a high price; goods which are abundant and for which there is little demand, a low price. This is what is meant by 'scarcity' in economics. It is the supply relative to the demand which determines the economic scarcity of a good. For example, the drawings and paintings of Pablo Picasso are quite numerous but there is a high demand for them so they command a high price. In contrast, I have myself produced a few drawings and paintings but even for this small number the market demand is zero and hence they command a zero price.

The economic problem exists because scarcity exists. Not everybody can have everything they want, so choices have to be made. The poor man has to choose between bread and potatoes, the rich man between a new yacht and a villa. Choices have to be made not only in consumption, however, but in all other situations characterised by scarcity – the individual has to decide how to allocate his time between work and leisure, the investor how to allocate his funds, the firm how to produce its goods and what and where to sell. All of these decisions have two things in common. Firstly, they are decisions based on the information about relative scarcities which is provided by the set of relative prices. Secondly, each decision is goal-orientated. It has some purpose to it. The consumer seeks to maximise his utility, the firm seeks to maximise its profits. In all cases, however, decisions are motivated by self-interest rather than by philanthropy. In pursuing their selfish ends, however, individuals inadvertently bring about an allocation of society's resources which is 'optimal'. They do good by doing well, since the price system channels and co-ordinates their myriad selfish actions in such a way that society as a whole benefits.

14.2 Market failure

If the analysis of the previous section is correct, then it does indeed seem that the market mechanism will produce an allocation of society's resources which is 'optimal' in the restricted sense that we have used this term. Indeed, advocates of the free market mechanism have used Pareto's analysis to support their contention that the greatest happiness of the greatest number can be secured if the state refrains from intervening in the market and simply allows market forces to rule. On the other hand, those who believe in some state intervention have pointed to the very restrictive – and unrealistic –

assumptions under which such a Pareto optimal allocation of resources will be produced. There are four key criticisms which can be levelled at these underlying assumptions.

1. Price not equal to marginal cost

In perfectly competitive markets price will be equal to marginal cost. Such markets are rare however. In most markets, in practice, price will diverge from marginal production cost (even assuming that marginal cost can be identified) and in many cases price will bear almost no relation to production costs – see for example section 8.4 on sailboard prices. The extent to which price could diverge from marginal costs obviously depends on the extent to which the firm enjoys monopoly powers. Monopolists – or to be more correct, oligopolists – are price makers rather than price takers, so their price need not reflect the element of economic scarcity embodied in the marginal cost concept.

2. Income distribution

A Pareto optimal allocation of resources is predicated upon a particular initial distribution of society's resources or, in other words, upon a particular distribution of income. Different income distributions will produce different Pareto optimal allocations of resources. In other words, there is not just one Pareto optimal allocation of resources but many Pareto optima – as many in fact as there are possible distributions of income. When consumers spend their income, each pound spent is like a vote cast for the production of a particular commodity. A pound spent on cakes is a vote for cake production. A pound spent on ale is a vote for ale production.

Suppose, for the purpose of this example, that society is composed of two groups, those who like cakes and a second group who like ale. If the cake lovers are rich and the ale lovers poor then the allocation of society's resources will be heavily biased towards cake production. If, on the other hand, the ale lovers become rich and the cake lovers poor then the resulting increased expenditure on ale would result in a shift of society's resources away from cake production and towards ale production. The allocation of society's resources which results from the operation of the market mechanism is therefore clearly dependent on the initial distribution of income.

3. Untraded goods

Some goods which affect consumers' utility are not traded. That is, not only are they not sold on perfectly competitive markets, they are not sold on markets at all. Thus, for example, a consumer's utility may be affected by the level of noise pollution to which he is exposed, by oil pollution on holiday beaches or by the level of street violence. None of these things are traded on markets. Hence the amount of society's resources devoted to producing them – or in this case controlling them – is not the result of a set of preferences expressed in the market. In other words, the consumer cannot vote for more resources devoted to reducing pollution by himself spending more money on reducing pollution. In summary, there is an area in which the market does not work.

4. Public goods

A further area in which the market works only imperfectly, if at all, is known as the *public good* area. The term 'public goods' as used by economists refers to certain goods and services often – but not invariably – supplied by the public sector rather than the market. Services such as policing, street lighting, roads and flood protection schemes can be considered as public goods. Because such goods possess the characteristics of *non-excludability* and *non-rivalness* (to be explained in section 17.3) they may not be supplied in the quantities which consumers' preferences would dictate because consumers cannot effectively express their preferences by purchasing or not purchasing the good in question.

Two related conclusions follow from the foregoing analysis. Firstly, the operation of the market mechanism may not produce a Pareto optimal allocation of resources because of the ability of some sellers in oligopolistic markets to set prices which diverge from marginal cost. Secondly, even if the allocation of resources in society were Pareto optimal there might be some citizens, or indeed a majority of citizens, who would prefer a different allocation of resources – for example, one which allowed for a different distribution of income and which allocated resources to areas which the market mechanism did not adequately serve.

Questions

14.1 A Pareto optimal allocation of resources is one where:
   (a) nobody can benefit from a redistribution of resources.
   (b) resources cannot be transferred from one use to another without causing a reduction in somebody's welfare.
   (c) resources cannot be transferred from one use to another without causing a reduction in society's welfare.

14.2 Say which of the following are correct. A Pareto optimal allocation of resources:
   (a) cannot be achieved under a planned system.
   (b) is automatically achieved in a market system.
   (c) is never achieved in reality.
   (d) could be achieved if prices conveyed information about relative scarcities.

14.3 Suppose the price of aluminium rose relative to the price of nylon. Which of the following statements are correct?
   (a) The government would have to instruct firms to use less aluminium.
   (b) Manufacturers would try to use nylon rather than aluminium where it was feasible to do so. The demand for

        aluminium would go down.

(c) Products which used aluminium would become more expensive. People would buy less of them so the demand for aluminium would go down.

(d) Only those consumers who were concerned about environmental issues and who knew that aluminium was becoming scarce would economise on its use. The rest would not.

14.4 In a market system, in pursuing their selfish ends individuals 'do good by doing well'. Why was this not true of Al Capone (the gangster who was so successful in America in the 1930s)?

(a) It was true. Al gave people what they wanted.

(b) Because the statement does not apply to things like alcohol and gambling.

(c) Because people were not free to choose whether they dealt with Al Capone or not.

(d) Because, by acting selfishly, people cannot possibly do good.

14.5 Market failure occurs because:

(a) not everyone has heard of the concept of Pareto optimality.

(b) the distribution of incomes is unequal.

(c) market prices do not always reflect the true resource costs involved.

15 The distribution of income

15.1 The distribution of personal incomes

The market mechanism rewards success and punishes failure. Small wonder then that the distribution of income which results is unequal. In this section we examine just how unequal that distribution is. We then go on to examine the extent to which the distribution is changed by the systems of taxation and cash grants. Finally we examine the distribution of wealth.

The distribution of income

In Table 15.1 we divide the population of households in the UK into quintile groups, each group containing 20 per cent of the total distribution. They are then ranked from highest to lowest. If the distribution of income were completely equal the top quintile group would receive 20 per cent of total income, as would the next quintile group and so on down to the lowest quintile group who would also receive 20 per cent of total income. Clearly, however, the distribution of income is not equal. As can be seen, the top quintile received more than 50 per cent of total income whereas the bottom quintile received less than half of 1 per cent of total income.

Note that Table 15.1 refers to what the CSO calls 'original household income'. Before proceeding therefore we should define what this means. Note first that the distribution of income which we

Table 15.1 Distribution of original household income (percentages accruing to each quintile group, UK, 1986)

top fifth	50.7
next fifth	26.9
middle fifth	16.4
next fifth	5.7
bottom fifth	0.3
	100.0

Source: derived from *Social Trends* 19, 1989. CSO data from *Family Expenditure Survey*.

are considering relates to *households* and not to persons. Statistics on the distribution of personal income would be meaningless because some individuals – children and especially infants – have very little or no income. Statisticians are therefore compelled to use households rather than persons as the unit being studied. This is not entirely satisfactory however, since some households will contain just one person, often a pensioner, whereas others will contain two or more adult income-earners and dependent children. This fact alone would lead us to expect an unequal distribution of household income.

Secondly, we should consider what is meant by the term 'income'. The basic distinction we want to make is between pre-tax and post-tax income but we also want to take account of receipts of cash grants, such as unemployment benefit and possibly even the receipt of income-in-kind such as free schooling and health care. The CSO defines four categories of income: original income, gross income, disposable income and final income.

'Original income'

Households receive income from various sources, but principally from employment (including self-employment) and from investments (dividends, etc.). Income from occupational pension schemes (but not state pensions) is also defined as part of *original income*, as are alimony, and gifts.

'Gross income'

For some households transfer payments, such as state retirement pensions or unemployment benefit, represent by far the most significant part of income received. The addition to original income of these cash payments yields what the CSO calls *gross income*.

'Disposable income'

Most households pay income tax and those in employment will also pay the employees' National Insurance Contribution (NIC). The deduction from gross income of income tax and employees' NIC yields *disposable income*.

'Final income'

The CSO then performs a statistical adjustment to the figures for disposable income to produce what it calls *final income*. This

Table 15.2 Distribution of original, disposable and final household income (percentage accruing to each quintile group, UK, 1976 and 1986)

	Income in 1976			Income in 1986		
	Original	Disposable	Final	Original	Disposable	Final
Top fifth	44.4	38.1	37.9	50.7	42.2	41.7
Next fifth	26.6	24.1	24.0	26.9	24.1	23.9
Middle fifth	18.8	18.2	18.0	16.4	16.9	17.0
Next fifth	9.4	12.6	12.7	5.7	11.0	11.4
Bottom fifth	0.8	7.0	7.4	0.3	5.9	5.9
	100.0	100.0	100.0	100.0	100.0	100.0

Source: as for Table 15.1.
Note: column totals may not sum to 100 because of rounding errors.

adjustment deducts payments of indirect taxes such as VAT and rates (or the Community Charge) and adds the imputed benefits to households from government expenditure on certain services such as education and the National Health Service.

Armed with these definitions we can now approach Table 15.2 which shows original, disposable and final income for 1976 and 1986. The most striking and perhaps surprising feature of Table 15.2 is that the distribution of income has become more unequal. This is true whether one considers original, disposable, or final income. Moreover the trend towards inequality has been at both ends of the distribution. That is, the rich have got richer and the poor have got poorer.

The second salient but perhaps unsurprising feature of Table 15.2 is that the tax-benefit system does redistribute income. There is a significant difference between the distribution of original income and the distribution of disposable income. Note however, that there is very little difference between shares of disposable income and final income. The reason for this is that although income in kind, such as spending on the NHS, has some slight redistributive effect, indirect taxes such as excise duties and rates are mildly regressive – that is, they take a larger proportion of low incomes than they do of high incomes.

Table 15.3 presents a more detailed analysis of the effect which the

Table 15.3 Redistribution of income through taxes and benefits (percentage contributions to disposable income. Households. UK, 1986)

	Bottom fifth	Middle fifth	Top fifth
Earnings of main earner	—	77	81
Earnings of others in household	—	9	34
Occupational pensions, annuities	1	9	3
Investment income	1	6	6
Other income	—	2	1
equals *total original income*	(4)	(103)	(125)
plus benefits in cash			
contributory	50	9	1
non-contributory	46	6	2
equals *gross income*	(100)	(119)	(128)
minus income tax and NIC	—	−19	−28
equals disposable income	**(100)**	**(100)**	**(100)**
minus indirect taxes	−25	−29	−21
plus benefits in kind			
Education	10	8	4
NHS	26	9	4
Other	6	2	1
equals *final income*	(118)	(90)	(87)

Source: derived from *Social Trends 19*, 1989, HMSO. Percentages are rounded, hence they may not sum.

tax-benefit system has on the distribution of income. For simplicity of exposition only the bottom, middle and top quintiles are shown.

As can be seen the bottom quintile has (almost) no income from employment. Almost all their disposable income comes from benefits in cash. Benefits in kind also constitute a significant fraction of their final income.

In the top quintile the picture is reversed. Virtually all their original income comes from employment. Benefits in cash contribute almost nothing to disposable income, but income taxes take a significant slice of gross income.

As might be supposed differences in household income are partly explained by differences in household composition. As Table 15.4 shows households in the bottom quintile are likely to contain fewer

Table 15.4 Average numbers per household (bottom, middle and top quintiles, UK, 1987)

	Bottom	Middle	Top
Average number of persons	2.4	2.9	2.4
of which: adults	1.7	2.1	2.0
of which:			
economically active*	**0.3**	**1.4**	**1.7**
retired	0.7	0.4	0.2
economically inactive, not retired	0.7	0.3	0.1

* 'Economically active' comprises employees, the self-employed and others not in employment but who were seeking or intending to seek work, but excluding those away from work for more than 1 year.
Source: derived from *Social Trends 21*, 1991, HMSO.

persons than those in the middle or top. Overwhelmingly, however, the main difference is that households in the bottom quintile are likely to contain few or no economically active persons. That is, they are either past retirement age or, if below retirement age, they are economically inactive, in the sense that they are neither working nor seeking work.

The market mechanism, as we said at the outset, rewards success. 'To each, according to his contribution' might be the maxim of the free market. This is tempered to some extent by a different ethic – 'to each according to his needs' – since the system of benefits in cash has some redistributive effect. But not much.

15.2 The distribution of wealth

The data necessary to compile statistics on the distribution of income are collected annually by the Inland Revenue and by a sample survey called the Family Expenditure Survey. Data on the distribution of wealth are however not readily available and therefore any statistics relating to the distribution of wealth should be treated with caution.

A parade of dwarfs

We know however that the distribution of wealth is very unequal, much more unequal than the distribution of income which we discussed in the previous section. It is sometimes difficult, when presented with the raw data, to get a feel for the degree of inequality. Because of this the economist Jan Pen suggested an expositional device which consisted of relating each person's income to his height. He would then arrange for the entire population to file past the observer in one hour, starting with persons receiving the least income (the shortest) and ending with those receiving the most (the tallest). What the observer saw was a parade of dwarfs . . . and, in the last few moments, a few giants. Had the parade related to wealth rather than income, the dwarfs would have been even smaller and the few giants who flashed past in the closing seconds even taller.

You cannot take it with you

The only time in a person's life when he is forced to reveal his wealth is when he dies. Bizarre as it may seem, this is the source used to compile data on the distribution of wealth. When a person dies the property he leaves is known in legal terms as his *estate*. Statisticians use the estates of dead people to paint a picture of the wealth of the living. Clearly this 'mortality multiplier' method, as it is known, is beset with difficulties and potential anomalies. If a few very wealthy young people die, estimates of the distribution of wealth among the living show a marked increase in inequality. Lysteria in the potted meat sandwiches at a royal garden party would significantly increase measured inequality.

The definition of wealth

In addition to the problem of acquiring data there is the problem of defining what is meant by wealth, and of evaluating the worth of the

Table 15.5 The distribution of wealth, UK

	1976	1988
Marketable wealth		
percentage of wealth owned by:		
most wealthy 1%	21	17
most wealthy 5%	38	38
most wealthy 10%	50	53
most wealthy 25%	71	75
most wealthy 50%	92	94
Marketable wealth less value of dwellings		
percentage of wealth owned by:		
most wealthy 1%	29	27
most wealthy 5%	47	50
most wealthy 10%	57	63
most wealthy 25%	73	80
most wealthy 50%	88	93

Note: the statistics relate to persons aged 18 and over.
Source: *Social Trends 21*, derived from Inland Revenue data.

assets. Some assets, such as stocks and shares, are marketable and are easy to place a value upon. Other marketable assets, such as real property and land, are more difficult to value unless they are sold. Some authors argue that non-marketable wealth such as occupational and state pension rights should also be included in a definition of wealth.

Table 15.5 relates to marketable wealth only. If one were to include occupational and state pension rights, the distribution would appear more equal, though the argument for the inclusion of such rights – particularly state pension rights – is unconvincing.

Table 15.5 has two salient features. Firstly, as we have already noted, the distribution of wealth is more unequal than the distribution of income. Secondly, unlike the distribution of income which is becoming more unequal, the distribution of wealth appears to be becoming more equal. The single most important factor in promoting greater equality seems to have been the increase in home ownership. In 1987 almost a third of all personal sector wealth was in dwellings.

15.3 Regional inequalities

We saw in the previous section that a market system produces inequalities in the distribution of income between households. Market systems are often characterised, too, by inequalities in the distribution of income between regions of the same country though such inequalities occur also in planned economies. In the UK there is a 'North–South divide'. The North is poorer than the South. While one could debate where the 'North' starts and the 'South' ends it is clear from Table 15.6 that certain regions such as the South-East, East Anglia and the South-West are more prosperous than other regions such as the North, Wales and N. Ireland.

Table 15.6 GDP per capita, by region, 1988 (index – UK average = 100)

South East	122
East Anglia	98
South West	95
East Midlands	93
Scotland	93
North West	92
West Midlands	91
Yorks and Humberside	91
North	87
Wales	83
N. Ireland	75
UK average	100

Source: *Regional Trends 25*, 1990.

GDP ('Gross Domestic Product') is a measure of the output of goods and services in a country, or within a region. GDP per capita is therefore a measure of the 'standard of living' of the inhabitants. Thus what these statistics show is that people in the South-East tend to be 22 per cent better-off than the UK average whereas people in N. Ireland are 25 per cent worse off than the UK average. Therefore people in the South East are almost 50 per cent better-off than people in N. Ireland.

GDP is of course a very imperfect measure of the standard of living. It reflects only those goods and services which are subject to economic transactions – those goods and services, in other words that are produced and sold directly to consumers or supplied to them indirectly via some governmental agency such as the National Health Service or the local education authority.

We should not be surprised to find that other indices of the *material* standard of living correlate highly with gross national product per capita. One such index of the material standard of living is the ownership of certain consumer durables.

Table 15.7 Percentage of households with selected durable goods (regions ranked by income per capita) 1986–87

	Dishwasher	Telephone	Video	Washing machine
South-East	11	89	46	78
East Anglia	9	85	37	83
South-West	9	85	38	81
East Midlands	6	82	44	88
Scotland	6	81	42	88
North-West	5	81	41	82
West Midlands	5	80	39	82
Yorks and Humberside	4	80	38	86
North	3	75	40	88
Wales	5	77	35	82
N. Ireland	7	72	30	81

Source: *Regional Trends 25*, 1990.

In Table 15.7 the regions are ranked according to income per capita. As can be seen the percentage of households owning dishwashers and videos correlates very highly with income per capita. The same is true of most other durable goods such as cars and refrigerators. Note however that some goods, such as washing machines, do not fit the general pattern since significantly fewer households in the affluent South-East and South-West own washing machines than in the poorer East Midlands and North. Given the statistical regularity observed

Table 15.8 Share ownership by region (percentage of adults owning shares or unit trusts (1989) (regions ranked by GDP per capita)

South-East	34
East Anglia	21
South-West	29
East Midlands	29
Scotland	18
North-West	19
West Midlands	21
Yorks and Humberside	21
North	18
Wales	27

Source: *Regional Trends 25*, 1990.

earlier this is quite puzzling. Other indices such as share ownership correlate with income per capita in the way that we would expect, with the affluent South-East having a significantly higher number of households owning shares than other regions, as Table 15.8 shows.

Table 15.9 Educational attainment by region (percentage of school leavers with GCSE grades A-C (regions ranked by GDP per capita) 1988) (females in parentheses)

	English	Mathematics
South-East	39.5 (52.0)	39.6 (34.3)
East Anglia	34.5 (50.7)	37.2 (32.5)
South-West	38.2 (53.3)	38.7 (34.5)
East Midlands	33.4 (45.3)	33.9 (28.8)
Scotland (see text)	42.4 (55.8)	47.9 (51.3)
North-West	33.1 (46.9)	34.2 (28.6)
West Midlands	32.7 (46.8)	32.6 (26.9)
Yorks and Humberside	29.9 (41.9)	31.4 (25.0)
North	29.3 (41.0)	31.3 (25.8)
Wales	30.7 (45.3)	35.4 (33.3)

Source: *Regional Trends 25*, 1990.

Indices of the material standard of living therefore correlate highly with indices of GDP per capita, as we would expect. What is perhaps more surprising is that other indices of the 'quality of life' which relate to less materialistic notions of well-being also correlate with GDP per capita. In Table 15.9 for example the association between educational attainment and material affluence is clear. Regions with higher GDP per capita record significantly higher pass rates at GCSE. The more affluent the region the more likely a pupil is to achieve a high grade at GCSE.

15.4 A note on statistical regularity

W. Sawyer once described statistics as 'the search for pattern'. Careful scrutiny of the statistics in Table 15.9 reveals an intriguing pattern. Study them for yourself for a moment and then read on.

As noted earlier pass rates correlate with income per capita. But it is also clear that in every region girls do better than boys in English, and by a significant margin (roughly 12 per cent). In mathematics the picture is reversed. In every region in England and Wales boys do better than girls, again by a significant, but smaller, amount, (roughly 4 per cent). We have discovered a pattern.

Scotland is another country

The pattern we have discovered is a type of 'explanation'. It does not explain the underlying processes which give rise to these differences but the discovery of the statistical regularity, in itself, goes some way towards improving our understanding. It teaches us what to look for. Girls do better than boys in English, and worse than boys in maths. If we know what to expect, the unexpected stands out.

Scotland is a region of the UK which has a separate educational system, hence the data for Scotland are not comparable with those for the rest of UK. In English (which the Scots speak a variant of) educational attainment is some 10 per cent higher, for both boys and girls, than we would expect on the basis of GDP per capita. This is either because the Scottish educational system is superior to that in England and Wales or simply because the examinations are easier. Inasmuch as Scottish girls score roughly 12 per cent higher than Scottish boys, however, the statistical regularity noted previously is still present. In mathematics, however, the results come as a complete surprise. Contrary to the pattern noted elsewhere, *girls do better than*

Table 15.10 Age adjusted mortality and disability rates (regions ranked by GDP per capita) (rate per 100 000 population, 1987)

	Heart disease	Cancer	All causes	Disability*
South-East	354	285	1055	121
East Anglia	350	285	1033	123
South-West	359	269	1014	124
East Midlands	397	185	1125	131
Scotland	479	328	1324	131
North-West	441	324	1253	131
West Midlands	410	303	1171	141
Yorks and Humberside	426	303	1194	148
North	446	330	1268	162
Wales	422	302	1179	160
N. Ireland	480	286	1267	—

* The Office of Population Censuses and Surveys categorises the severity of disability on a ten point scale. The figures given here include all disabilities, and are standardised for age. They are the rate per thousand population.

Source: *Regional Trends 24*, 1989.

boys. This is so surprising that we could legitimately claim to have 'discovered' something – though we know not what – about mathematics education in Scotland. There is something sufficiently interesting here to warrant further investigation, but not now as we have to get back to our story.

We have seen that GDP per capita correlates not just with indices of the material standard of living, but also with things such as educational attainment. It also correlates with mortality and disability rates as Table 15.10 shows.

The first three columns of Table 15.10 show the age adjusted death rates by heart disease, cancer, and all causes. As can be seen at any particular age you are more likely to die of heart disease if you live in the North than in the South. You are also more likely to die of cancer. In fact, you are more likely to die. While you are alive, as the last column shows you are much more likely to suffer disability. If one were to calculate what is known as the rank correlation coefficient between this index of disability and GDP per capita it would be 100 per cent – GDP per capita 'explains' in a statistical sense all the variation in disability rates between regions. Finally, readers in N. Ireland, if there are any, can take a crumb of comfort from the fact that they are no more likely to die of cancer than those in the South-East – but this is probably because they will already have died from heart disease.

Table 15.11 Increase in inequality (total personal income (£ per head) by region) UK average = 100

	1982	1986	1988
South-East	113.5	115.9	117.0
East Anglia	94.6	98.2	96.1
South-West	97.9	98.1	101.1
East Midlands	96.9	95.8	93.2
Scotland	96.2	94.6	95.9
North-West	95.3	93.2	92.5
West Midlands	91.2	92.0	90.1
Yorkshire and Humberside	93.5	93.5	92.3
North	95.2	92.2	89.9
Wales	89.1	86.8	83.9
N. Ireland	83.6	74.8	81.5
Total	100.0	100.0	100.0

Source: *Regional Trends No.25*, 1990, Table 12.5.

An increase in inequalities

GDP per capita is a convenient summary statistic. To the experienced economic statistician the predictive power of variations in GDP per capita to 'explain' variations in other indices of the standard of living is well known, and it comes as no surprise to find the correlations we have observed.

Table 15.12 Government expenditure on Regional Preferential Assistance to Industry 1979–89 (£m at constant 1985 prices. Great Britain)

79/80	80/81	81/82	82/83	83/84	84/85	85/86	86/87	87/88	88/89
965	977	1012	1042	710	663	578	711	508	526

The figures shown are in real terms. That is, they are inflation-adjusted.
Source: derived from *Regional Trends*, 1990. Figures deflated using the implied deflator for fixed capital formation, taken from *UK National Accounts*, 1990, Table 1.7.

What is perhaps slightly more surprising is that regional inequalities are increasing in the UK. As Table 15.11 shows, over the latter half of the 1980s the degree of inequality between the regions has increased, and by a significant extent. The South-East in particular has become relatively richer whereas most of the regions have become relatively poorer.

15.5 Will the market mechanism reduce inequalities

The last ten years have of course been a period in which greater reliance has been placed on the market mechanism. Expenditure on policies designed to reduce regional inequalities has been cut back. Table 15.12 shows that in real terms assistance to industries in less favoured regions fell by almost a half.

The rationale for this policy of non-intervention has been that the market mechanism, left to its own devices, will tend to reduce and in the long run eliminate regional inequalities in income per capita. The

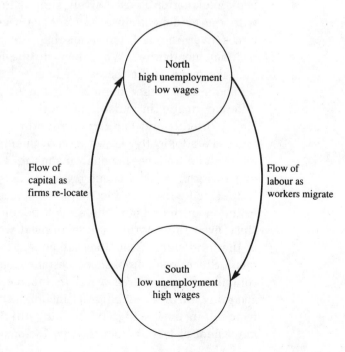

Figure 15.1

text-book argument which supports this argument focuses on flows of factors between regions in response to regional differences in the prices of these factors. Suppose there are two regions – 'North' and 'South' as in Fig. 15.1. The North is characterised by relatively low income per capita and relatively high unemployment rates. In the prosperous South in contrast, unemployment rates are much lower and consequently there are labour shortages in some industries.

If the market for labour works in the way that competitive markets are supposed to do, then the excess demand for labour in the South will cause the price of labour – that is, wages – to rise. In the North, high rates of unemployment depress wages. It follows therefore that *wage costs* will be higher in the South than in the North. In pursuit of these lower costs firms will move North, relocating their factories to areas where wages are lower. In short, there is a movement of capital from South to North. This increases job opportunities in the North, raising output and income (GDP) in the region.

For their part workers are attracted by the higher wages in the South. They therefore migrate in pursuit of these higher wages, reducing unemployment rates in the North as they do so.

In summary labour will flow from North to South and capital will flow from South to North. These flows result from the market incentives provided by regional differences in wage rates and profit rates. These flows will reduce the inequalities that gave rise to them, eventually eliminating the inequalities altogether. Clearly, this text-book explanation is excessively simplistic. It is moreover at variance with the evidence, since as we have seen the freer play of market forces over the last ten years has increased rather than reduced regional inequalities. Why, then, do the flows of capital and labour not take place as the theory predicts?

Labour is a rather immobile factor of production. Migration to a different region in pursuit of work involves the loss of (perhaps) family, friends and familiar surroundings. Nevertheless, labour does move. Paradoxically, however, movements of labour may exacerbate rather than reduce regional inequalities in income. When labour migrates from a low-income region it takes purchasing power with it, further reducing the income of that region. This will affect the residents of the region who are left behind – shopkeepers will suffer since even those formerly unemployed would have spent something in the local shops. Now they are gone. Their spending has gone with them. Since local shopkeepers, estate agents, builders, gardeners and solicitors have suffered a fall in income, they in turn reduce their spending, further reducing the income of the local community. Thus regional income will tend to fall still further as a result of the movement of labour from the low income area, exacerbating regional inequalities. Economists refer to this as a *multiplier* effect.

Moreover, the theory, illustrated in Fig. 15.1 implicitly assumes that labour is a homogeneous factor. Labour is non-homogeneous however. A skilled carpenter is not a perfect substitute for an accountant or a chemist. Unemployed labour in the North may not possess the skills for which there is high demand in the South. Firms moreover may rely on specific skills only available in their existing location in the South. A pool of unemployed labour in the North, and lower wages, may not provide sufficient attraction if that labour does not possess the requisite skills.

Capital is a more mobile factor. In fact, it is very mobile and willing to move not just to different regions, but to different countries, sometimes on the other side of the globe. Therein lies the fault with the theory illustrated in Fig. 15.1. Some way off the diagram, off the page in fact, lie other countries with wage costs that are not only lower than those in the South of Britain but are lower than those in the North too. Countries such as Taiwan, Korea and Thailand where wages are not only low but there is a plentiful supply of pliant labour. The market mechanism does work in the sense that capital will flow from the South. But it flows not to the North but to these low-waged countries overseas.

16 Planning

16.1 Economic planning in peace and war

State planning stands in contrast to the market as a mechanism of resource allocation. In this chapter we shall look at planning in two distinct, though related, contexts. Firstly, we shall consider the way resources were allocated in the centrally planned or command economies of the Soviet type. Secondly, we shall look at the planning methods used in capitalist economies in wartime, the focus of our study being the British economy in the Second World War. These two examples of planning, though distinct, in fact share the common features that they do not use prices and profitability as a means of indicating where resources should flow. In a market system, as we have seen, the myriad decisions of economic agents – firms and consumers – are co-ordinated by the unseen hand of the price mechanism. Decisions are decentralised but the basic questions which have to be resolved – what is to be produced, by what method and for whom – are resolved because economic agents respond to price signals. Thus, ultimately the allocation of society's resources is the result of decisions which are decentralised and diffused. This is the way of the market.

In a planned system, in contrast, decisions are taken centrally by some state planning agency. This agency, in effect, dictates the way in which society's resources are allocated in pursuit of some objective which may be either the maximisation of economic growth (as in the case of centrally planned economies) or the winning of a war (as in the case of wartime economies).

It may seem strange that a book about the operation of market economies should discuss planning, which is in effect the antithesis of market allocation. There are a number of valid reasons for so doing, however. First, a sizeable proportion of the world's population – between a third and a half – have lived, at least until recently, in economic systems which are characterised by central planning: the Soviet bloc, China and many Third World countries. Second, in both the First and Second World Wars the combatants resorted to planning as a means of more effectively promoting the war effort. Third, a study, even a brief one, of the operation of economic planning gives an invaluable perspective to the study of the operation of market economies. The market economy does work; it does allocate resources, but there may be an alternative way of doing so – planning. Since planning was and remains a preferred development strategy in some countries and is used extensively by market economies in wartime, it will be instructive to consider the rationale for economic planning, the mechanisms involved and the experiences of such policies.

Two contemporary developments give increased importance to this chapter. The first occurred in the UK in the 1980s and it related to the way in which the provision of public services such as refuse collection, education and health care was organised. It came to be accepted by the government of the day that the provision of such services by a planning system (centralised or decentralised) was inefficient and that the substitution of quasi-market forces would increase efficiency, improve resource allocation and responsiveness to consumer wishes. Typical of this was LMS (local management of schools); the contracting out of local authority services such as refuse collection; and the introduction of trust status for NHS hospitals, freeing them from the control of Area Health Authorities. This is discussed in section 16.4

The second development, more significant in a global sense, occurred in the economies of Eastern Europe where a *volte-face* took place in the late 1980s. One by one in rapid succession these economies decided to abandon the command systems that they had used for 50 years and espouse the market. This is discussed in section 16.5.

16.2 Soviet planning

Words like 'socialist', 'communist' and 'Marxist' are all adjectives used loosely in the West to describe economies the essential feature of which is economic planning. Confusingly, however, these terms mean different things to different people. For example, in America the word 'socialist' is applied to many European countries, among them Sweden, France and even Britain, which are essentially capitalist in nature. They are capitalist because even though there may be some state-owned industries, most resources are privately owned and economic decisions are for the most part taken on the basis of market signals. In command economies, by contrast, the means of production tend to be owned by the state, and decisions about resource allocation are based on administrative fiat. Some centrally planned economies are more 'planned' than others, however. The USSR was probably the most centralised of the command economies. Even today there is comparatively little private ownership of productive resources and even though prices may be used as part of the allocative mechanism these prices do not necessarily reflect relative scarcities. By contrast,

Yugoslavia, which stands geographically and ideologically on the edge of the communist block, had introduced a sort of 'market socialism'. In this evolving system factories and other production facilities tended to be owned and run by workers' co-operatives and the decisions of the factory managers about what to produce, in what quantities and by what techniques, were based on market prices.

The history of Soviet planning

It is difficult to appreciate why Soviet central planning developed in the way it did without knowing something of the historical context within which it occurred. In 1917, the date of the Russian Revolution, Russia was a backward country whose attempts to industrialise had faltered. Between 1914 and 1921 war with Germany and the ensuing civil war had caused a catastrophic worsening of an already bad situation. Industrial output in 1921 fell to a third of what it had been in 1913.[1] Some recovery occurred under the New Economic Policy (NEP) instituted by Lenin in 1921 which reintroduced elements of the free market. However, Lenin's policy of reforms was reversed by Stalin when he came to power in 1928. The Stalin era, 1928–53, marks the period in which the full mechanism of state central planning was constructed. In 1928 Russia felt herself vulnerable, firstly because she was economically weak in comparison with the capitalist economies and secondly because, being the only communist country, she felt isolated and under threat. Thus it was imperative to build up her economic strength quickly to enable her to withstand the assault which she felt sure would come from the capitalist countries. The promotion of rapid economic growth requires that resources that would otherwise have been used to produce consumer goods be diverted into investment – investment in machines, factories, roads, communications, power generation and so on – as well as investment in the human capital required – the trained technicians, doctors, teachers, scientists and all the other specialists that an advanced industrial society requires.

In a market economy, as we have seen, the consumer is sovereign, in theory at least. Consumers ultimately dictate what is produced and they also dictate what proportion of annual output will be devoted to investment. They do this by refraining from consumption, that is, by saving part of their income, thus freeing resources to build up the economy's stock of capital goods. The rationale for central planning, then, was to remove from private individuals the ability selfishly to consume almost all of annual output. Central planning would lower consumption levels in the short term in order to increase the stock of capital assets in society and thereby raise production possibilities in the longer term. Thus during the Stalin era the proportion of Russia's resources devoted to investment (in heavy industry and infrastructure) was comparatively high. Consequently, the rate of economic growth was high in comparison to previously achieved Russian levels and in comparison to most capitalist countries at the same time. This then was the rationale for economic planning in the Soviet Union.

The nature of Soviet planning

A Soviet economic plan started from a set of macro aggregates – the target output of steel, of cement, of men's suits, of trained doctors, and so on. Each of the economic enterprises producing, say, steel was then given an individual production target, the production targets both at the individual (micro) level and at the aggregate (macro) level being related to past years' realised performance. Each of the individual enterprises was then allocated the resources deemed to be both necessary and sufficient to meet its production quota. At this stage inputs and outputs were decided upon in physical terms rather than in terms of the money values of those inputs and outputs. Thus, for example, the target output for steel would be X million tonnes rather than X million pounds' worth of steel; coal input into steel making would be Y million tonnes of coal rather than Y million pounds' worth of coal; and so on for all the other inputs including labour. The physical plan was then translated into monetary terms using prices deemed appropriate by the central planners. Each individual enterprise then purchased the inputs it had been allocated, at the prices decided upon by the central planners, and sold the output it produced, again at the prices decided upon by the central planners.

Note that in this system the performance (the efficiency) of an enterprise is gauged by its success in meeting its production target (which is based on previous achieved levels). Profitability was not a meaningful measure of efficiency, nor indeed was it a relevant concept since it depended on an arbitrarily imposed set of prices. Moreover, there was no incentive for the firm to economise on the use of the resources it had been allocated since if it were to do so the resulting surpluses (of income over expenditure) would be appropriated by the state and the firm's allocation of inputs for subsequent years reduced. The incentive to exceed current production targets was slight since this resulted in increased targets in subsequent years.

An evaluation of Soviet planning

The foregoing account of Soviet planning is based on methods used in the Stalin era, but the methods used up until 1991 were essentially the same. However, early attempts at planning were characterised by an emphasis on physical planning – the use of prices as part of the planning process was eschewed altogether. The measurement of output in physical terms (often in weight) frequently led to absurdities. Some of the stories which emanate from the Soviet Union about central planning in the Stalin era may be apocryphal, but the deficiencies of the system are well known and acknowledged by the Soviets themselves. A famous cartoon, much emulated even in the official Soviet press, shows a crane lifting an enormous button. The caption, which loses nothing in translation from the original Russian, reads: '. . . and with this single button we can fulfil our production quota for the next three years.'

The reforms of the 1950s reintroduced prices into the planning system but the prices used were not market prices in the sense that they did not reflect scarcity. That is, they did not reflect consumers' evaluation of the desirability or otherwise of the products, so that there was no incentive for producers to improve the quality of the goods produced. In the West goods which are perceived as being of higher quality command a higher price. In the Soviet system prices were administered centrally. The system therefore had an inbuilt inflexibility which did not readily permit price differentials between high-quality and low-quality goods. Moreover, innovation and technical change were, and are, extremely slow to occur in the Soviet system. Both in terms of techniques used to produce a given output and in terms of the range of outputs produced, the Soviet system was ossified. One of the strengths of a free enterprise system is its ability to exploit market opportunities, to fill gaps which entrepreneurs spot in the market and to create entirely new markets. Thus, for example, Sir Clive Sinclair created a market for cheap home computers with the ZX81 and Spectrum computers. The market did not exist before he created it. He also attempted to create another new market with the Sinclair C5 electric tricycle, which appears to have been a resounding failure. The essential point, however, is that the dynamic of the free enterprise system is based on the rewarding of success and the punishing of failure. This in turn is based on profitability. Profits flow from producing things which people are prepared to buy. The deficiencies of the Soviet system stemmed from the lack of any feedback mechanism from consumers to producers, a mechanism we referred to earlier as consumer sovereignty. In a market economy, as we noted in Chapter 14, consumers influence (and, arguably, determine) what is produced. They do this by the purchasing decisions they make. Prices are the link between the wishes of consumers and the actions of producers. In the Soviet system planners decided what was produced. There was no need for prices.

Prices of course did exist in the Soviet Union, both for producer goods and for consumer goods, but they did not necessarily reflect relative scarcity. Since prices were officially controlled rather than market determined, excess demand gave rise to shortages. These were choked off not by a rise in price but by queueing which then became merely an unofficial form of rationing. To get the good in question you had to be prepared to wait. Goods had a time price as well as a money price. Similarly, excess supply resulted in the production of surpluses – goods which could not be disposed of at the official prices – just as food surpluses are created under the European Community's Common Agricultural Policy.

The fact that consumer sovereignty did not exist even in a weak form in the Soviet system is not in itself surprising. The concept of the market as an allocative mechanism in which resources are allocated in accordance with consumer preferences – in short, the mechanism described in section 14.1 – is not a concept with which Marx would have been familiar. Marx, whose critique of capitalism inspired the creation of the Soviet system, predates those economists like Marshall, Jevons and Pareto who fully worked out the view of the price mechanism described above.[2] Thus, for Marx, planning must be better than no planning because no planning – that is, the market – was simply chaos. The idea that the function of prices might be to bring order out of chaos is not one that Marx would have heard of: nor, incidentally, is it an idea which would be acceptable to latter-day Western Marxists. Since the concept of optimal resource allocation is Paretian in origin, the concept of a misallocation of resources can only be understood within the framework of welfare economics which Pareto originated. Thus the economic inefficiencies of the Soviet system represent misallocations of resources only if one is first prepared to accept the framework of Paretian welfare economics. In other words, in pointing to the economic inefficiencies of the Soviet system and identifying these as misallocations of resources, we tend to assume implicitly that no such misallocations occur in a free market system. That is, we assume that a properly functioning market allocates resources 'correctly' or optimally. This is far from true, however, for the reasons set out in section 14.2 (and other reasons besides). Many people would question, for example, whether the resources devoted to advertising in a capitalist society really do fulfil a socially necessary or even socially useful function. Moreover, some of the most highly skilled and highly paid members of the labour force are engaged as accountants, lawyers and tax experts whose sole function is to minimise the contribution that companies make to the Exchequer through the payment of taxes. Two examples, it could be argued, of resource misallocations.

There is another significant failing of market economies to which planned economies are less susceptible, namely the cycles in economic activity which periodically produce deep recessions. In the depression years of the 1920s and 1930s, for example, and in Britain in the early 1980s and again in the early 1990s, resources lay idle – surely an extreme form of resource misallocation. However, although one could argue that recessions are endemic to a capitalist society, it could also be argued that they result from the application of incorrect policies at a macro level. In other words, governments could prevent

16.3 Planning in wartime

recessions from occurring by boosting the overall level of demand in an economy as and when necessary.

In the Soviet Union the rationale for central planning was to divert into investment those resources which would otherwise have been used up in consumption. Similarly, in wartime there is a need to divert resources into the production of munitions. Since society's productive potential is limited these resources must be drawn away from the consumption goods sector. The industries producing consumption goods will only produce what people are able to buy. Thus, people's ability to purchase consumer goods must be reduced. In the Second World War in Britain this was achieved in two ways. First, by raising income taxes so that post-tax incomes were reduced. Second, a system of rationing was introduced which limited demand to the reduced supply then available. In this way the government took command of those productive resources needed to produce munitions without at the same time generating demand inflation in the consumer goods industries.

The extent to which the government was able to divert resources is shown in Table 16.1 which, interestingly, casts doubt on the popular belief about the German economy being an all-out war machine. Throughout the course of the war, and particularly in the early stages, the British government was relatively more successful in diverting resources away from consumption than the German government.

The operation of the system of rationing and price controls in wartime Britain is something which has been well documented and may even be within the range of personal experience of some readers (rationing was finally brought to an end in 1954). The aspect of

Table 16.1 Civilian expenditure on consumption in Germany and the UK 1938–44 (indices based on constant prices 1938 = 100)

Year	Germany (pre-war area)	UK
1938	100	100
1939	108	100
1940	100	87
1941	97	81
1942	88	79
1943	87	76
1944	79	77

Source: N Kaldor, 'The German War Economy' in *Essays on Economic Policy*, Vol. II, Duckworth, 1965.

economic planning which we want to focus on here is the way in which the output of munitions was planned. The methods used resembled the techniques of Soviet planning. However, they were not in any sense modelled on Soviet experience, since literature documenting Soviet planning experience in the pre-war period was sparse. Rather, the techniques of planning evolved as the war progressed, with pragmatism rather than dogma being the guiding principle. There does not seem, moreover, to have been a single co-ordinated master plan for wartime production. Ely Devons,[3] one of the wartime planners in Britain, writes:

> In the early years of the war there was little attempt at the central direction of production. As far as I am aware no-one worked out, or attempted to work out, what resources would be left after meeting the minimum needs of the civilian population, and how these resources should be divided between the armed forces and the production of aircraft, army and naval supplies. It is true that general decisions were taken about the size of the Army, Air Force and Navy to plan for, but these decisions were by no means clear cut and did not in any case take account of the interrelation between the size of the armed forces and the production of munitions that would be needed for them. Each supply department was left to proceed with its plan for expansion in the light of the requirements that were put to it by the appropriate Service Department. It was only later, as the war proceeded, and these various plans came into conflict that a system of central direction to solve these conflicts was evolved; and by that time the general outlines of the plans of the various departments concerned were already determined, at least for a substantial period of time ahead. (Devons p. 73)

In fact, a system of separate committees was established, each one responsible for different aspects of the war effort. There was at first no central co-ordination between these various committees. Individuals on these committees, Devons writes, 'were often out of touch with what individuals on the other co-ordinating committees were doing.' Central direction emerged, however, through the medium of the production plans of the various departments:

> The main link and co-ordinating mechanism between the various allocating committees was provided by the production programmes of the individual supply departments. It was by the effect on the plans of the individual departments of the decisions of any one of these allocating committees, and the further reaction of these altered plans on the decisions of the other committees, that the whole planning process was kept in motion. Thus, if the manpower committee cut the allocation of labour to the Ministry of Aircraft

Production, as a result MAP would reduce its aircraft programme; this would, in turn, reduce MAP's requirements for steel, timber, building capacity etc., and these reduced requirements would be taken into account by the appropriate allocating committee at the next quarterly review. It might be that at such a review MAP's steel allocation was cut even further, and this would involve a further re-adjustment in its programme, which would again have its effects in MAP's demand for other factors. (Devons p. 74)

In today's terminology we would describe this as an iterative process. Of course, given the speed at which committees worked, the process of iteration had not been completed before action pertinent to the prior decisions of committees had already been taken. Often, however, some of the more cumbersome aspects of the formal planning procedures were overcome by *ad hoc* and informal consultative arrangements between individuals on related committees. Individual initiative made the system workable.

The wartime planners did not, of course, have access to the high-speed data processing capabilities of modern computers, but it is difficult to see that they would have been assisted in their task had such computers been available. In the post-war years mathematical techniques were developed to cope with complex resource-allocation problems involving interrelations between inputs and outputs, such as the situation described by Devons above. The most important of these techniques, input-output analysis, was developed by Wassily Leontief[4] in the 1940s and is used to some extent in the centrally planned economies today. The technique in effect speeds up the process of iteration by solving simultaneously a set of equations showing the interrelationships between all of the major inputs and outputs in an economic system. Had the technique been available to the wartime planners, however, the outcome would probably have been little different. The system of planning evolved as the war progressed and became more efficient as a result of human initiative and ingenuity. As Devons says, 'It would be quite mistaken to conclude that the process by which government economic planning operated in wartime in any way resembled the theoretical structures of the overall planners.'

While the divergence between practice and theory is undoubtedly a feature of all planning systems – using the term 'planning' in its widest sense – the reader should not take away the impression of British wartime planning as consisting of Whitehall civil servants muddling through in the face of an ultra-efficient German war effort organised from the centre and characterised by utter ruthlessness and superb organising ability. In reality very little central planning took place in Germany until the Speer administration took control of the production of munitions in 1942. The success of the Speer administration in increasing the output of munitions occurred rather late in the war and too late to affect the outcome. Table 16.2 gives some illustrative figures of British and German armaments production.

Table 16.2 Comparison of output of particular classes of armaments in Germany and the UK, 1940–44

	1940 Germany	UK	1941 Germany	UK	1942 Germany	UK	1943 Germany	UK	1944 Germany	UK
Military aircraft										
Fighters	3 100	4 300	3 700	7 000	5 200	9 800	11 700	10 700	28 900	10 500
Bombers	4 000	3 700	4 300	4 700	6 500	6 300	8 600	7 700	6 500	8 100
Other types	1 800	1 900	2 100	1 800	1 800	1 600	2 800	3 000	1 100	5 000
Trainers	1 300	5 100	900	6 600	1 200	5 900	2 100	4 800	3 100	2 900
Total (numbers)	10 200	15 000	11 000	20 100	14 200	23 600	25 200	26 200	39 600	26 500
Bombs (filled weight '000 tons)	n.a.	48	245	143	262	241	273	309	231	370
Tanks	1 600	1 400	3 800	4 800	6 300	8 600	12 100	7 500	19 000	4 600
Heavy guns (75 mm and over)	6 300	1 900	7 800	5 300	13 600	6 600	38 000	12 200	62 300	12 400
Light guns (over 20 mm and under 75 mm)	n.a.	2 800	3 400	11 400	9 600	36 400	8 100	25 800	8 400	3 600
Small arms:										
Infantry rifles ('000)	1 350	81	1 358	78	1 370	594	2 244	910	2 585	547
Infantry machine guns ('000)	170	30	320	46	320	1 510	440	1 650	790	730

Note: United Kingdom figures refer to UK production only. German figures include all deliveries to the Wehrmacht.
Source: N. Kaldor, 'The German war economy', in *Essays on Economic Policy*, Vol. II, Duckworth, 1965.

Probably the most important of the munitions production programmes was that concerned with aircraft. In Britain this was the responsibility of the MAP (Ministry of Aircraft Production). The MAP's responsibilities covered not just those factories assembling the airframe itself but also those factories manufacturing the principal component parts – the engines, undercarriages, propellers, turrets, etc. Obviously components had to be manufactured in the correct quantities for the number of completed aircraft coming off the production line. In addition, the requirements for spare parts had to be satisfied. The problem of co-ordination between the component manufacturers and the airframe manufacturers was solved via the MAP using the medium of the production plan referred to earlier. Each of the individual representatives on the co-ordinating committee knew the planned output of Spitfires, Hurricanes, etc., and the likely demand for spare parts for the next quarter. From this the component manufacturers could estimate the requirement for components. In the event that the planned output of, say, propellers was insufficient to meet the planned requirements for them, then a combination of two things would happen. Either planned requirements for propellers would be reduced by scaling down the planned output of aircraft or more resources would be diverted away from other areas and into propeller production.

The MAP was actively instrumental in the resource allocation programme at all levels. It would have been possible of course to leave it to the market as is done in peacetime, but there were considerable drawbacks with such a system. Consider how such a system would have worked. The MAP would have issued contracts to aircraft manufacturers to purchase given numbers of aircraft at prices which the MAP determined. The manufacturers themselves would then have been free to enter into contracts with the component suppliers to purchase components that would do the job as cheaply as possible.

The drawbacks of such a system are twofold. Firstly, the speed of adjustment of the output of components in response to changes in the output of final aircraft, and vice versa, would almost certainly have been slower if it had relied upon price signals to indicate relative scarcities. Certainly there was a widespread belief that this was the case and a widespread acceptance therefore that the MAP should intervene. The MAP, that is, had to be seen to be doing something actively to promote the war effort rather than just leaving it to the market. The second drawback of leaving the aircraft manufacturers to purchase the components they required at the best prices they could obtain was that the contract price of the aircraft (paid by the MAP to the aircraft manufacturer) would determine the quality of the components fitted to it. In effect, the price would determine the specification of the aircraft. The higher the price the better the specification.

> For example, an extra £1000 for a Spitfire would enable the Spitfire manufacturers to command the best Merlin engines, and a reduction of the price for the Hurricane would have forced manufacturers of the Hurricane to engine their aircraft with second best Merlins. (Devons p. 68)

Now it might have been possible for the MAP to set the relative price of Spitfires and Hurricanes in such a way that this outcome was achieved (assuming this was what the MAP desired). But it was much easier to achieve this outcome if the MAP *directed* the output of the engine manufacturers in the way that it saw fit. The desired allocation of resources (in this case engines) was achieved more quickly and with a greater degree of certainty through a system based on the physical direction of resources rather than through a mechanism in which producers responded to prices.

We began this chapter by defining planning as being a system of resource allocation which stands in contrast to a market allocation. The reader may by now be aware, however, that to present the situation as a choice between two stark alternatives – planning or the market – is misleadingly simplistic. In producing a complex manufactured product such as an aircraft, co-ordination of the various aspects of production (in other words, planning) is a technological necessity. The problems of co-ordination in aircraft production in peacetime are no less acute than in wartime. They are simply less urgent. Companies like British Aerospace are the modern-day equivalent of the MAP. They have production plans, extending several years into the future, for the various types of aircraft they produce. These plans must be co-ordinated with the planned production of components, whether these components are produced in-house (within BAe itself) or by independent suppliers. The process of planning is no different from that carried out in wartime except that it is carried out by different people – BAe employees rather than Whitehall civil servants. The only substantive difference is that the resource cost of this indispensable planning – the salaries of the planners – is incorporated in the price of the aircraft rather than paid out of general taxation.

16.4 Planning versus the market: Mrs Thatcher's Britain

In Britain in the 1980s – the decade that corresponds to Mrs Thatcher's premiership – a gradual but fundamental shift occurred in public attitudes towards the planning-versus-the-market debate. Certain services such as education and health care had for many decades been provided publicly and paid for out of general taxation. The debate is not so much as to whether such services should be provided publicly as to how the provision of such services should be organised – what role should market forces play in the provision of such services?

Historically the provision of services such as education had been organised by planning agencies such as Local Education Authorities under the overall control of a central government department called the Department of Education. Similarly health care was organised by Area Health Authorities under the overall control of the Department of Health. There had always been widespread public acceptance that some inefficiencies occurred in the organisation of these services – as there is under any planning system, or indeed under any system. However it came to be accepted by government – and this view was imposed on the electorate – that the introduction of 'market forces' would improve the overall efficiency of the provision of such services.

Thus it was for example that in education each school was given its own budget with much greater freedom than before to spend this income in the way that it saw fit. The proportion of the school's income devoted to staffing, to the purchase of books, to the upkeep of buildings and so on was to be decided by the Board of Governors of the school (in effect strongly guided by the head teacher) rather than by the Local Education Authority. The school would purchase these goods and services paying market prices for them (though the price of teaching labour was set by government) endeavouring to get the best value-for-money from its expenditures in the same way as a household or firm. Moreover the school's income would be determined by its 'output' – the number of children on its roll. This in turn would depend upon the extent to which consumers (children and parents) endorsed the product being offered by enrolling at the school rather than at some alternative school in the neighbourhood. In short, schools would become more responsive to consumer wishes and would utilise the resources at their disposal in a more efficient manner.

In health care too hospitals could opt to become self-governing trusts with much more autonomy than had been the case when they were under the control of the Area Health Authority. Their success in generating income would depend upon the extent to which consumers of health care – patients and general practitioners acting as agents for the patients themselves – wished to purchase the services the hospital was offering. These services would be 'bought' and 'sold' in a competitive environment, each hospital being in competition with others for custom. The competitive environment would promote increased efficiency in the use of resources.

In areas such as refuse collection and street cleaning the local authority who was responsible for this had previously carried out the work necessary using its own directly employed labour. Henceforth the local authority would contract out this work to private firms, issuing contracts which would specify the standard to which the work should be performed and the penalties which would be invoked if the work was not performed satisfactorily. Such contracts would be competed for and would normally be awarded to the firm quoting the lowest price. The contracts were for a fixed term and would normally not be renewed if the firm failed to fulfil its contractual obligations. Other local authority services were contracted out in a similar way – the provision and maintenance of football pitches, swimming pools, parks and gardens and so on.

The most fundamental change which took place in the 1980s was perhaps not directly in the way that these services were provided. In the case of refuse collection for example the work which was contracted out may well have been performed by the same individuals and the same vehicles (in different livery) as those previously employed. The fundamental change was in terms of the public's attitude. Increasingly it came to be accepted not just that non-market systems were inefficient and unresponsive to consumer demands but that 'market' systems were more efficient and more responsive to consumer demands. There was a presupposition that market allocation was better than non-market allocation.

This was the fundamental shift of emphasis. In effect non-market systems were guilty unless proved innocent. Having followed the arguments in this chapter readers can judge for themselves whether such a presupposition seems reasonable. Certainly it would not have seemed reasonable to the wartime planners for whom central direction of resources seemed self-evidently to be a preferred option for getting the job done.

16.5 Planning versus the market: Eastern Europe

We saw in section 16.2 that Soviet planning began after the Russian Revolution in 1917 and became entrenched in the inter-war era. After the Second World War the Soviet Union imposed her preferred system on those neighbouring countries which she had 'liberated' forming them into a protective buffer between herself and Western Europe. These countries – Poland, Czechoslovakia, Hungary, Rumania, Albania, Yugoslavia . . . and East Germany – formed CMEA (the Council for Mutual Economic Assistance), otherwise known as the COMECON countries. All of these countries instigated a form of state planning, though there were significant differences between individual cases. In essence however they were all command economies to a lesser or greater extent.

By the late 1980s the Soviet Union's grip on her satellites was loosening and there was talk in the Soviet Union itself of reform and the re-introduction of market forces. In the event the dismantling of the command systems in Poland, Czechoslovakia, East Germany and Rumania occurred suddenly, swept along by political reform. CMEA was officially brought to an end on 1 January 1991 a fact which went unnoticed and unremarked.

The countries of Eastern Europe which opened up their economies to market forces have begun to experience an economic renaissance. The birth pangs are distinctly unpleasant however. Unemployment in the former East Germany rose from approximately zero to over 40 per cent in 1991 as uncompetitive firms closed down. The market must indeed seem harsh particularly to those insulated for so long from its realities. The market as we have seen rewards success and punishes failure. You cannot have one without the other.

Notes

1. Dalton, G., *Economic Systems and Society*. Penguin, 1974.
2. Alfred Marshall 1842–1924. (His famous *Principles of Economics* was published in 1890); William Jevons 1835–82; Vilfredo Pareto 1848–1923; Marx's *Das Kapital* was first published in 1867.
3. Devons, E., 'Economic planning in war and peace', in *Essays in Economics*. Greenwood Press, 1980.

4. Leontief, W. W., *The Structure of the American Economy 1919–1939* (2nd edn). OUP: Fairlawn, N. J., 1951.

Questions

16.1 'What's in a name?' The words we use to describe economic systems are not value-free. They reflect, to a lesser or greater extent, approval or disapproval of that system. Study the following two lists of names:

price system	central planning
capitalism	socialism
free enterprise	state planning
market mechanism	communism
private enterprise	planned economy
free-market system	command economy

Now re-arrange each list so that it starts with terms which reflect approval of the system and finishes with terms which reflect disapproval of the system.

16.2 In Bogravia, an Eastern European satellite of the USSR, consumers wishing to buy a car must put down their names on a waiting list and pay a deposit. The most sought-after model is the Lada 1200, for which there is a four-year waiting list. There are no demonstration models in the showroom, only photographs. Which of the following statements are correct?

(a) The size of the waiting list is evidence that the price charged is too low. The price should rise to choke off the excess demand.

(b) By keeping the price down the authorities ensure that everyone who wants a car can buy one.

(c) The price of the Lada in Bogravia reflects what the Bogravian consumer thinks about the desirability of the product.

(d) At least it's better than just giving cars to members of the Communist Party.

(e) The Lada is a technically advanced car so everyone wants it.

(f) The Lada is a copy of a model that Fiat stopped making in Italy years ago.

(g) There are no waiting lists for cars in Britain.

What could you predict about the price of second-hand (nearly new) Ladas in Bogravia?

17 State intervention in market economies: public spending

17.1 A welfare economics framework?

In Chapter 14 we looked at a theoretical model of the way in which resources are allocated by the market, and in Chapter 16 we looked at planning both in the context of Soviet-type economies and in the context of wartime capitalist economies. A *mixed economy* such as that of the UK is fundamentally a market economy but with a significant amount of state intervention. This intervention takes a number of broad forms, namely:

1. spending on goods and services
2. spending on income maintenance programmes, e.g. unemployment benefit
3. state ownership and control of certain industrial resources, e.g. nationalised industries
4. legal controls on the behaviour of firms.

Within a Paretian welfare economics framework these forms of intervention can be seen as ways of tackling the various forms of market failure identified in section 14.2. Thus the framework of welfare economics sketched out in Chapter 14 forms a sort of overarching theory which can be used to explain and justify these various forms of state intervention. The modern tendency, however, is to place less emphasis on the overarching theory of welfare economics and to adopt a more piecemeal approach to the analysis of intervention. The reason for this may be a suspicion that the all-encompassing nature of welfare theory explains everything, but in such broad generalities as to explain nothing. A second reason, possibly, is the acknowledgement that the all-pervasive existence of market failure in the real world makes a Pareto optimal allocation of resources impossible to attain no matter how much one tries to patch up the system with bits of intervention here and there. We shall adopt the piecemeal approach, though recognising that all forms of state intervention do have a welfare-theoretic base.

In this chapter we shall look at public spending (the first two forms of intervention mentioned above). In Chapter 18 we shall consider the third form of intervention mentioned above – nationalised industries. The final form of intervention mentioned is mostly concerned with policy towards monopolies and mergers, which we considered earlier in section 9.10.

17.2 Public spending: transfer payments

Table 17.1 presents an analysis of public spending in the UK broken down into broad categories. As can be seen, over one-quarter of government spending is on transfer payments. The major expenditure in this category is on retirement pensions, unemployment benefit and supplementary benefit, but also included are things like maternity benefit, child allowances, student grants, family income supplement and death grant. From the cradle, as you might say, to the grave. Such transfer payments constitute the cash part of the income maintenance programme which all market economies provide to a greater or lesser extent for their citizens. The non-cash part of the income-maintenance programme is the income-in-kind provided by free health care, education, and so on. The objective quite clearly is to redistribute income in favour of those on low incomes and to prevent their standard of living slipping below some 'acceptable' level.

Table 17.1 Analysis of UK public spending 1990–91 (%)

Social Security (transfer payments)	26.3
Education	12.4
Health	12.5
Defence	9.9
Law and order and protective services	5.1
Environmental services	3.5
Other functions	18.4
Debt interest	8.2

Note: the total does not sum to 100 per cent because of statistical adjustments and rounding errors.
   Source: *Autumn Statement*, 1990, February 1991, HMSO.

Approximately three-quarters of government spending – that is, that part of total government spending which does not go on transfer payments – is on goods and services. The rationale for the public provision of certain goods and services is related to the 'public good' characteristics of certain goods. These characteristics, which were mentioned in section 14.2, are non-excludability and non-rivalness. We shall first explain the meaning of these terms in section 17.3 and then consider in section 17.4 the extent to which they provide a rationale for public provision.

17.3 Non-excludability and non-rivalness

'Non-excludability' means that those who do not pay cannot be excluded from consuming the good in question. Thus defence of the realm is a non-excludable public good. Even if you pay no taxes at all, and thus make no contribution towards the cost of provision, you cannot be excluded from enjoying the benefits of being defended. Neither of course can you choose not to consume the good in question. Whether you pay for it or not – and whether you like it or not – you consume the benefits of living under the nuclear umbrella. Declaring your house and garden a nuclear-free zone does not alter this basic fact.

'Non-rivalness' is the second characteristic of public goods. It means that if a good or service is provided for one person then it can be provided for everyone at no extra cost. In other words, the goods are not rivals in consumption. Radio and television broadcasts are an example of a non-rival public good. By tuning to a particular broadcast I do not diminish the signal strength in any way. My consumption in no way diminishes the supply available to my neighbours.

Radio and television broadcasts are also intrinsically non-excludable public goods of course, though attempts are made through the legal system to render them excludable. In other words, in Britain at least, the law requires you to purchase a television licence in order to use a television set. The enforcement of the law is difficult, however, since broadcasts are intrinsically non-excludable – television sets work just as well whether you have paid your licence fee or not. Thus, in order to catch and prosecute the 'free riders' – those who do not pay their television licence fee – the authorities are forced to incur substantial administrative costs: the cost of advertising campaigns designed to persuade people to buy a licence and the cost of TV detector vans to catch those who do not. When attempts are made to render excludable those goods which are intrinsically non-excludable, the administrative and other costs of so doing are often large. Roads, for example, are by their nature more or less non-excludable. In Britain, however, cars used on public roads must be licensed but, as with the television licence fee, evasion is widespread. However, it is certainly possible – as with continental motorway tolls – to devise systems for making some kinds of roads excludable.

17.4 Public spending: goods and services

The market will fail to provide an adequate supply of public goods – those goods which possess to some degree the characteristics of non-excludability and non-rivalness. Table 17.2 presents a more detailed analysis of government spending in Britain in 1989. It can be seen from this table that some of the areas of public spending can be explained in terms of the 'public good' argument. Defence, for example, which now consumes about 10 per cent of total public spending, is a pure public good. If the government did not provide it, no one else would because no private-sector company is capable of 'selling' £21 bn worth of defence to the 57 million consumers in the UK. Defence is either provided for everyone or for no one. It cannot be divided up into 57 million separate lots and sold to individual

Table 17.2 Detailed analysis of public spending – central and local government 1989 (%)

Social Security	32.8
Education	14.0
Health	14.5
Defence	12.0
General public services (parliament, tax collection, etc.)	5.2
Police	2.6
Fire	0.6
Law courts	1.4
Prisons	0.8
Housing and community amenities (e.g. sewage)	4.4
Recreational and cultural affairs (e.g. libraries, museums)	1.8
Agriculture, forestry, fishing	1.2
Transport and communication	4.1
Other economic affairs and services	3.1
Current grants abroad	1.3
Total expenditure excluding debt interest	*100.0*

Note: total does not sum because of rounding errors.
  Source: derived from UK National Accounts, 1990, HMSO Table 9.4.

consumers, because each consumer would choose to be a 'free rider'. If they had a choice, no rational consumer would pay.

Although the public-good argument explains why defence is not provided by the market, it cannot, of course, be used to justify so much – or so little – public expenditure in this area. The decision to devote 10 per cent of public spending to defence is essentially a political decision. It does not result from a set of consumer preferences expressed in the market in the same way that the quantity of washing machines produced ultimately depends on the purchasing decisions of consumers. Hence where the market fails because of the existence of public goods there is no mechanism whereby consumers can express their preferences, that is, make known their views, except by the very imperfect means of voting for a political party in an election.

Some of the other areas of public spending shown in Table 17.2 are goods or services which possess the characteristics of non-excludability and/or non-rivalness to a greater or lesser extent. For example, most of the expenditure on environmental services – roads, parks, coastal protection – comes under this heading. No private company could have 'sold' the Thames Flood Barrier to the millions of consumers who could potentially have benefited from it. Thus if it were not provided by the government and financed out of general taxation it would not have been provided at all.

It is clear that two of the largest spending areas – education and health care – are not really public goods at all. Between them these two areas comprise about one-quarter of total public spending, yet they are neither non-excludable nor non-rival. A hospital bed occupied by a psychiatric patient cannot simultaneously be occupied by a heart transplant patient. They are rival goods. Resources devoted to screening for cervical cancer cannot simultaneously be employed in finding a cure for AIDS. Similarly, because health care and education are essentially personal services they are excludable by their nature. Schools and colleges can decide which students to admit and which to exclude. Doctors decide which patient is to receive a transplanted kidney. There are exceptions of course. For example, some of the output of the Open University (the broadcasts) is a pure public good and fluoridation of the water supply (to prevent dental decay) constitutes a non-excludable good. The bulk of the output of the education and health-care sectors is both excludable and rival, however. The implication of this is that there is no reason in principle why both education and health care could not be provided by the market. The existence of private health care and private schools in Britain bears witness to this fact. Moreover, some countries have a much smaller state provision of education and health care than we do in the UK (though some have much larger). Since the provision of health care and education cannot be justified in terms of the public-good argument, some other justification is required. This is provided by the *merit good* argument. Certain goods and services are so important, it is argued, that every individual should be able to consume an adequate amount of them no matter what his income. In effect, by subsidising certain goods, or by providing them at a zero price to the consumer, the state attempts to persuade consumers to consume a larger quantity than they would do if they were forced to pay the full cost of provision. This argument extends to a range of goods like school meals, libraries, museums and the arts, as the following conversation between two high-ranking civil servants illustrates. (Bernard, a naive young personal assistant, has been questioning the rationale for public subsidy of the opera, which only the rich seem to benefit from. He suggests that football should be subsidised too . . .)

Sir Humphrey Appleby: . . . and what about greyhound racing? Should dog tracks be subsidised as well as football clubs for instance?

   Bernard: Well, why not if that's what the people want?

   Sir Humphrey: Bernard, subsidy is for *art*. For culture. It is not to

be given to what the people want. It is to what the people don't want but ought to have. If they want something they'll pay for it themselves. No, we subsidise education, enlightenment, spiritual uplift – not the vulgar pastimes of ordinary people.
(Extract from *Yes Minister – the Middle-Class Rip-off*)

In addition, certain goods and services provided by the state give benefit not just to the direct recipient of the good in question but to society at large. For example, inoculation against communicable disease benefits the patient himself but also those with whom he is likely to come into contact. In this case *positive external benefits* are said to exist and their existence can be used to justify the provision of treatment below cost or at zero price.

Finally, some areas of public spending, particularly that on education and health care, can be considered as investment spending – in this case investment in human capital. The return yielded by this investment is in the form of a more productive workforce. It is argued that through ignorance or myopia individuals will tend to underinvest, preferring immediate consumption benefits. The state, taking a longer view, channels resources away from immediate consumption (by taxing people's incomes) and towards investment in those areas which increase the productive capacity of the economy in the longer term.

Questions

17.1 State which of the following constitute expenditure on goods and services, and which are transfer payments:

unemployment benefit
supplementary benefit payments
student grants
teachers' salaries
salaries of social workers
spending on the school dental service
spending on research (e.g. the Economic and Social Research Council)

17.2 Consider the extent to which the following are either non-excludable or non-rival or both:

television broadcasts   McDonald's hamburgers
the M1 motorway   the pavement outside McDonald's
the River Thames   navigation buoys

17.3 The Arts Council receives considerable amounts of public money. How can this be justified?

18 Public corporations

In section 17.1 we identified a number of broad areas of state intervention in market economies. One of these was the ownership and control of certain industrial resources – the nationalised industries. It is to this form of state intervention that we now turn.

The term 'public corporation' is the official designation given to bodies that are publicly owned (i.e. state owned) yet are outside the sectors controlled directly by central government or by local authorities. Most public corporations engage in commercial activities but are independent of the government and parliament in the day-to-day management of their commercial and financial affairs, though they are subject to constraints on their borrowing. Table 18.1 gives a list of public corporations in existence at 31 December 1989.

Table 18.1 Names of public corporations in existence at 31 December 1989

	Commencing or vesting date
Audit Commission	1983
Bank of England Banking Department	1946
British Broadcasting Corporation	1927
British Coal (formerly NCB)	1947
British Railways Board	1963
British Shipbuilders	1977
British Technology Group (see text)	1981
British Waterways Board	1963
Civil Aviation Authority	1972
Commonwealth Development Corporation	1948
Covent Garden Market Authority	1961
Crown Agents & Crown Agents Holding & Realisation Board	1980
The Crown Suppliers	1976
Electricity Council (together with the CEGB and Area Electricity Boards)*	1958
English Industrial Estates Corporation	1986
Highlands and Islands Development Board	1965
HMSO	1980
Independent Broadcasting Authority	1972
Land Authority for Wales	1976
Local authority airports	1987
Local authority bus companies	1986
London Regional Transport	1970

	Commencing or vesting date
New Town Development Corporations and Commission	1946 and various later dates
Northern Ireland Housing Executive	1971
Northern Ireland Transport Holding Company	1968
North of Scotland Hydro-Electric Board*	1943
Passenger Transport Executives	1969 and various later dates
Pilotage Commission	1979
Post Office	1961
Royal Mint	1975
Scottish Development Agency	1975
Scottish Special Housing Association	1937
Scottish Transport Group	1969
South of Scotland Electricity Board	1955
Trust Ports in Northern Ireland	1974
United Kingdom Atomic Energy Authority	1986
Urban Development Corporations	1981, 1987, 1988

* Privatised in 1990 (Area Boards) and 1991 (National Power and Powergen).
  Source: UK National Accounts, 1990, HMSO, explanatory notes to Chapter 6.

As can be seen, the public corporations form a heterogeneous group whose only common feature is their status as commercially independent but publicly owned corporations. The histories of these corporations, and the reasons for their existence, are as varied as their trading activities. Many, such as British Coal (formerly the National Coal Board) were set up by the post-war Labour government. Others, such as London Regional Transport, were set up to administer functions previously carried out by local authorities. Some were set up as regulatory bodies to cope with newly emerging needs – for example, the Independent Broadcasting Authority and the Civil Aviation Authority. Others, such as the Bank of England and the Post Office, had been in existence as government departments for many years before being officially reclassified as public corporations.

Up until quite recently an official distinction was made between the terms 'nationalised industry' and 'public corporation'. The distinction was somewhat arbitrary, however, since corporations such as the Royal Mint and HMSO are essentially trading corporations in the same sense as British Coal and British Rail.

As a group the public corporations formed a significant sector of the national economy. In 1983 they accounted for 10.7 per cent of GDP and 16 per cent of Fixed Capital Formation (Investment). They employed about 1.7 million people (about 7 per cent of the labour force). However, the size of this sector shrank as the Conservative government proceeded with its plans to privatise large parts of the public sector. By 1989 the remaining public corporations accounted for only 4.6 per cent of GDP and 5 per cent of investment. Table 18.2 shows some of the major corporations which have been reclassified to the private sector.

Table 18.2 Major reclassifications to the private sector

British Petroleum	1979/83/87
British Aerospace	1981
Enterprise Oil	1984
British Telecom	1984
Trust Ports in Great Britain	1985
British Gas	1986
British Airways	1987
Royal Ordnance	1987
BAA	1987
National Bus Company	1988
Local Authority Bus Companies (7)	1988/89
British Steel	1988
General Practice Finance Corpn.	1989
Regional Water Authorities, Welsh Water Authority and Water Authorities Association	1989
Area Electricity Boards	1990
National Power, PowerGen (formerly the CEGB)	1991

Source: derived from *UK National Accounts*, 1990, HMSO, explanatory notes to Chapter 6.

Some of the more newsworthy 'privatisations' are missing from the list shown in Table 18.2. The reason for this is to do with the activities of the British Technology Group (itself a public corporation). Formerly known as the National Enterprise Board this has acted as a sort of state holding company for shares bought from the private sector or acquired in some other way. Thus for example the Group has held shares in Rolls-Royce, ICL (computers), Jaguar and Rover. When these shares were returned to the private sector the resulting transaction did not strictly speaking result in a change in the legal status of the company, since these companies had never had a legal existence as public corporations. Nevertheless transactions such as the sale of Rolls-Royce to the public in 1987 are normally regarded as part of the government's privatisation programme even though for the reason outlined above it does not appear in the official list of reclassifications.

18.2 Reasons for nationalisation

This chapter will be principally concerned with various aspects of the privatisation debate. It is first necessary, however, to consider the reasons why the present nationalised industries were originally taken into public ownership. As we have already indicated, these reasons vary from case to case. On a general level, however, it is well known that Clause 4 of the Labour Party's Constitution talks of 'the public ownership of the means of production, distribution and exchange' as a specific political objective. Taken literally, this means nationalising everything, and while some members of the Labour Party would still support this objective, most would not. More usually, the Clause was interpreted to refer to the nationalisation of certain key industrial and commercial sectors – the 'commanding heights' of the economy. This provided the justification, if not the rationale, for the post-war acts of nationalisation.

The economic case for public ownership of certain industries rests on a number of general principles. Keynes, the acknowledged founder of modern macroeconomics, talks in his *General Theory*[1] of the stabilising influence that a sizable public sector would have on the economy. It is well known that a market economy without a significant public sector is prone to suffer cycles in economic activity which periodically produce booms and slumps. This is principally because the investment behaviour of private-sector firms is very volatile. In periods when the growth in sales appears to falter, firms cut or delay their investment in new productive capacity. The reduction in investment demand which this brings about induces a further decline in demand. The economy enters a recession from which it will not automatically extricate itself. The investment spending of the public sector would be less volatile, Keynes argued, and this would tend to damp down the oscillations in economic activity. Moreover, control of the public enterprise sector would allow it to be used by the government for countercyclical demand management. That is, investment spending in the public sector could be boosted to take up the slack in private-sector demand when necessary. This then is the macroeconomic case for a public sector in general and, by extension, the case for public ownership of key industrial sectors.

In addition, certain of these key industrial sectors are what are known as *natural monopolies*. That is, they are industries which can only be run efficiently if one firm supplies the whole market. To allow competition between rival firms would result in wasteful duplication of services. Examples of natural monopolies are electricity distribution (it would not be sensible to allow rival companies to erect transmission lines for electricity), gas distribution, postal deliveries, the railways, water supply and sewage disposal. If such a monopoly were in private hands, it is argued, it could operate against the public interest. A monopolist who is pursuing the objective of profit maximisation will use his market power to raise prices and restrict supply. Since by definition barriers to the entry of new firms exist, super-normal profits will continue to accrue to those private individuals who own the monopoly firm. Therefore, it is argued, the private sector monopolist should be taken into public ownership so that prices can then be controlled and output expanded.

Moreover, many of the natural monopolies are thought to have some strategic significance, in the sense that they are important to the defence and security of the state – for example, energy supplies and communications. This reinforces the case for some state control of such industries. Ownership, through nationalisation, ensures this overall control. In addition to their strategic significance, these industries also form an important part of the infrastructure of the economy – transport, communications, energy supplies, and so on. Since infrastructure is an important prerequisite for the growth and development of the economy, the state may wish to direct investment resources into those areas as a means of promoting economic growth in the economy as a whole.

The foregoing arguments apply to many of the industries which have been taken into public ownership. The specific circumstances of each individual case are as important as the general case for public ownership, however. For example, in 1948 the railways were nationalised because they were then in poor condition and would not have been able, in private hands, to attract the necessary investment capital for modernisation. Many of the nationalised industries had an equally inauspicious start in life. In 1967, for example, the British Steel Corporation was formed from 13 separate steel companies which were 'already in a difficult and deteriorating position. In 1957–58 they had earned a net profit of over £400 m.; by 1962–63 this had fallen to around £200 m., and during 1967–68, which was the Corporation's first year, the figure was less than £60 m. This represented a return of only 0.5 per cent on net assets at replacement cost.'[2]

The British Steel Corporation came into existence because the government of the day wished to increase concentration in the industry as a means of promoting efficiency. The government was instrumental in the mergers which gave birth to BSC. Similarly, the government was instrumental in promoting the merger activity in the motor industry which eventually produced British Leyland in 1968. BL was taken into public ownership in 1975. In 1988 renamed the Rover Group it was sold back to the private sector, its shares being sold at a knockdown price to British Aerospace plc. British Aerospace itself had been formed in 1977 as a result of a government-sponsored merger between Hawker Siddeley and the British Aircraft Corporation, firms which had both received substantial amounts of government money in the past. In 1979 the incoming Conservative government began divesting itself of the BAe shares which it owned, the final tranche being sold in 1985.

18.3 Reasons for privatisation

It is probably true to say that the Labour Party never really knew what to do with the nationalised industries – how they should be regulated, what pricing and investment policies they should pursue, and so on. Mrs Thatcher, however, when she came to power in 1979, knew exactly what to do with them. The Conservative government's plans for the nationalised industries became increasingly clear in the early 1980s, as the following three quotations show.

> It remains our purpose, wherever possible to transfer to the private sector assets which can be better managed there. (Sir Geoffrey Howe, Chancellor of the Exchequer, Budget speech, 9 March 1982)

> Privatisation represents by far the most effective means of extending market forces, and in turn of improving efficiency and the allocation of resources. (Lord Cockfield, then Minister of State, Treasury, 19 November 1981)

> It must be right to press ahead with the transfer of ownership from the state to private enterprise of as many public sector businesses as possible ... The introduction of competition must, whenever possible, be linked to a transfer of ownership to private citizens and away from the state. Real public ownership – that is, ownership by the people – must be and is our ultimate goal. (Mr Nicholas Ridley, Financial Secretary to the Treasury, 12 February 1982)

From these statements, one is left in no doubt that the intention was to privatise large parts of the public sector, particularly public corporations, and the rationale for so doing rests on the following two propositions: firstly, privatisation ensures competition, and secondly, competition ensures efficiency.

Privatisation ensures competition?

The first of these two propositions is clearly wrong, or at least is correct only in a restricted context. A nationalised industry that monopolises the market which it serves and is returned intact to the private sector is still a monopoly. A state monopoly has merely been replaced by a private-sector one. In the market for its product there has been no increase in competition as a result of privatisation. The term 'liberalisation' has been coined to refer to the introduction of competition into an erstwhile protected monopolistic industry. Clearly, privatisation does not ensure liberalisation. The two things are quite distinct. Moreover, while it is relatively easy to privatise an industry, it may be much more difficult to liberalise it. Some of the existing and former nationalised industries are natural monopolies, as we have already noted. It is absurd to suggest that these industries could be split up into atomistically competitive firms – indeed, any sort of competition is wasteful in industries such as water supply and electricity distribution because scale economies are such an important feature of those industries. Thus the privatisation of British Telecom did not in itself increase competition in the industry since it was sold off as a single entity. The statutory monopoly of BT had been rescinded some years earlier and this did more to liberalise the industry than was achieved by privatisation *per se*. Similarly, British Gas was sold off as a single entity. It was argued that to split it up would have been neither economically desirable nor feasible.

Although it is clearly wrong to equate privatisation with an increase in competition in the market for its product, a privatised industry is in a sense exposed to competition on the Stock Market. That is, its shares are in competition with the shares of all other companies and those shares reflect the profitability of the company. Nationalised industries, on the other hand, are not subject to the discipline of the market. They can never suffer the ultimate sanction – liquidation – since their losses will always be made good by the government. It is in this sense, and in this sense only, that privatisation *per se* exposes the industry to competition: what may be termed capital market competition.

Although the foregoing applies whether or not the industry is a monopoly, it loses much of its force if the firm faces no competition in the market for its product and if barriers to the entry of new firms exist – that is, if the firm is a monopolist – since in this case the firm can make profits, not by increasing efficiency and cutting costs, but by raising prices. A firm's Stock Market valuation, that is, the price of its shares on the Stock Exchange, reflects not its efficiency but its profitability. Efficiency and profitability are two different things.

Competition ensures efficiency?

The second proposition on which the justification for privatisation rests – that competition ensures efficiency – is also open to question. Even if we assume that the industry can be liberalised, such liberalisation will clearly not result in a market structure which is anything like a perfectly competitive market. Rather, it will be an oligopolistic market. As we saw in Chapter 9, the behaviour of firms in oligopolistic markets may be competitive, but it may also be collusive. If competition does emerge, it is unlikely to be price competition: non-price competition is much more usual.

We cannot, however, make any general statements on the basis of our analysis alone about the efficiency of firms in oligopolistic industries. A crucial problem is that we have not yet defined what efficiency is. The debate about the efficiency of nationalised industries relative to private-sector firms is, however, a debate which predates the current spate of privatisations. Nor is the debate confined to the UK, since all market economies have some state-owned industries. What we shall do in section 18.5 is to summarise the evidence that has been collected on this issue. Before we can do this, however, we need to say something about the pricing strategies adopted by nationalised industries and the objectives they pursue.

18.4 Pricing strategies in nationalised industries

The pricing strategies pursued by nationalised industries and the objectives they pursue are clearly related issues. If a private-sector company pursues profit maximisation, this has clear implications for the prices it will charge. They will be profit-maximising prices, not necessarily in the sense that the firm consciously equates marginal cost to marginal revenue, but in the sense that the firm feels its way by a process of trial and error towards prices that maximise the firm's profits. For a nationalised industry, however, particularly a monopolistic one, the pursuit of maximum profit is not necessarily an appropriate objective.

With the growth of the nationalised industry sector in the post-war period it was recognised that guidelines needed to be laid down governing the nationalised industries' pricing and investment strategies. Economists at the time were closely wedded to the idea of *marginal cost pricing* for nationalised industries. Prices, they argued, should be set equal to the marginal production cost of the good or service in question. The reason for their advocacy of marginal cost pricing stemmed from a rather literal interpretation of the Pareto welfare analysis set out in section 14.1. Recall that, according to this analysis, if all goods were sold on markets where price was equal to marginal cost, then a Pareto optimal allocation of society's resources would result. Therefore, argued the economists, nationalised industries should set their prices equal to marginal costs, since this would lead society as a whole to gain the maximum benefit from the operation of these industries.

Limitations of marginal cost pricing

The guidelines for pricing and investment were set down in a series of government White Papers in 1961, 1967, and 1978. (A White Paper is a document which lays down in general terms the policy to be followed.) For a number of reasons however, it came to be realised that a strict adherence to the marginal cost pricing principle was neither desirable nor feasible. These reasons stemmed both from developments in the theory of welfare economics itself and from an increasing realisation of the impracticality of applying the policy prescriptions which emanated from it.

On the theory side, economists recognised that nationalised industries operated in an environment where most firms' prices were not equal to marginal cost. If nationalised industries set price equal to marginal cost when prices were above marginal cost in the private sector, this would lead to a misallocation of society's resources. Consider the following hypothetical example of an economy in which there are only two sources of energy, both indigenous. The oil industry is in private hands and the gas industry is state owned. Prices are set equal to marginal cost for gas, but are above marginal

Table 18.3 Example: energy pricing

Private sector Oil	Public sector Gas
$P > MC$	$P = MC$

cost for oil. Table 18.3 summarises this. Consider the choice facing the consumer who is considering how to heat his home in winter. He will base his decision on the set of relative prices – in this case the price of oil relative to the price of gas – but in this instance relative prices do not reflect relative scarcities. The price of gas is too low relative to the price of oil so that the price ratio between the two does not reflect the relative cost of producing gas in comparison to the cost of producing oil. Because prices for gas are 'too low', demand for gas will be higher than it would otherwise have been. Too large a proportion of society's resources will flow into gas production, and too small a proportion into oil production. Recognising this, economists developed the general theory of the 'second best'. In a first-best world (in which all other prices are equal to marginal cost) nationalised industries should also set price equal to marginal cost. But in a second-best world, where in the private sector price exceeds marginal cost, nationalised industries should emulate the behaviour of private-sector firms. In other words, if prices in the private sector exceed marginal cost by 10 per cent then nationalised industries should set their prices on the same basis. In this way a Pareto optimal allocation of resources is still assured, even in this second-best world.

Although the general theory of the second-best clears up a problem in welfare theory, it leaves untouched the thorny problem of how marginal cost is to be measured. It is not at all clear what 'marginal cost' means in practice. Economists know what it means in theory. It is the first derivative of the total cost function. Less mathematically, it is the increase in total costs which results from the production of one extra unit of output. In the real world, however, there are *indivisibilities*. For example, in British Rail's case, the marginal cost of carrying an extra passenger when there are still empty seats on its trains is virtually zero. When the train is full, however, the marginal cost of carrying an extra passenger is the cost of putting an extra coach on the train, or of running an extra train. To adhere strictly to marginal cost pricing would result in most passengers paying almost nothing, and one extremely unfortunate passenger paying a very high price indeed. In addition, in calculating marginal costs some account must be taken of capital costs. In electricity generation, for example, the short-run marginal cost of power generation is the fuel cost alone. But if prices to the consumer took into account only fuel costs, then the industry would not be raising sufficient revenue to cover the depreciation of its generating capacity, nor to pay for new capacity. A related point is that firms which are subject to substantial scale economies cannot hope to cover all their operating costs if they set price equal to marginal cost. To see why this should be so, consider Fig. 18.1, which shows a typical declining cost firm (or industry). The downward sloping long-run average cost (LRAC) curve indicates that unit costs fall as the level of output rises. Such cost conditions are typical in capital-intensive industries such as electricity generation and telecommunications. It can be demonstrated (see section 5.3) that if average costs are declining then marginal cost must be less than average cost, as in Fig. 18.1. If the firm sets price equal to marginal cost and charges a price of P_1, then losses will result. This is because the firm's total revenue which is equal to the rectangle OP_1CD is less than its total costs represented by the rectangle $OABD$. (Remember that total revenue is equal to the revenue per unit, OP_1, multiplied by the number of units sold, OD. Similarly, total costs are the costs per unit, OA, multiplied by the number of units produced OD.) The firm therefore makes losses equal to the rectangle P_1ABC.

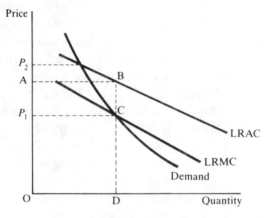

Figure 18.1

In order to 'break even' the firm must set price equal to average rather than marginal cost and charge a price of P_2 (Figs 18.1 and 18.2). At this price and with output restricted to OZ, both total revenue and total cost can be represented by the rectangle OP_2YZ. This seems to mean that the firm is making zero profits. If we remember, however, that our definition of cost includes a normal return to capital, what this really means is that the firm is making zero *super-normal* profits.

Controls on pricing and investment

For the reasons set out above, successive White Papers on the nationalised industries have tended to move away from an advocacy of marginal cost pricing. In its place they have substituted the

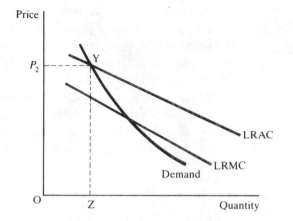

Figure 18.2

requirement that nationalised industries should set their prices in such a way that the industry meets the *financial target* imposed upon it. This financial target is in the form of a prescribed rate of return on the value of the assets employed in the industry. This rate of return can obviously be varied from time to time by the government. A problem exists, however, in that the *valuation* of the assets employed in the industry is by no means straightforward. Different approaches produce different estimates of the value of assets and it is not possible to say objectively which is 'correct'. The major area of disagreement centres around whether assets should be valued at their historical cost (minus an allowance for depreciation) or at their replacement value. The latter would normally give a much higher value.

In addition to financial targets, nationalised industries are now also subject to two additional controls. Both these controls affect the industry's investment, and therefore, indirectly the prices it can charge. The first requirement is that an investment project can only be undertaken if it will yield the required rate of return (RRR). This RRR is normally 5 per cent in real terms (that is, after allowing for inflation and using standard discounted cash flow techniques). Additionally, the borrowing which the industry undertakes to finance its investment is subject to an external financing limit (EFL). This effectively puts a ceiling on the amount of capital that the industry can raise on the capital market in any one financial year. The implication of this is considered in more detail in section 18.6.

18.5 The efficiency of public-sector industries

We saw in section 18.3 that the advocates of privatisation argued that the efficiency of the nationalised industries would be increased if they were transferred to the private sector. Implicit in this view is the belief that nationalised industries are inherently less efficient than similar industries in private hands. It also implies, in particular, that the record of the nationalised industries in Britain shows evidence of inefficiency.

In this section we shall review some of the evidence on the relative efficiency of public and private sector firms. We have already noted that profitability is a poor measure of efficiency. Profits depend, among other things, on the prices charged and these have often been held artificially low in nationalised industries as part of government anti-inflation policy. An alternative measure of efficiency therefore needs to be found, and several writers have used 'productivity' indices as yardsticks. Labour productivity can be calculated by dividing output by labour input. That is:

$$\text{output per employee} = \text{labour productivity} = \frac{\text{value of output}}{\text{labour input}} \qquad [18.1]$$

The denominator in the expression 'labour input' can be measured by the number of employees. The numerator, however, is measured in value terms, rather than in volume terms. (It would be possible to measure output in volume terms if it were homogeneous – for example, tons of coal – but comparisons of labour productivity in different industries would not then be possible.) This immediately casts doubt on the validity of the index as a true measure of efficiency since variations in prices will affect the value of output and hence labour productivity.

A more serious objection is that other factors of production in addition to labour are involved in the production process. The most important of these is, of course, capital. Capital-intensive industries, like telecommunications and electricity generation, therefore have high levels of labour productivity in comparison to labour-intensive industries like postal services, but this says nothing about their relative efficiency.

A better measure of efficiency would take account of both the labour and capital used in production. These factor inputs would perforce have to be measured in value terms. Although the value of labour input can be measured quite simply by the wages bill, the value of capital input is much more difficult to determine. Usually some arbitrary assumption is made. For example, the value of capital input is equal to 10 per cent of the value of the industry's capital stock. In this way a (somewhat questionable) measure of the value of total factor inputs is obtained and from this a measure of *total factor productivity*, so called, can be derived. Thus:

$$\text{total factor productivity} = \frac{\text{value of output}}{\text{value of labour input} + \text{value of capital input}}$$

Alternatively, the *rate of growth* of either labour productivity or

Table 18.4 Rate of change of productivity in selected nationalised industries (% per annum)

	Output per head		Total factor productivity	
	1968–78	1978–85	1968–78	1978–85
British Rail	0.8	3.9	n.a.	2.8
British Steel	−0.2	12.6	−2.5	2.9
Post Office	−1.3	2.3	n.a.	1.9
British Telecom	8.2	5.8	5.2	0.5
British Coal	−0.7	4.4	−1.4	0.0
Electricity	5.3	3.9	0.7	1.4
British Gas	8.5	3.8	n.a.	1.2
National Bus	−0.5	2.1	−1.4	0.1
British Airways	6.4	6.6	5.5	4.8
UK manufacturing	2.7	3.0	1.7	n.a.

Source: quoted in J. Vickers and G. Yarrow, *Privatization: an economic analysis*, 1988, Cambridge (MIT Press). The studies on which this is based are those by Pryke (1981) and Molyneux and Thompson (1987).

total factor productivity can be used. This overcomes – or sidesteps – many of the practical difficulties involved in making efficiency comparisons on the basis of observed productivity *levels*. Table 18.4 shows the rate of growth of productivity of certain selected nationalised industries in comparison with UK manufacturing industry generally.

No definitive conclusions can be reached from this table. In general it appears that industries that did badly in the earlier period fared rather better in the latter. However the performance of industries such as telecoms, gas and electricity showed little change.

Some authors are critical of the use of the sort of 'productivity' measures used in Table 18.4. Such measures they argue are meaningless because they are influenced by the price movements of both inputs and outputs. This argument has particular force in the case of industries that have some monopolistic power and are therefore able to influence these prices.

A further difficulty is apparent from Table 18.4, namely that the nationalised industries do not form a homogeneous group. British Telecom, British Airways and British Gas apparently secured large increases in 'productivity'. These three industries were in a particularly favoured position, however. They are capital-intensive industries and during the period studied, improvements in technology enabled large improvements in productivity to be secured. British Airways, for example, benefited from the introduction of wide-bodied jets; British Gas benefited from the exploitation of North Sea gas; and British Telecom from the general advances in electronics. Moreover, the demand for the output of these industries was increasing. The electricity industry was similarly favoured, though not to the same extent, as demand was not increasing as fast and unit costs were rising. In contrast, most of the other nationalised industries were suffering a decline in the demand for their output. Costs were, in most cases, rising, necessitating price increases which further depressed demand.

The only conclusion that emerges from Table 18.4 is that some nationalised industries did 'better' than the average for manufacturing industry generally, and others did 'worse'. Those that did better were the industries with generally favourable demand and cost conditions. Those that did worse had unfavourable demand and cost conditions. No general conclusion can therefore be reached about the relative efficiencies of public ownership versus private ownership, even if we accept the view that 'productivity' indexes do in fact measure efficiency.

Some writers argue that a more satisfactory approach to the general question of whether public ownership affects efficiency is to compare the performance of public and private sector firms operating in the same industry. Opportunities for doing this are relatively rare, but Millward[3] reports the results of a number of such studies. In Canada there are two main railway companies, the publicly owned Canadian National and the privately owned Canadian Pacific, operating in competition with each other over many routes. The major conclusion Millward draws is that there is no significant evidence that productivity is lower in Canadian National than in Canadian Pacific. A study of Australian airlines where a public firm Trans-Australian Airways coexisted with a private firm (Ansett Transport Industries) produced broadly similar conclusions. Millward's third case study is that of electricity supply in the United States, where a large number of firms, some public and some private, supply the nation's power. Because of its relevance to the general issue of whether public ownership affects efficiency, this industry has been subject to scrutiny by a number of authors. In reviewing these studies, Millward concludes that 'none of the cost studies support the proposition that public electricity firms have lower productivity or higher unit costs than private firms', allowing for differences in factor prices and the size of plant. Similar conclusions emerge from studies of unit costs in areas such as water supply and refuse collection. (Economists, as Millward once remarked, always end up talking rubbish.)

18.6 Privatisation and the PSBR

The empirical studies of the previous section were all addressed to the central question of whether public as opposed to private ownership materially affects the managerial efficiency of firms. At the very least, one could conclude that there is no strong evidence to support the proposition that privatisation *per se* will increase efficiency. Since the British government and Treasury are presumably familiar with this evidence, their support for privatisation must therefore be explained in one of two ways. Either their interpretation of the available evidence is different from the one we have made, or they are motivated by factors we have not yet considered. This second possibility leads us into a consideration of two possible motives. First, a general ideological desire to roll back the frontiers of the state, which we shall discuss in the next chapter. And second, the impact which privatisation has on the Public Sector Borrowing Requirement (PSBR), which we discuss below.

A full analysis of the PSBR takes us into the realm of macroeconomics and hence is outside the scope of this book. Broadly speaking, however, the PSBR is equal to the financial deficit of the public sector, which is composed of central government, local authorities and public corporations. The financial deficit of the public corporations sector is the excess of its expenditure over its income in any one year. This excess is met by borrowing from the public, that is, from private individuals and financial institutions, by the issue of bonds and other debt instruments.

The Public Sector Borrowing Requirement, of which the Public Corporations Borrowing Requirement forms a part, was a key target of Mrs Thatcher's macroeconomic policy. The objective was to reduce it to as low a level as possible, because it was seen as a burden on the economy. Whether or not this is a sensible interpretation of the PSBR will not be considered here. However, given that the government pursues the objective of reducing the PSBR, privatisation is an excellent way of doing so.

This follows for three reasons. Firstly, any public corporation which is incurring a deficit adds an equivalent amount to the government's spending and hence to its borrowing requirement. Secondly, and more importantly, borrowing by public corporations to finance future investment is treated as part of the PSBR even though this borrowing is really little different from the borrowing which private-sector firms undertake to finance investment. Because they are treated differently, however, borrowing by a nationalised BT, for example, increases the PSBR and is a 'burden' on the economy. Borrowing by a privatised BT does not increase the PSBR and is not a burden on the economy. This seems nonsensical but, like all sophistry, there is a grain, but only a grain, of truth in it. Private-sector companies, the argument runs, are ultimately subject to the discipline of the Stock Market. Investments must produce a return which in the long term is no less than the average return in the company sector generally. If not, the company's shares will fall in value and it will eventually be taken over or go into liquidation. Public-sector companies, on the other hand, are not subject to such discipline. Although their investments are required to earn a specified return, they do not suffer a fall in their Stock Market valuation if they fail to do so. Their investments are, in a sense, underwritten by the government. They cannot go bankrupt. This therefore is the argument which is used to justify the inclusion of public corporations' borrowing as part of the PSBR and to view it as 'a burden on the economy'.

Clearly the smaller the public corporations sector, the smaller the 'burden' it can impose on the economy. This, in part, is the rationale for privatisation. It is also the rationale for the imposition of External Financing Limits on the nationalised industries which we mentioned earlier.

The most important reason for privatisation, however, if one takes a cynical view, is that the proceeds from the sale of public assets reduce the PSBR directly. The sale of BT raised £3.9 bn, British Gas over £5 bn. By 1990 privatisation proceeds were exceeding £10 bn per annum (about 5 per cent of total government revenue).

18.7 Regulating the newly privatised monopolies

Many of the former public corporations which were privatised by Mrs Thatcher's government were natural monopolies. Companies like BT and British Gas were sold off intact and they therefore became private sector monopolies. In contrast, before it was sold off, the Central Electricity Generating Board was split up into National Power (with roughly 70 per cent of the assets) and PowerGen (with 30 per cent), the objective being to introduce some sort of competition into the industry. When the Area Electricity Boards were sold off however they retained for all practical purposes a local monopoly, as did the Regional Water Authorities when they were privatised.

Because of the monopoly or near-monopoly position of some of these newly privatised companies, and the threat that this posed, the government established regulatory bodies whose job was to oversee the activities – and particularly the pricing behaviour – of such companies. The first of these was OFTEL (the Office of Telecommunications). BT who had a near-monopoly position in the market for telecoms was compelled to fulfil certain obligations such as the maintenance of the 999 emergency service, and to keep its price increases below the rate of inflation according to some *RPI-minus-x* formula (where x was set at 3 per cent). Notwithstanding this however BT made large profits in the period following privatisation, as did British Gas and the Electricity and Water companies which led some writers to argue that these companies were abusing their market power. Moreover the efficacy of the regulators like OFTEL, OFGAS, and OFWAT was questioned. It came to be realised that the regulation of private sector monopolies was just as difficult as ensuring the efficiency of such industries when they were in the public sector.

Where possible structural changes were proposed which would have the effect of introducing a greater degree of effective competition. In telecoms for example the 'Duopoly Review' sought to encourage other firms to enter the industry by licensing other operators. It was envisaged that one such was British Rail who, if they were allowed to connect into BT's local network, would provide trunk routes by laying optic fibres alongside their existing track.

Notes

1. Keynes, J. M., *The General Theory of Employment, Interest and Money.* 1939.
2. Pryke, R., *The Nationalised Industries: Policies and Performance since 1968.* Martin Robertson, 1981, p. 183.
3. Pryke, R., *Public Enterprise in Practice*, MacGibbon and Kee 1971, and Pryke (1981) op.cit.; Millward, R. *et al.*, *Public Sector Economics.* Longman 1983.

Questions

18.1 Which of the following statements are correct?
  (a) All nationalised industries are public corporations but not all public corporations are nationalised industries.
  (b) The public sector stands in contradistinction to the private sector.
  (c) Public limited companies (plcs) are part of the public sector.
  (d) Plcs are part of the private sector.
  (e) Public corporations are state-owned enterprises.

18.2 In 1983 the public corporations accounted for 16 per cent of total investment but only 10.7 per cent of output. Suggest reasons why this discrepancy exists.

18.3 Consider the extent to which the nationalised industries (listed in Table 18.1) constitute 'natural monopolies'.

18.4 Which of the following necessarily results from the privatisation of a nationalised industry?
  (a) Selling off assets brings a windfall gain to the Treasury.
  (b) Privatisation increases competition in the industry.
  (c) Privatisation increases efficiency in the industry.

18.5 How might one best measure 'efficiency' in the operation of a nationalised industry which monopolises the market which it serves? An 'efficient' industry is one which:
  (a) achieves a specified output level at least cost;
  (b) uses the minimum amount of resources to produce a particular output;
  (c) charges low prices;

(d)   achieves the highest profits;

(e)   has the greatest return on assets employed;

(f)   none of the above is a satisfactory definition of efficiency.

18.6   Suppose state-owned industries compete with private-sector companies whose prices exceed marginal cost. What does the theory of the second-best advocate about prices in the state owned industries?

(a)   The nationalised industries should still set price equal to marginal cost.

(b)   The state-owned industries should merely try to cover their total costs.

(c)   Prices in the state-owned industries should be above marginal cost.

(d)   The ratio of price to marginal cost should be the same in the nationalised industries as it is in the private sector.

(e)   Nationalised industries should behave commercially and try to maximise profits.

18.7   The Central Electricity Generating Board had a 'merit order' of power stations. Stations with low fuel costs per unit of electricity generated – that is, low marginal costs – were at the top of the merit order. Hydro and nuclear stations have low marginal costs, followed by coal-fired and oil-fired stations. Given that electricity demand varies during the day, explain why 'off-peak' electricity is sold to the consumer more cheaply than 'on-peak' electricity?

18.8   The following could all be used to try to measure the 'efficiency' of a nationalised industry. What are the drawbacks of each of these measures?

(a)   profitability

(b)   labour productivity, i.e. $\dfrac{\text{value of output}}{\text{labour input}}$

(c)   rate of return on capital employed

(d)   total factor productivity

19 The producer, the consumer and the state

This is a concluding chapter only in the sense that it comes at the end of the book. It does not purport to come to any conclusions. The issues are too complex, the questions are too large and an introductory textbook is not the appropriate forum within which to state any conclusions, definitive or otherwise. It is not an indictment to say, as George Bernard Shaw did, that if all the economists in the world were laid end to end they still would not reach a conclusion. Rather it is a reflection of the complexity of the issues involved.

Nor does this short chapter attempt to summarise what has gone before, since any summary would be overly superficial. What it does do is to restate and highlight some of the issues raised in this book. The reader can if he wishes form his own conclusions. Be warned, however. If you think you know the answers it is probably because you do not fully understand the question.

An undercurrent in this book, implicit up to now, has been the relationship between the three *dramatis personae* in the economic system – the producer, the consumer and the state. The form of the relationship between these three characterises the mixed economy. On the one hand we have presented a model – that of Pareto welfare theory – which portrays the individual consumer as being sovereign. Producers – that is, firms – merely respond passively to his wishes. There is no need for the state to intervene except in those few areas of market failure, principally those areas concerned with pure public goods like defence. Clearly this view is untenable, however. Producers do not passively respond to consumers' wishes. Rather they shape and manipulate those wishes through advertising and through the exercise of market power. Typically markets in the real world are not atomistically competitive. They are oligopolistic, and virtually the whole of Chapter 9 was devoted to the study of cases in which producers attempted to use and abuse their market power. The pursuit of self-interest by such firms does not, as Pareto claimed, lead to an allocation of resources which is optimal in any sense. It does not lead to the greatest happiness of the greatest number. There is a need for state intervention to curb the power of large firms when that power is abused. Chapter 11 reinforced these caveats.

Market failure – in the sense of externalities and public goods – is characterised in a Pareto model as a minor blemish on an otherwise perfect system. In fact market failure runs through that system, touching every part. Externalities are all-pervasive in an industrialised, urbanised society. The public-good area is of major significance, shaping as it does the physical and social environment within which individuals live out their lives. The market mechanism cannot by definition provide an adequate supply of those public goods like universal health care and education and environmental services which become more important as society becomes more affluent. Again, there is need for state intervention in the provision of public goods and to address the problem of externalities.

There is, I would guess, an overwhelming consensus that some state intervention in these areas is both appropriate and desirable. There never can be any consensus, however, in deciding exactly how much state intervention is desirable. To what extent should private producers be free to pursue their self-interested, and indeed selfish ends? To what extent, indeed, should society's productive resources be in the untrammelled hands of private individuals, free to pursue those ends? And to what extent should the state intervene to correct for market failure? These questions are of course – as if you had not already realised it – political. Economics is political economy. It can never divorce itself from that no matter how much it pretends to be an objective, value-free science.

There is of course a political tide in Britain. That tide, which has been running in Britain for several years, has been referred to as 'rolling back the frontiers of the state'. It is about shifting the emphasis of our mixed economy away from increasing reliance on state intervention and towards greater reliance on market forces. Supply-side economics, it is sometimes called. What characterises this policy is the view that an economy actually functions better – that is, is more productive – if individuals both as consumers and producers are motivated by the rewards and punishments that are an essential feature of the market mechanism. This view is, of course, based on a particular interpretation of how the market mechanism works, a view which is open to challenge. In this book we have tried to give an analysis of how that market mechanism works. The reader should by now be aware that our analysis is not characterised by a world of competitive markets where price is determined by demand and supply (whatever that is), where producers passively respond to consumers' wishes and in which market failure is only a minor defect.

We have not set out in our analysis to persuade the reader into accepting any particular view about the appropriate role of the state. We shall not have failed, however, if the reader has been brought to a more informed agnosticism.

Answers to selected questions

Chapter 2

2.1 (a) demand is inelastic
   (b) demand is elastic
   (c) unit elasticity

2.2 The *availability of substitutes* is the most important factor, but things such as the proportion of income spent on the good in question will also affect the elasticity of demand.

2.3 (a) The demand for salt is very inelastic because only a tiny fraction of the weekly grocery bill is spent on salt. If the price of salt doubled or trebled the amount purchased would scarcely be affected at all.

   (b and c) The demand for cigarettes is inelastic, which is one of the reasons why the Chancellor of the Exchequer imposes high taxes on them. The demand for a particular brand is highly elastic however since there are dozens of rival brands which are almost perfect substitutes.

   (d) There are a number of substitutes for first-class letter services including second-class letter services, telephone, fax and courier. The closer these substitutes are perceived to be in the mind of the consumer, the more readily will he switch to an alternative form of communication.

2.4 In the short run the other factors of production – the coal-fired boilers for example – are fixed. In the longer run however, following an increase in coal prices, domestic consumers and electricity generating companies can scrap their coal-fired boilers and switch to an alternative fuel, such as gas or oil. (In fact the generating companies already possess a number of dual-fired stations capable of using different fuels depending upon relative prices.) In the very long run if coal and other fossil fuels became very expensive it would pay firms to invest in new technologies such as solar, wind, bio-mass, and nuclear.

2.5 (a) These are substitutes (supposedly) hence the cross price elasticity will be positive. This is not borne out by the statistical evidence however. Table A2.8 below shows that the estimated coefficients are not significantly different from zero. This either means that the statistical techniques used to estimate the parameters are wrong or that shoppers in Sainsbury's really do not perceive butter and margarine as substitutes – some individuals will never buy butter in preference to low-cholesterol margarine because they believe butter is an unhealthy food. Others take the opposite view but neither will be swayed by small changes in relative prices.

Table A2.8

Cross price elasticity demand	With respect to the price of	Probable range of coefficient
butter	margarine	−0.71 to +0.11
margarine	butter	−0.99 to +0.21

Source: *Household Food Consumption and Expenditure*. Annual Report of the National Food Survey Committee, HMSO, MAFF, 1990, Table 5.3. These estimates are based on survey data from 1982 to 1989. They appear to show that the response of consumers is indeterminate.

    (b)   These are complementary goods, hence a negative cross price elasticity.

2.6   The price of substitutes such as electricity, oil, and coal has also increased, in some cases by more than the increase in gas prices. Incomes have also risen and since gas is non-inferior this would also lead to an increase in demand.

2.7   Percentage change in price = 5 per cent, percentage change in demand = 20 per cent, so the price elasticity of demand would appear to be 4.

    However one would want to know what the other filling stations in the vicinity are doing. Are they matching price cuts or are they allowing this filling station to poach all their customers? And is Friday a typical day, or is demand always higher on Fridays than on other days?

Chapter 3

3.2   Only the perfectly competitive firm is a price taker. All of the others face a downward sloping demand curve and hence have some discretion in setting prices.

3.3   Firms in perfect competition face a perfectly elastic demand curve. This implies that they can sell as much as they like (at the ruling price). There is no point in advertising therefore. For the industry as a whole however advertising may be a sensible strategy.

3.5 Perfectly competitive markets are characterised by *homogeneity* of the product. Such homogeneity enables consumers to check prices more easily, since they can compare like with like. Perhaps the EC's desire for standardisation can be explained in terms of the desire to promote competition. Consumer protection is sometimes cited as the rationale though it is unclear why consumers need protecting from non-standard cauliflowers.

3.6 If rivals follow suit the increase in demand will not be as great as it would otherwise be, so demand is less responsive (less elastic) than it would have been. The correct response is (b).

Chapter 4

4.1 (a) This will increase the demand for the raw material (cocoa) pushing up its price, *ceteris paribus*.

(b) This will cause the supply curve to shift to the left – less will be offered for sale at each price than previously. Hence equilibrium price rises.

(c) The increase in the price of coffee will cause a shift in the demand curve to D' as in Fig. A1. If the supply curve remains unchanged this will lead to an increase in the quantity traded and an increase in price. However the new high yield strain will shift the supply curve to the right increasing the quantity traded still further but depressing price. Whether the final equilibrium price P_1 is greater than or less than the original price P_0 will depend upon how much each curve shifts. In our diagram the increase in supply swamps the induced rise in demand so price falls. Whatever happens the equilibrium quantity must rise.

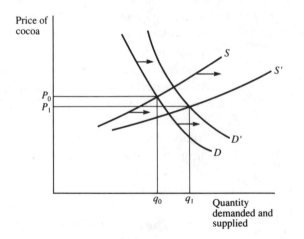

Figure A1

4.4 (a) This will increase the demand for housing generally and hence push up house prices everywhere including Ealing.

(b)   In effect loans for house purchase become more expensive. Thus people will become more reluctant to borrow money for house purchase. This will reduce demand, depressing prices.

(c)   Improved transport links will make Ealing more attractive increasing the demand for houses there.

(d)   This will expand the supply of new houses which will tend to reduce house prices, *ceteris paribus*.

(e)   These are substitutes. A rise in the price of a substitute will cause consumers to switch to a (cheaper) alternative so house prices in Ealing will receive a further boost.

(f)   This is a supply side effect which will tend to increase house prices.

(g)   A demand side effect which tends to increase house prices.

Chapter 5

5.5   Its revenues of £5100 cover all its variable costs and make some contribution to its fixed costs. If it closed in the winter its losses would be £1000 per month whereas if it stays open its losses are only £900 per month. Hence it is better to stay open provided of course that its revenue in the summer is such that on a year round basis it makes a profit.

Chapter 6

6.4   This depends on the extent to which the amount of other work the skilled workers can perform is reduced by the time they spend training apprentices. If all of their time is taken up as instuctors then the real cost to the company of such a training scheme would be the value of the output these workers would have produced had they not been engaged in training.

Chapter 10

10.1   (a)   Yes, Alphaland does.

(b)   In Alphaland the opportunity cost of one unit of clothing is one-tenth of an appliance. In Betaland it is one-ninth of an appliance.

(c)   The cost of one appliance in Alphaland is ten units of clothing, whereas in Betaland it is only nine units of clothing. So Betaland has a comparative advantage in appliance production.

(d)   It must be Alphaland.

(e)   Clothing, because it has a comparative advantage there. The cost of one unit of clothing is one-tenth of an appliance, but in Betaland it is one-ninth (one-ninth is more than one-tenth).

(f)   The closure of the Alphaland factory results in the loss of 1000 appliances. However 50 000 man-hours are 'freed' by this which will make an extra 10 000 units of clothing.

If it reduces clothing output from its Betaland factory by 10 000 units this will free 70 000 man hours which can be used to produce

$$\frac{70\ 000}{63} = 1111 \text{ appliances}$$

So it can get an extra 111 units of domestic applicances.

(g) It's still Betaland. The general increase in wage rates in Alphaland has not altered the fact that it has a comparative advantage in appliance production.

(h) Close down all its factories in Alphaland.

(i) The table of input requirements measured in money units would look like this:

	Alphaland	Betaland
clothing	6	7
appliances	60	63

As a result the company would close down all the Betaland factories and move to Alphaland.

Note that neither the change in the exchange rate nor the change in the wage rate affects the comparative advantage which Alphaland has in clothing production *vis-à-vis* appliance production.

However when the input requirements are expressed in money terms, changes in *prices* (of currencies and/or labour) can substantially alter the picture, even though these changes have got nothing to do with real resources.

Chapter 17

17.1 Unemployment benefit, supplementary benefit payments and student grants are transfer payments.

The salaries of teachers, however, represent expenditure on goods and services. These would be included when calculating GDP whereas transfer payments would not. Similarly one wishes to include the output of the social work 'industry' as part of the output of the economy (GDP). Since one cannot measure this directly – inputs to this industry are taken to represent outputs – so the salaries of social workers would be included in GDP.

Spending on research would be treated in the same way. Note however that much of this expenditure finances maintenance grants for postgraduate students. The paradox is that mainten-ance grants for undergraduate students are treated as transfer payments.

17.2 Television broadcasts are non-rival. If you tune in to watch *Neighbours* the signal strength is not diminished. The supply of *Neighbours* available to everyone else is not reduced.

Broadcasts are also non-excludable. In the UK you are

supposed to purchase a receiving licence (costing £71) if you have a TV. But in fact the TV works just as well if you don't have a licence. Legally TV broadcasts are excludable, but they are intrinsically non-excludable. It is technically possible to make them excludable, by scrambling them, and forcing would-be consumers to purchase or rent a decoder.

The M1 motorway, like any public road, is non-excludable. You do not have to pay directly to use the road. Like any non-excludable good the M1 tends to suffer from over-use (congestion) since prices are not used to choke off excess demand. The M1 is non-rival when uncongested, but rival when congested. The presence of other road users reduces the utility that I get from the road, because it reduces my average speed.

The River Thames is non-excludable and rival and hence suffers from pollution since some users (upstream) are imposing costs on users downstream by using the river to discharge effluent, etc. In recent years the legal system has been used to render it excludable (by prohibiting the discharge of certain wastes) and the level of pollution has fallen.

Incidentally, the Thames Barrier (a flood prevention scheme for London) is a classic non-excludable, non-rival public good. The tramps in Cardboard City are protected from flooding even though they pay no tax. How lucky they are.

McDonald's hamburgers are a pure, private good. If you don't pay, you don't get. And you cannot have mine because I've eaten it.

The pavement outside McDonald's is non-excludable and covered with hamburger wrappers.

Navigation buoys are non-excludable and non-rival. Like lighthouses, a classic public good. We all pay for them through our taxes.

Index